Pluralism, Racism, and Public Policy

Edited by
Edwin G. Clausen and
Jack Bermingham

Pluralism, Racism, and Public Policy
The Search for Equality

G. K. Hall & Co.   Boston, Massachusetts

Library of Congress Cataloging in Publication Data

Main entry under title:

Pluralism, racism, and public policy.

   Bibliography:
   Includes index.
   1. United States–Social policy–Addresses, essays,
lectures. 2. Pluralism (social sciences)–Addresses,
essays, lectures. 3. Racism–United States–Addresses,
essays, lectures. 4. Equality–Addresses, essays, lectures. I. Clausen, Edwin. II. Bermingham, Jack.
HN65.P54   305.5′0973   81–4454
ISBN 0-8161-9041-0   AACR2

This publication is printed on permanent/durable acid-free paper.
MANUFACTURED IN THE UNITED STATES OF AMERICA

Contents

Acknowledgments

This volume is actually the result of the efforts of many people, agencies, institutions, and departments. The California Council for the Humanities in Public Policy and the National Endowment for the Humanities funded an overall project investigating public policy designed to aid minorities overcome social injustice in California. Part of that project was a conference on racism, pluralism and public policy in the United States. This volume is a result of that conference, therefore the Council and NEH indirectly provided for the compilation of these articles. A special debt of gratitude is owed to Bruce Sievers, Executive Director, and Phyllis Quan, Planning Coordinator for the California Council, for their kindness, generosity, and infinite patience.

The History Department, Social Process Research Institute, Department of Black Studies, Center for Black Studies, and Public Historical Studies, all of the University of California at Santa Barbara, contributed invaluably to this project. Ms. Helen Nordoff, Assistant to the Chairperson of the History Department, constantly assisted in times of need. Bob Davis, Contracts and Grants officer, somehow brought humor into the bureaucracy, and without his careful scrutiny our efforts would have been much less fruitful. It is almost impossible to measure the value of Mrs. Hilda Cooper, who somehow managed not only to type this manuscript in an incredibly short time but also to cast a sharp editorial eye as she proceeded.

Robert O. Collins is actually responsible for the ultimate completion of the project of which this volume is indirectly a part. He guided the project through some turbulent times. Donald Miller, a colleague and true friend, provided periodic and incisive criticism at various stages in the development of the volume.

The editors are immeasurably in debt to many Chinese and African professionals who now reside in this country for the vast amount of time they contributed to all phases of our project. They provided much of the commentary and insight that prompted our decision to compile this anthology. Their dedication to seeing racism become a thing of the past is immense, as measured by their enthusiasm over and hours spent on this project. We sincerely hope that this volume will in some way contribute to the eventual realization of their desire for real cultural pluralism in the United States.

Lastly, the editors would like to express their sincere appreciation to G. K. Hall, and especially to Eric Sakai and Ara Salibian, for the editorial services they performed. The style of several articles is measurably improved because of their assistance.

Introduction

On August 3, 1979, local fisherman Billy Joe Aplin was killed in Seadrift, Texas, a normally quiet fishing village of 1,000 people. Two Vietnamese refugees were indicted for murder, while homes of other Vietnamese residents were firebombed and three of their fishing boats burned.[1] Many of the Vietnamese fled the town, gradually returning only after the overt violence ceased. Yet tension remains between the white and Vietnamese communities. Whites complain that the refugees fish longer hours for less money, thus making it difficult for others to compete with them. The Vietnamese fishermen are accused of selling their catch for less and for disregarding an unwritten agreement concerning the distances between crab traps. Other whites want to know: "Why can't they be Americans? Why don't they become like us?"

The question of why this tension developed and exists sparks controversy among observers of minority experiences in America. Answers to the question fall into two general categories. First, racism is identified as the cause of such tension. Whites feel antipathy for "nonwhite" minorities and certain developments trigger a "dormant" racism that leads to overt tension. Second, class and economic competition is presented as the root of the problem. The American type of social and economic system creates natural tension as people compete for the spoils the country offers.

People who believe that tension between whites and minorities is caused by racism often suggest that the values of democracy and equality have two sides: democracy and equality for white people and exclusion and equality for all others. They maintain, in fact, that America has defined itself as being "a white man's country."[2] Incidents like the ones in Seadrift only become understandable when people realize that the United States is fundamentally racist, built upon the assumption of white power and superiority. Any challenge to that assumption, real or imaginary, results in overt repression and direct violence.

Analysts who feel that a person's social and economic background primarily determines an individual's "place" in American society reject the idea that racism is the basic reason for tension between whites and minorities.

They do not totally discount racism as an important characteristic of American society, but rather maintain, as one scholar persuasively argues, that "once ideology arises it alters profoundly the material reality and in fact becomes a partially autonomous feature of the reality."[3] For such scholars, racism as a state of mind and racism as economic exploitation merge to form a basic feature of United States society. Therefore any discussion of white-minority relations must proceed from an understanding that both racism (ideology) and class (material conditions and background) influence such interaction, and in turn determine a person's social and economic position in society.

Both the racist and the materialist approaches to understanding minority experience in the United States emphasize that that experience has been based on a power relationship between the oppressed minorities and the dominant whites. The significant difference between the two approaches involves the origin of the relationship: the former points to the importance of culture and thought, while the latter stresses economic competition and social background. Implicit in both approaches is a belief that the significance of cultural pluralism is its emphasis on an acceptance and appreciation of cultural diversity in society. Cultural pluralism is viewed as a positive step towards achieving equality because it assumes cultural parity: all different cultures in the society have an equal right not only to survive but to flourish.

People who identify racism as the fundamental cause of the oppression suffered by many of America's minorities have been successful in devising and winning passage of legislation designed to enact cultural pluralism. The legislation has been directed primarily towards two areas: an end to discrimination and an end to racism. Since the Brown decision in 1954, we have had a plethora of laws, statutes, and court decisions that promote equal opportunity for all citizens, regardless of their cultural or ethnic heritage. Discrimination is prohibited, legally, in all walks of public life: in education, employment, property relationships, and social interaction in public places. Such laws seek the fulfillment of cultural pluralism by banning discriminatory action against any person based on cultural or ethnic distinctiveness.

In the attempt to eliminate racism, the primary focus has been on education. Two approaches have been taken. First, there has been a push to correct stereotyped images of minorities in the schools and in textbooks assigned to students. Attempts have been made to portray positively all cultures in the society, especially those of minorities who have been subjected to racism. Cultural heroes of Blacks, Chicanos, Native Americans, Asian Americans, and others are presented alongside the traditional heroes of white society. Legislation also prohibits barring any student from any level of education because of his or her ethnic or cultural heritage.

The second approach is to implement special education programs designed specifically for minorities. These programs now abound. All attempt both to preserve cultural heritages and to teach skills necessary for an equal chance to "succeed" in American society. Here, in an attempt to allow for the development or continuation of self-confidence and self-esteem, the emphasis is on the minorities themselves. These programs attempt to mollify the effect racism has on both the physical and psychological life of minorities. Programs such as English as a second language and bilingual/bicultural education seek to reestablish confidence and pride in one's ethnicity, while at the same time teaching the skills necessary to function in a predominately white society.

Although there are critics who wish an end to public policy designed to preserve cultural diversity,[4] most experts conclude that these local, state, and federal programs are of great benefit to society in general and minorities in particular.[5] These same proponents often acknowledge the inadequacy of these laws and programs as presently constituted. The most trenchant criticism comes from people who feel that such piecemeal legislation, often reflecting a belief in the traditional liberal values of capitalism and its attendant "Lockean" political philosophy, has not solved the dilemma of institutional and structural inequality.[6] These critics reject the belief that education is a panacea for the difficulties faced by minorities. They feel that the only way cultural pluralism can be fully achieved is by total change in the economic and social fabric of society. Cultural pluralism can only be attained when people start from a position of equality, not simply a position of equal opportunity. Such critics do not desire an end to laws and programs that oppose racism and seek cultural pluralism. Indeed, many such people feel that these measures must remain in force and perhaps even be expanded. But what they do argue is that a person's future, especially if the person belongs to a minority, will not be determined primarily by ability, "special" education programs, or "innate" motivation.[7] There is the distinct belief that there is an intricate, and at times subtle, connection between the total environmental and class context in which a person grows up and the final social, professional, and economic status achieved by that individual.[8] People who come from middle- to upper-class backgrounds and have been taught to believe in capitalism, liberalism, and American democracy generally have a far better chance of maintaining that background or of achieving it if they are recent immigrants.[9]

As directors and principal investigators of a project investigating cultural pluralism in California, we found such criticism of current attempts to promote cultural pluralism and end racism to be valid.[10] The project investigated the backgrounds of Chinese and Africans who immigrated to the United States in the last fifteen years and who are currently professionals in California. Through this investigation we sought further knowledge concerning the relationship between a person's socioeconomic background and race and that person's ability to be occupationally and economically mobile in this society.

The results were twofold. First, we found that special programs do serve a valuable purpose by helping a minority person or immigrant develop certain skills necessary for equal opportunity in American society. Second, "success" in America currently means abandonment of cultural pluralism, because these immigrants' social and economic background leads to their acceptance of the values and customs of white America. People who did not have the requisite economic and educational background prior to arrival continue to suffer from privation and inequality.[11]

This volume emphasizes these criticisms of public policy designed to help achieve cultural pluralism. The contributing authors value cultural pluralism. They also feel it has not been achieved because neither laws nor legislators recognize the need to develop true equality and pluralism through a fundamental alteration of the socioeconomic foundations of this country. Many of the arguments were originally presented in attenuated versions during a conference on "Pluralism, Racism, and Public Policy," held in Santa Barbara, California, in February, 1979.[12] The participants analyzed the relationship between multi-culturalism and racism, class, and power and how these are reflected in public policy. The papers presented assessed current laws and programs designed to redress past injustices, their efficacy, and possible courses of action, and considered the issue of cultural pluralism as only a partial solution to racism and minority oppression in American society.

The focus of the conference was on Chinese Americans, Chinese immigrants, Black Americans, and African immigrants. This anthology has the same focus, and much of the discussion addresses itself to the experiences of those groups, the public policy that affects them, and criticism of that policy.

The book is divided into three parts. The first stresses the importance of a person's social and economic background in shaping values and beliefs that affect life in the United States. Three of the articles in Part I are about Chinese Americans or recent Chinese immigrants and the historical relationship between the United States and China as a force shaping the experiences of Chinese in American society. The other two articles also assess the role of environment, while conveying a sense of comparative struggle that has in part helped to determine the status of recent African immigrants and Black Americans in the United States. The articles present a clear picture of cultural diversity. They also suggest that if public policy is truly to guide America towards equality for all citizens, much more must be done than the establishment of programs promoting plurality. All five articles have very practical implications for public policy designed to benefit these ethnic groups.

The second section contains articles discussing specific programs, the evolution of laws underlying them, suggestions for the improvement of current policy, and the need to pursue new strategies for combating racism. To some extent, all of the authors are concerned that public policy does not attempt to correct structural and institutional inequality. Like the contributors to the first section, they tend to emphasize that socioeconomic background will determine a person's future in American society. If laws and programs are to correct injustices, they must be broadened to eradicate gross social and economic disparities.

The concluding section presents a gloomy view of current public policy designed to eliminate inequality. One article questions the effectiveness of antidiscrimination legislation in general, while another suggests that the people who make policy may indeed themselves exhibit a kind of unconscious racism. Both believe that only when these problems are overcome can the society proceed towards something approximating true racial equality. The final article argues that racism's continued presence is a result of an unequal white-minority power relationship. Correction of racial inequality is therefore possible only when there is a change in the structure of political and economic power in the United States.

All the articles accept cultural pluralism as something not only to be accepted, but fostered. The authors are skeptical or critical of the success of policy that has only sought to apply that pluralism to society's norms and institutions in an attempt to counter discrimination. They do feel that progress has been made towards heeding the warning that "People who shut their eyes to reality simply invite their own destruction, and anyone who insists on remaining in a state of innocence long after that innocence is dead turns himself into a monster."[13] But as this volume suggests, acknowlment of cultural pluralism does not signal an end to racism.

Notes

1. The two Vietnamese accused of murder have been acquitted, but the animosity and tension continue to exist.
2. Winthrop Jordan, *White Over Black: American Attitudes Toward the Negro, 1550-1812* (New York: W. W. Norton, 1968), p. xiii.
3. Eugene Genovese, *In Red and Black* (New York: Vintage Books, 1972), p. 32.
4. For examples, see Stephen Rosenfeld, "Bilingualism and the Melting Pot," *Washington Post,* 27 September, 1974; A. Tully, "American Education is Raped," *Albuquerque Journal,* 7 October, 1974; and Lawrence A. Cremin, *The Genius of American Education* (Pittsburgh: University of Pittsburgh Press, 1965), who implies that such programs are harmful to the coherence of the United States.
5. Rupert Trujillo, "Bicultural Education: A Necessary Strategy for American Public Education," in *A Relook at Tucson '66 and Beyond* (Washington, D.C.: U. S. Government Printing Office, 1973), p. 21; Henry Casso, *Bilingual/Bicultural Education and Teacher Training* (Washing-

ton, D.C.: National Education Association, 1976); and Mario D. Fantini, *Public Schools of Choice: A Plan for the Reform of American Education* (New York: Simon & Schuster, 1973).

6. See Richard de Lone, *Small Futures: Children, Inequality, and the Limits of Liberal Reform* (New York: Harcourt Brace Jovanovich, 1979).

7. Ibid.

8. See Edwin Clausen, "The Politics of Success: Mobility and Post-Liberation Chinese Professionals in America," *Asian-American Political Culture,* ed. Douglas Lee (Santa Barbara, forthcoming).

9. Ibid.

10. The project was entitled, "To Faciliate Inclusion and Mobility: The Chinese and African Immigrant Connection." It was funded by the California Council for Humanities in Public Policy and the National Endowment for the Humanities. We produced a five-part television program, convened a conference discussing racism, pluralism, and public policy. Many of our findings will be discussed in Edwin Clausen and Jack Bermingham, *Opportunity and Equality: Environment, Education, and Ethnicity in American Society* (Washington, D.C.: University Press of America, 1981, forthcoming). For a brief discussion of the project, its methodology and purpose, see Edwin Clausen and Jack Bermingham, "Social Issues and Public History: Immigrants and Integration in California," *The Public Historian* 1, no. 3 (Spring 1979):51–57.

11. For what constitutes the "right" background, see Clausen, "The Politics of Success," and Clausen and Bermingham, *Opportunity and Equality.*

12. This conference was sponsored and funded by the California Council for the Humanities in Public Policy, the National Endowment for the Humanities, and the Black Studies Department, the Center for Black Studies, and the Public Historical Studies Program of University of California, Santa Barbara.

13. James Baldwin, *Notes of a Native Son* (New York: Bantam Books, 1968), p. 148.

Part I

Pluralism, Racism, and Class:
Inequality in America

Introduction

The five essays in the following section emphasize the importance of an individual's socioeconomic background to the formation of values and beliefs conducive to social and occupational advancement in American society. Within this context the articles collectively consider six important issues.

First, the historical exclusion of Blacks and Chinese from fundamental American rights implicitly denies the plural character of American society. Second, exclusion and denial served as an impetus for a complex and often ill-understood struggle for equality. Third, representatives from these minorities with special status or class backgrounds were prominent in this struggle. Fourth, the legal victories that ultimately gained "equal rights under the law" have not produced basic changes in American society and societal attitudes. Fifth, these accomplishments and failures help illuminate the significance of the status and class background of immigrant Chinese and Africans in America. If the immigrants gain the necessary educational and/or professional experience and develop a value system compatible with America's, they may become what American society defines as "successful." Sixth, the remaining institutional racism in the United States still limits advancement for even these new immigrants. Chinese and African Americans who have achieved professional mobility may encounter obstacles to promotion or appointment to positions which would enable them to make policy. For new immigrants and minority Americans who come from a lower socioeconomic environment, there is often poverty and despair.

Sucheng Chan outlines part of the Chinese American experience, emphasizing the importance of Sino-American relations to that experience. Her essay concentrates on the legal, economic, political, and social exigencies that confronted residents of Chinese heritage in the United States. She maintains that the nature of Sino-American relations helped define life for Chinese in the United States and the types of difficulties they faced at different times. Chan also describes the evolution of the Chinese American community and its social tensions, which have been exacerbated by discrimination in American society.

Edwin Clausen's article examines Chinese immigrants who arrived in the United States after Liberation in China in 1949 and who are currently professionals in American society. He relates their story, using their own observations about themselves and their perceptions of America. Significantly, their status and class background were important in forming values that promoted economic and professional success in American society.

Todd Carrel, a journalist, reports on the life of recent Chinese immigrants from a different socioeconomic background: former Red Guards from the People's Republic of China who have arrived recently in San Francisco. Their motivation and positive self-image help them overcome the socioeconomic and educational obstacles which they encounter as new immigrants. They live austerely, buoyed by the belief that diligence and forbearance will help them change their lives. They are both critical of and pleased with American society, having developed certain values that in some ways are similar to those of their adopted country.

William Edwards examines the civil rights movement after the 1954 Brown decision. He concentrates on the "unfinished agenda" that has yet to win fundamental economic changes which would provide real opportunities for economically deprived Blacks. The legal gains which were crucial to all Americans, especially minorities, did not alter the basic economic framework of America. Power did not change hands, and the plural character of the society was recognized in rhetoric only.

Finally, the essay by David Chanaiwa demonstrates that there is a new group of Black Americans: recent immigrants from Africa. Although small in number, these new residents may be important in changing the misconception that Blacks in the United States come from a "backward" homeland. The similarity of these Africans to their Chinese counterparts confirms the importance of status and class backgrounds as determinants of future status.

Sucheng Chan

Public Policy, U.S.-China Relations, and the Chinese American Experience: An Interpretive Essay

Public policy has probably affected the lives of Chinese Americans more than those of any other immigrant group in the United States.[1] Public policy has controlled, restricted, and discriminated against immigrants of Chinese ancestry, as well as their American-born children, in almost all facets of life. At the local level, public policy in the form of municipal ordinances and law enforcement practices has discriminated against Chinese Americans in the areas of residence, education, opportunities for earning a living, culture and life-style, social interaction, and access to social services. At the state level, public policy has affected the lives of Chinese Americans through discriminatory taxation policy, the passage of anti-Chinese laws, statutes, and state constitutional articles, denial of due process in the courts, and occupational restrictions. At the national level, public policy has been used to restrict and finally halt immigration, to deny Chinese Americans the right to citizenship through naturalization, and to deny them franchise and, consequently, participation in political life. Both houses of Congress, agencies of the executive branch, and the Supreme Court have all participated in building up a web of institutional barriers to full equality for persons of Chinese ancestry in the United States. Finally, prior to 1949, treaties were negotiated between China and the United States which aimed at securing more rights for Americans in China on the one hand, while denying Chinese in America a fair treatment on the other. Who are the Chinese Americans and what have they done to provoke so much negative public policy at so many different levels?

The Chinese Americans presently residing in the United States are not a homogeneous population. The group is differentiated by the normal factors which divide any population into socially stratified levels and into subgroups with regional variations. More importantly, however, the Chinese American population varies according to the date and circumstance of arrival of its component subgroups. Historically, there have been four streams of immigrants. The dates when particular immigration laws were passed distinguish the four periods of immigration.

The first period of Chinese immigration was from 1849 to 1882. The beginning of the period is marked by the influx of several hundred Chinese immigrants who came in the wake of the California Gold Rush. Really large-scale immigration began in 1852 with the arrival of some 20,000 Chinese during that year alone. The majority of the immigrants who came during this thirty-year period were married male laborers from Kwangtung province in southeastern China. The end of the period is marked by the passage of the Chinese Exclusion Law in 1882.

The second period dates from 1882 to 1943. During this sixty-year period, immigration was highly selective. Legally, only merchants, students, diplomats, temporary visitors, and children of Chinese holding American citizenship could enter. The repeal of the Chinese exclusion laws signaled the end of this period. The repeal was at best a token gesture, for thereafter, only 105 persons of Chinese ancestry could enter the United States per year.

The third period, between 1943 and 1968, saw the arrival of several thousand Chinese immigrants under special legislation. The largest portion of them entered as refugees from communism. The fourth period, from 1968 to the present, has seen the arrival of a more demographically normal population, including Chinese from Hong Kong, Taiwan, and the People's Republic of China. The largest number of persons immigrate as families. Children, young adults, and middle-aged and older persons have come. They represent a wider range of occupational backgrounds and geographic origins. Immigration today, however, is by no means unregulated. The current immigration laws have clearly established priorities regarding who may enter. In general, members of nuclear families and persons with certain professional skills receive preference.

During each of the four periods, public policy has influenced the mode of adaptation of Chinese immigrants to American society. The level, range, and aim of public policy measures have changed from one period to the next. This article will survey briefly for each period the kind of immigrants who came, how their lives were affected by public policy measures, why those particular public policies came to be enacted and implemented, and the international context (in terms of U.S.-China relations) in which immigration and public policy formation took place. Before looking at the history of Chinese immigration into the United States, however, it will be useful to discuss briefly Chinese international migrations in general.

Chinese Immigration in Historical Perspective

There have been extensive internal migrations in Chinese history. In addition, Chinese from the southeastern seaboard of China began emigration overseas as early as the seventh century. The first group of emigrants went only as far as the Penghu Islands and Taiwan, sailing across the relatively narrow Taiwan Straits. In the fifteenth century, following the famous voyages of Cheng Ho,

Chinese from Fukien and Kwangtung provinces began to emigrate to various parts of Southeast Asia. The Chinese called Southeast Asia "Nanyang," the Southern Ocean. A floruishing trade between China and Southeast Asia developed. Some Chinese merchandise was transshipped from Southeast Asian ports and carried across the Indian Ocean to India, the Middle East, and even to the island of Madagascar. Merchandise was also transshipped from Manila and carried across the Pacific Ocean to Mexico on ships of the Manila Galleon. In the early part of the nineteenth century, when European colonialists stepped up the pace of colonizing Southeast Asia and exploiting the natural resources of the region, Chinese emigration increased dramatically. Some Chinese emigrants were laborers, while others were merchants. Within decades, Chinese merchants in Southeast Asia came to dominate retail trade in the entire area. In the process of emigrating to Southeast Asia, certain modes of transportation, labor recruitment and placement, and other supportive networks were developed among the Chinese migrants. When Chinese began to make the much longer voyage across the Pacific Ocean to the Americas, they made use of an already well-established network of services facilitating emigration.[2]

The attitude of the Chinese government toward emigration was negative, for both political and cultural reasons. After the Manchus conquered China and established the Ch'ing dynasty in 1644, many persons still loyal to the preceding Ming dynasty escaped to southeastern China, or even overseas. The Ch'ing government disapproved of emigration because it did not wish to have a group of potential rebels outside the geographic limits of its control. Because the Chinese looked inward and were usually more concerned with China's inner Asian frontiers than with lands across the seas, people who emigrated were considered to be disloyal to the Chinese Empire. Section 225 of the Fundamental Laws of the Ch'ing Dynasty forbade emigration on pain of death.[3] Those who did emigrate were afraid to return home. They feared they would be subjected to extortion by officials at the ports of return, or they feared social ostracism by their own kinsmen.[4]

It was the European powers which finally induced the Chinese government to allow its subjects to emigrate. In 1859, a local official, the governor of Kwangtung province, permitted the British and the French to recruit indentured laborers from his province.[5] After China's defeat at the hands of the British and the French in the Arrow War, a convention was signed which stated that:

> as soon as the ratification of the treaty of 1858 shall have been
> exchanged, His Majesty the Emperor of China, will by decree,
> command the high authorities of every Province to proclaim
> throughout their jurisdiction, that Chinese, choosing to take service
> in the British colonies or other parts beyond the sea, are at perfect

liberty to enter engagements with British subjects for that purpose
and to ship themselves and their families on board any British
vessel at any of the open ports of China.[6]

In 1868 the United States government played a role in further eroding the
Chinese government's reluctance to allow the emigration of Chinese. An
article included in the Burlingame Treaty recognized the inalienable right
of man to change his home and allegiance. In 1893, an imperial edict repealed
Section 225 of the Fundamental Laws of the Ch'ing Dynasty. Now Chinese
who had gone abroad could return home without penalty. The Fundamental
Laws themselves were revised in 1910.

Chinese emigrated to Latin America and North America as well as Southeast Asia. A smaller number also went to Australia. The Chinese who went to
Latin America suffered the worst abuses. Between 1847 and 1874, Chinese
contract laborers, called "coolies," were shipped to Cuba, Peru, Trinidad,
British Guiana and Jamaica, where they worked on plantations, on railroads,
in guano beds and at other forms of hard menial labor. Mortality rates both
on board ship and after arrival were high. Some coolies were treated worse
than slaves, for their employers did not consider them to be an investment
as chattel slaves were. A coolie who was worked to death was simply replaced
by another. The sum of money an employer had to pay to procure a new
coolie was smaller than that paid by a slave owner to purchase a slave. Conditions were so shocking that international public opinion played a role in
seeking ways to reduce some of the abuses of the trade. The Chinese government carried out an investigation of the trade to Cuba and Peru in 1874. In
1873, the British colonial government in Hong Kong halted the further
emigration of contract laborers from Hong Kong to points within the British
empire. In 1874, the Portuguese colonial authorities in Macao closed the
coolie trade also, but a nefarious traffic doubtless continued.[7]

Chinese emigration to the United States began a year after the commencement of the coolie trade to Latin America. The contemporaneity of the
two streams of migration has led to some confusion regarding the status of
Chinese emigration to the United States. Although some American captains
sailing under foreign flags participated in the coolie trade, they could not
bring any contract laborers directly to the United States because an American
law forbade American vessels to engage in the trade. Most Chinese immigrants
to the United States came under the credit-ticket system. Agents for potential
employers advanced the emigrants' steamship fares, and the debt so incurred
would be repaid out of deductions from the emigrants' wages after arrival in
the United States.

The intense controversy surrounding Chinese immigration into the United
States has made it difficult to ascertain the true status of the Chinese immigrants who came in the nineteenth century. Because the anti-Chinese spokes-

men called Chinese immigrants "coolies," those who defended Chinese immigration made a point of stressing the free character of Chinese immigration.[8] A separate but related debate involved the alleged motivations of the Chinese immigrants. The term "sojourner" was used to characterize Chinese immigrants, and they were contrasted with European immigrants, who were depicted as having come to the United States to settle. Sojourners were said to be here only to earn money, after which they would return to China to enjoy easy lives. As sojourners, Chinese immigrants were attacked for having no desire to contribute to the development of American society, and were seen as a perpetually foreign, indigestible and harmful body of American society.[9]

The term sojourner is not useful analytically because of its emotive connotations. It is extremely difficult to determine, in retrospect, the motivations of a group of people who left us few records of their personal lives. A brief comparison of Chinese immigrants to both the "old" and the "new" European immigrants will be instructive. Aside from the fact that the bulk of the "old" immigrants came from the British Isles, Germany and northern Europe while the "new" immigrants originated primarily from southern and eastern Europe, the "new" immigrants were frequently attacked for being less able to assimilate into American culture. Italians, Slavs, and Russian Jews, for example, were seen as clinging more tenaciously to their cultures of origin. I would like to suggest that perhaps the difference between the two waves of European immigrants lies less in cultural differences than in structural changes which occurred in the world economy and in transportation technology during the late nineteenth and early twentieth centuries. With the advent of steamships, passage across the Atlantic became safer and more convenient. Fares were cheaper relative to wages to be earned. Thus, ties to the countries of origin could be maintained more easily, because repeated oceanic crossings became more feasible. Prior to the advent of steamships, migration was a more irreversible decision. In the period between 1880 and 1920, however, migration was not necessarily an irreversible decision. One could cross the ocean, try out one's fortunes, and *then* decide to settle permanently in America or to return home.

The latter part of the nineteenth century also saw the rise of what has been called the "Second Industrial Revolution" in the United States economy. Manufacturing industries became larger and ownership and control became more concentrated. Mergers and trusts became more common forms of corporate organization. Each time the economy went into a recession, more small firms were bankrupted. In order to survive, firms had to be able to compete in national as well as international markets. A new class of corporation managers came into existence. The rapid maturation of the American capitalist industrialized economy required a larger, increasingly mobile, disciplined, and easily controlled labor force. Immigration provided a flexibility in the size of the labor force which domestic workers alone could not have provided. Many of the "new" European immigrants who came between 1880 and 1920 were migrant laborers. Their migrant status, however, was influenced not only by their own proclivities but by the changing demands of the American economy.

Some students of European immigration have tried to show that an economic interdependence existed between the United States and the emigration regions of Europe. Countries on the opposite shores of the Atlantic Ocean are said to have formed an integrated "Atlantic Economy."[10] The pace of industrialization in Europe was not rapid enough to absorb the surplus labor supply generated by changes in Europe's agrarian sectors. In contrast, the United States—and to a smaller extent Canada and some of the Latin American countries—suffered from a labor shortage. In the United States, the rural-to-urban migration was insufficient to create a labor supply to fill the needs of her burgeoning industries. European migration was an attempt by those with labor power to sell, and those with capital to establish industries and to hire labor, to redistribute factors of production in order to maximize their respective returns. Redistribution occurred both domestically and across the ocean.

A study of European immigrant destinations has shown that precise factors influence the *kind* of work a particular immigrant group can find and eventually specialize in, and *where* such work may be found.[11] These factors are related primarily to the state of economic development in the area in which a particular immigrant group settles. To survive in any particular region, an immigrant group must be able to find a particular economic niche into which members of the group are accepted. In other words, they must be able to serve as a factor of production in a particular sector of the economy where their labor power is needed. This line of analysis views immigrants not as amorphous waves of people but as groups coming in response to specific needs in the American economy.

In many ways, Chinese immigrants to the United States resembled the "new" European immigrants more than the "old" European immigrants. Chinese immigrants who came to the western United States from 1849 to 1882 can also be best characterized as migrant laborers. Although it is doubtful that the kind of systemic economic interdependence which is said to have existed between certain parts of Europe and the United States also existed between the American and the Chinese national economies, it is possible to argue that a certain amount of reciprocity did exist between the *local* economies of California and Kwangtung province. (Almost all of the Chinese emigrants came from Kwangtung province; those who came to the United States settled largely in California.) Geography and the existing state of transportation technology made this so. Kwangtung province is surrounded on three sides by mountains. There are only two passes leading to its neighboring provinces. Transportation out of the province was easiest by water, both along the coast, and inland by way of the Pearl River and its tributaries. Similarly, California is separated from the other western states by the Sierra Nevada mountains. The western states, in turn are separated from the rest of the United States by the Rocky mountains. The completion of the transcontinental railroad did not immediately solve the problems posed by California's distance from markets and sources of labor supply.

By contrast, although the Pacific Ocean was vast, it did provide a transportation route for the export of products and the importation of labor. In 1880, it took an average of only twenty-six days to cross the Pacific from Hong Kong to San Francisco. Steamship fares averaged between forty and fifty dollars for steerage passengers. This was cheaper than railroad fares from the east coast to California (except during those periods when railroad companies engaged in cutthroat competition in the form of rate wars). Thus, labor could be recruited more cheaply and more readily across the Pacific Ocean than overland across the Rocky Mountains.[12] Taking these facts into consideration, one can see that the oft-cited "cheapness" of Chinese labor resulted from a combination of at least four factors: the relative cheapness of ocean transportation; the relatively abundant labor supply in China; the higher wages in California, which made Chinese laborers seem cheap even though Chinese laborers frequently were paid higher wages than white workers on the east coast; and, only in part, the much-touted willingness of Chinese immigrants to work for low wages.

A final point to be noted is that even though many of the Chinese migrant laborers may indeed have had sojourner mentalities, the realities of life in the Pearl River delta made it impossible for all those who wished to return home to do so. Although the city of Canton was a trade center, it did not industrialize in the Western pattern. Those peasants driven off the land by the destruction of land and crops during the Opium War (1839–42), the T'aip'ing Rebellion (1851–64) and various local uprisings, and by rapacious landlords found jobs in Canton mainly in the economic infrastructure supporting trade. They worked as porters, boatsmen and ricksha coolies. They did not, for the most part, work in factories. Neither China's declining cottage industries nor her large-scale enterprises (salt production and distribution, mining, and armament manufacturing) operating under government-licensed monopolies, was able to provide sufficient employment to her landless peasants. The developing California economy absorbed some of them, but many more settled in America than were intended.

1849–1882: Chinese Pioneers in a Hostile Environment

Chinese immigrants who came to California and eventually dispersed to work in all the western states were true pioneers. They represented the first mass of immigrants from Asia to the Pacific coast. (They were preceded to the New World by a group of contract laborers taken to Cuba in 1847.) They often entered into employment which was unfamiliar to them.[13] They were required either to learn new skills, or to adapt creatively the knowledge which they had brought with them to new and different conditions.[14] Many of the enterprises in which they found employment were themselves pioneering ventures. Large numbers of Chinese worked in those sectors which represented the very foundations of the western economy: gold mining in the 1850s, railroad building in the 1860s, extensive agriculture (grain cultivation) and manufacturing in the 1870s, and land reclamation and intensive farming in the 1880s.[15] The nature of the work available necessitated a migratory existence. Some of the Chinese pioneers settled in scattered localities. In this period, they were not ghettoized and could be found in places all over the western United States.

Since the Chinese immigrants came primarily to work, their work relationships and work environments formed the center of their lives. From this fact two consequences followed. First, social relations and the social hierarchies found within the growing Chinese American communities were strongly influenced by the economic positions of individuals and sub-groups. Second, when the anti-Chinese movement became virulent, much of its venom was directed at undermining the Chinese immigrants' ability to earn a living. The anti-Chinese forces assumed that if the Chinese could not earn a living, they would stop coming.

The fascination of students of Chinese American community organization and structure with the array of family and district associations has meant that vertical divisions along linguistic, clan and regional lines have been emphasized almost to the exclusion of any consideration of the horizontal division of the Chinese American population along class lines.[16] There has been little analysis of the relationship of economic power to social prestige or political power.[17] For example, even though the Chinese Six Companies (officially known as the Chinese Consolidated Benevolent Association) was organized as an umbrella organization for district associations, the power of the Chinese Six Companies came not only from its control of the immigrant population on the basis of ancient ties of regional affinity but also from its ability to place new immigrants in jobs, to keep track of their whereabouts, to collect contributions, and to refuse to issue departure certificates for the return trip to China until all of those persons' debts had been paid.[18] Long-standing ties of kinship, language and regional affinity on the one hand, and economic superordinate and subordinate relationships on the other are not mutually-exclusive factors. In rural China, the family and the clan were in fact cooperative work groups and economic units of production, consumption, and distribution.[19] These traditional social network patterns were transplanted to countries in which Chinese immigrants settled. However, for many of the early immigrants working in isolated localities, the social relations encountered in their daily lives existed more in the form of a two-tiered dyad than in the form of a complex network. The most common relationship was that between a labor boss or contractor and his gang of workers. The power which the superordinate member of the dyad held over its subordinate members was based on the former's economic control over the latter. The laborer had to work, or he starved. He could not rely on family and kin to provide alternative means of support should he lose his job due to a hostile relationship with the labor contractor. A Chinese immigrant in America who lost his job did not have the option of returning to subsistence farming as he might have done in China. He was a wage earner—a hired laborer—and those who were in a position to provide him with employment controlled his life and freedom of movement.

To escape such a state of dependence, many Chinese immigrants attempted to attain the status of independent entrepreneurs. A few succeeded, but discriminatory laws and mob violence severely limited the Chinese immigrants' chances for upward mobility. The proverbial Chinese restaurant, laundry, or grocery store were among the few avenues open. An interesting irony in public policy towards Chinese immigrants is that while much hateful rhetoric was directed against Chinese "cheap labor," in reality it was at those times when Chinese immigrants attempted to move *out* of laborer status that legal obstacles were thrown in their way.

The anti-Chinese movement originated in the gold mines of California. American miners early developed the notion that gold, as part of the natural wealth of the land, should be reserved for native-born Americans. Foreigners —even those who were white—were not welcome.[20] California's Foreign Miners' Tax, first imposed in 1852, was an expression of this sentiment. Although all foreign miners were supposed to be liable for this tax, tax collectors soon made a practice of collecting it only from Chinese miners. Moreover, tax collectors extorted extra sums for themselves, roughed up and even killed some Chinese miners, and together with white miners, made it impossible for Chinese to work good claims.[21] Many of the early Chinese miners were independent prospectors. Perhaps it was this status which irked the white miners, for Chinese immigrants were allowed in the mining camps as cooks, woodgatherers and laundrymen—that is, as wage-earning laborers—but they were harassed whenever they assumed the status of independent entrepreneurs or prospectors. After placer mining gave out, large mining companies moved in with heavy hydraulic equipment to extract the gold buried deeper in the mountain sides. Many of these mining companies, including some owned by Chinese entrepreneurs, hired Chinese to work for wages. It would be interesting to study to what extent mob violence against Chinese miners subsided after Chinese miners shifted from independent prospector to wage-earner status.

Similarly, in fishing, manufacturing, and agriculture, California's laws prevented Chinese immigrants from attaining independent entrepreneurial status. Between 1860 and 1864 Chinese fishing boats had to pay a special tax; in the 1870s, a law was passed regulating the size of mesh in fishing nets so as to affect primarily Chinese immigrant fishermen. Laws passed in 1880, 1901, 1915 and 1917 curtailed various facets of Chinese immigrant entrepreneurship in shrimping.[22] In manufacturing, Chinese-made goods were boycotted, and union labels were first used as an anti-Chinese device.[23] An 1880 act prohibited the issuance of licenses to aliens ineligible to vote.[24] Chinese immigrants who worked in agriculture did so mainly as hired hands or as tenants. Few attempted to buy land. Had they done so—as Japanese immigrants were to do in the early years of the twentieth century—it is likely that an Alien Land Law would have been enacted in California several decades before 1913.[25]

Since so much of the political rhetoric directed against this first group of Chinese immigrants attacked them for being "cheap labor," it is easy to come to the conclusion that Chinese immigrants were disliked because they were laborers per se. They fact that the 1882 Chinese Exclusion Law barred the further immigration of laborers had helped to strengthen the image that the anti-Chinese movement was directed entirely against Chinese "cheap labor."[26] In reality, an analysis of the local and state legislation which was passed against the Chinese will reveal that a more complex set of factors was at work. In my reading of the latter and the spirit of California's anti-Chinese legislation, it appears that the main thrust of these laws was directed at preventing Chinese immigrants from moving out of laborer status and into independent entrepreneurial status.

In the American economic system, there is a fundamental difference between the status of wage-earners and that of independent entrepreneurs. The income of wage-earners is fixed; they have little control over their working conditions. Even with continual hard work and frugality, the amount of wealth which can be accumulated from wages is limited. In contrast, the American capitalist system rewards entrepreneurship by permitting the making of large profits. Profits are said to be returns for risk-taking. Those who engage in business as independent entrepreneurs risk failure and may become bankrupt; on the other hand, they also have a chance at making a great deal of monty. That chance is not open to hired laborers. Many of the anti-Chinese laws were aimed at keeping Chinese immigrants at hired laborer status only. Seen in this light, the Chinese immigrants' love of gambling, and the participation of some prominent Chinese in underworld activities, may be better understood: having been shut out of legitimate channels to accumulate wealth, they turned to less legitimate means.

There was a contradiction in the public policy directed toward Chinese Americans in the nineteenth century, however. While local and state governments were busy trying to squelch the development of capitalistic enterprises by Chinese immigrants, the federal government evolved a policy which discriminated against laborers (both skilled and unskilled) and favored merchants. Why was this the case? The answer, I think, lies in the different perspectives of the different levels of government.

State and local governments were most concerned with controlling the Chinese in their midst. When they discovered that economic discrimination did not drive the Chinese out, they resorted to means to "contain" the population which was already here, and to push for national legislation which would prevent their further immigration.[27] Segregation and harrassment were two of the means used to "contain" the Chinese immigrant population. Residential segregation became legally sanctioned when an 1880 California law empowered the board of trustees, board of supervisors, or other municipal authorities

> to pass and enforce any and all acts, or ordinances, or resolutions
> necessary to cause the removal without the limits of such cities and
> towns, or city and county, of any Chinese now within or hereafter
> to come within such limits, provided that they may set apart certain
> prescribed portions of the limits of such cities, or towns, or city and
> county, for the location thereon of such Chinese.[28]

The segregation of Chinese schoolchildren—regardless of their citizenship status—was stipulated in California's Political Code in 1885, 1891, 1893, 1903, 1909, 1917, 1921, and 1927.[29] Chinese children were put into the same category as "children of filthy or vicious habits, or children suffering from contagious or infectious diseases." (Black children had been segregated earlier. Native American Indian children also had to attend separate schools.)

Chinese immigrants were harrassed in many different ways.[30] For example, the San Francisco Board of Supervisors passed an ordinance forbidding the rental of quarters with less than 500 cubic feet of air per person. Living quarters in Chinatown were crowded. Many Chinese were arrested for violating this ordinance. At one point, the jail became so crowded that *it* violated the ordinance. Moreover, most of the buildings in Chinatown were not owned by Chinese. Yet the landlords were not made culpable. Other city ordinances discriminated against Chinese laundries, Chinese methods for carrying merchandise (in two baskets suspended at the ends of a pole slung across the shoulder), and the wearing of the queue. Persons thought to be facilitating the immigration of Chinese were also penalized. For example, the master of any vessel bringing in persons who could not become citizens was liable to a fifty dollars per person capitation tax.[31] Other ordinances passed during this period were later declared unconstitutional, but while they were in effect the lives of Chinese immigrants were subject to much harrassment. Probably even worse than the many ordinances and laws was the wanton use of violence against Chinese residents. Chinese were stoned in the streets, their wares upset, and their stores vandalized. There were even incidents of arson and murder, but the culprits were seldom apprehended. Even when they were, they were never convicted. Chinese testimony against white persons was not accepted in court.[32]

Because Chinese were denied the right to naturalization, they could not vote. Thus, they had no political leverage.[33] Even the 1868 Burlingame Treaty, designed specifically to promote Chinese immigration, contained a clause which exempted naturalization as a right to be enjoyed by Chinese immigrants.[34] In 1878, the San Francisco Circuit Court denied naturalization to a Chinese petitioner named Ah Yup, thereby setting the precedent for the denial of citizenship to Chinese immigrants.[35] The 1882 Chinese Exclusion Act confirmed the denial of citizenship.[36]

Several theories have been offered for the existence of the anti-Chinese movement. These include the national existence of negative Chinese stereotypes,[37] the use of the anti-Chinese movement as a political football in bipartisan party politics,[38] and the use of the anti-Chinese movement to consolidate and build the white labor movement.[39] Each of these theories has validity. In my opinion, the linking of the anti-Chinese movement to the rise of the labor movement seems most persuasive. In particular, one must remember that the period of initial Chinese mass immigration saw the decline in status of the workman. It has been estimated that in 1780, approximately eighty percent of the working population in the United States was self-employed as independent farmers or as skilled journeymen. By 1800, however, only thirty-seven percent of the working population were self-employed entrepreneurs. In contrast, the percentage of wage employees had risen from an estimated twenty percent in 1780 to sixty-two percent in 1880.[40] Three-fifths of the working population was therefore dependent on an employer for its living. These people had little control over their wages or their working conditions. The labor movement arose out of the sense of powerlessness felt by skilled craftsmen who fought to retain some measure of control over their working lives. In their struggle against their employers, their position was an unequal and definitely weaker one. They saw the Chinese as "tools of the capitalists." While there were many strikes, especially in the 1880s, few were successful. Probably in their frustration, they found it easier to pick on the helpless Chinese immigrants.

Had the anti-Chinese movement been based only on the fear of economic competition by the white working class, however, it probably would not have resulted in the enactment of national legislation. A careful reading of the Congressional debates prior to the passage of the 1882 Chinese Exclusion Law, and the subsequent exclusion laws, reveals that a greater fear was at work. As I interpret the tone of the debates, the anti-Chinese movement's emotional force was linked not only to the bitterness resulting from the

Civil War, but also to the need to rationalize the history of persecution of Native Americans.

At the time that the anti-Chinese movement was picking up national support, the United States was winding up the last phase of its Indian Wars. The supporters of Chinese exclusion were quite frank about their views. Senator Miller of California, for example, after a long recital of how, through four thousand years of history, the Chinese people had been "under training" for survival, said that the Chinese who survived were those who had "adapted to the smallest needs of human life, with a capacity for physical endurance equal to that of the most stalwart races." He said that "competition with such a machine by the free white man is impossible," that the call for Chinese exclusion went beyond a question of economics: it was, indeed, a call for self-preservation. "National safety demands an intelligent discrimination," he said. "It is not numbers that are needed; quality is of more importance than quantity. One complete man, the product of free institutions and a high civilization, is worth more to the world than hundreds of barbarians. Upon what other theory can we justify the almost complete extermination of the Indian, the original possessor of all these states?"[41]

Senator Grover of Oregon spoke in a similar vein. In response to Senator Hoar of Massachusetts, who opposed Chinese exclusion and who had invoked the noble sentiments of the Declaration of Independence and the Constitution, Senator Grover insisted that the founding fathers had not intended the non-white races to be included as recipients of the inalienable rights of man. "If they were intent on missionary labors in building up and sustaining a government devoted to the elevation of the colored races of mankind, why did they not seize upon the opportunity when this continent was occupied, and rightfully occupied by the red man, to devote their great zeal and enterprise in civilizing and instructing him?" Moreover, he argued, "this will appear the more clearly when we consider the treatment of the African by the very men who founded our Government. They never invited the African here as a voluntary immigrant. They neither endowed him with lands nor the ballot, nor did they grant him the right of citizenship . . . On what ground, then, can it now be claimed that the hereditary policy of this Government requires us to open our ports to the admission of all races of mankind without discrimination . . . ?"[42]

Those who wanted Chinese exclusion had no qualms about their racism. Frequently, it is said that racism is based on the ideas of superiority which the racists have with regard to themselves. They see those they discriminate against as inferior. In the debates on Chinese immigration, however, it appears that mixed with allegations about the Chinese people's inferiority—"degradation" was the word used—was a fear based on their superiority. The Chinese were feared for their superior ability to survive and, perhaps even more so, for their large numbers. Over and over again, the size of China's population was invoked, giving rise to images of "hordes" and "tides."

While the reasons for the anti-Chinese movement may be found in the social history of the United States, the reasons why such a movement was *possible* must be sought in the history of the U.S.-China relations. The federal policy which finally emerged with regard to Chinese immigration was one which was discriminatory towards the Chinese laborer, and selectively favorable to the Chinese merchant (although in time, the implementation of this policy wrought enormous hardship on Chinese merchants, too). Why did the United States want to continue to allow the merchant to come? It was because its primary concern in its relations with China was trade. When Chinese migration to the United States began, the United States was relatively insignificant vis-à-vis the European powers. The federal government was wary of offending China. As the nineteenth century wore on, however, even though opponents of Chinese exclusion warned that exclusion would have adverse effects on America's China trade, it became increasingly clear that China was so weak that there was little she could do to retaliate against any insults to her national honor. By 1882, it was apparent that the United States could have her cake and eat it, too—that is to say, to continue to enjoy most-favored-nation status in China, particularly in the two areas of trade and Christian proselytization, *and* to simultaneously enforce a policy of exclusion against Chinese immigration.

In the early years of U.S.-China relations, the main vehicle for their interaction was the China trade. American commercial and naval presence predated the formal establishment of diplomatic relations by many decades.[43] The first Treaty of Peace, Amity and Commerce between the two countries, signed in 1844 at Wanghsia, was directed toward securing for Americans commercial and extraterritorial rights equal to those won by Great Britain in the Treaty of Nanking.[44] The second treaty, signed in 1858, together with two conventions signed the same year, gave the United States additional rights, including the right of the United States Minister to China "to visit and sojourn at the Capital of His Majesty the Emperor of China," the right to trade and reside in the additional treaty ports opened in 1858, and the right to proselytize Christianity without persecution or harrassment.[45]

Neither the 1844 nor the 1858 treaty mentioned emigration or immigration. In fact, it was not until the Burlingame Treaty of 1868 that "the inherent and inalienable right of man to change his home and allegiance, and also the mutual advantage of the free migration and emigration of their citizens and subjects from the one country to the other" was recognized.[46] This article was an explicit repudiation of the Ch'ing Dynasty law which forbade emigration. Within a few years, however, Anson Burlingame—who was in the interesting position of having served as the United States Minister to China for six years and was then invited by the Chinese government to serve as its envoy on the first Chinese mission to foreign powers—came under severe criticism for having "sold out" the interests of his own country by promoting Chinese immigration into the United States.[47] Twelve years after the Burlingame Treaty, the United States sent three commissioners to China to negotiate a treaty to modify the Burlingame Treaty. The Treaty of 1880 stipulated that

> Whenever in the opinion of the Government of the United States, the coming of Chinese laborers to the United States, or their residence therein, affects or threatens to affect the interests of that country . . . the Government of China agrees that the Government of the United States may regulate, limit, or suspend such coming or residence, but may not absolutely prohibit it.[48]

The Treaty of 1880 served as a "green light" to several senators to support the Chinese exclusion bills which were introduced in Congress in 1882. For example, Senator Garland and Senator Cameron had both voted against the exclusion bills introduced in 1879 because they felt any such bill was a violation of the treaty with China then in force (the Burlingame Treaty). Having secured a modification of the Burlingame Treaty by the Treaty of 1880, these senators now felt they could support the suspension of Chinese immigration with a clear conscience.[49] Senator Hoar's argument that the 1880 Treaty had been "forced" upon China was of no avail. Thus, the weak international position of China, which made some of her statesmen take an accommodationist stance, made it possible for American lawmakers to enact a defensible discriminatory law.

At the same time, Chinese laborers were victims of class prejudice. China's statesmen, who negotiated the 1880 treaty, were members of the elite. They were primarily concerned with China's *national* honor. They fought hard to get the phrase "but not absolutely prohibit" included in the text of the treaty.[50] This phrase was a face-saving device. So long as what Americans called "the better classes," specifically identified as officials, teachers, students, merchants, or travellers, could continue to enter, the Chinese officials were willing to sacrifice the interests of the laborers. American lawmakers showed their own variant of class prejudice: they would sanction the immigration of those groups of Chinese who could help to promote American interests in China. Officials, students, teachers, and travellers who became familiar with American society would, presumably, act as spearheads for the spread of American civilization when they returned home. Merchants, on the other hand, would help to promote trade between the two countries. It is perhaps one of the great ironies of history that the vast markets and great profits visualized for the China trade seldom materialized. The China trade never exceeded 4 percent of the total foreign trade of the United States. The huge population of China and its potential as consumers of American- and European-produced goods continues to lure businessmen with dreams of profit. At the same time, the sheer number of Chinese is an object of awe and fear.

1882-1943: A Repressed Minority Turns Inward

The years between the end of the nineteenth century and the beginning of World War II are perhaps the least familiar years in terms of the evolution of the Chinese-American community. Mass immigration had stopped, and those who remained in America became increasingly ghettoized into urban Chinatowns. The pioneers who had fanned out all over the western and northwestern parts of the North American continent were forced by the mob violence which erupted in numerous places to retreat to the relative safety of urban ghettos. The *implementation* of public policy previously formulated became more important than new laws in affecting the lives of the Chinese-American communities. Internationally, China continued to lose bits and pieces of her tenuous sovereignty. At one point, certain segments of the Chinese people, together with some of the Chinese in America, rose up in protest of the repressiveness of American public policy towards even the "exempt classes" of immigrants, but the protest died out and did little to change that policy. During this period, the United States rose to ascendancy in the Pacific Basin, annexed Guam and Hawaii, and colonized the Philippines. She was concerned about the turn of events in China during the 1911 Revolution and during Chiang Kai-shek's Northern Expedition of 1926-28.[51] Increasingly, however, her main attention in East Asia was directed at Japan, another rising world power. On the home front, policymakers were concerned about Japanese immigration. The Chinese-American communities took advantage of the relative decline of public scrutiny and learned to survive by becoming a silent minority. It was not until Japan's invasion of China in the late 1930s that a flurry of publicly-noticed activities took place among the members of this repressed minority.

In 1880, the census counted 105,465 persons of Chinese ancestry in the United States. In 1890, the number was 107,488. The slight increase was due to the influx of almost 40,000 Chinese immigrants in 1882, just prior to the Exclusion Law going into effect. Thereafter, we see a decline. There were 89,863 in 1900, 71,531 in 1910, 61,639 in 1920, 74,954 in 1930 and 77,504 in 1940. The increases in the 1920-30 and 1930-40 decades derive from the birth of second-generation Chinese Americans. In terms of new immigration, this period saw the entry of both legal and illegal immigrants. The largest proportion of legal immigrants consisted of the children of Chinese who held American citizenship. Prior to the denial of the right of naturalization to Chinese immigrants, a very small number of Chinese immigrants had succeeded in their petitions for naturalization, mainly in the eastern states. Those persons of Chinese ancestry born in the United States also had citizenship status. After the 1906 San Francisco earthquake, when official records were destroyed, quite a number of Chinese claimed to have been born in San Francisco. Since very few Chinese women had emigrated during the first period between 1849 and 1882, many of the men who had chosen to reside in the United States, and who could legally do so under the various immigration laws, returned to China from time to time to visit their wives. Out of the small nucleus of persons of Chinese ancestry holding American citizenship grew the only consistent source of growth from immigration in the Chinese-American population. Children born in China of those persons with American citizenship could be admitted as derivative citizens. In the period 1920-40, for which statistics exist, 71,040 persons (usually minors) with derivative citizenship were admitted. In contrast, the total number of aliens who entered (including reentries) for the same period was only 66,039.[52]

This source of immigration gave rise to certain abuses. Chinese-American citizens returning from visits to China usually reported the birth of children. By so reporting, they created "slots" for the future admission of these minors. "Slots" soon became negotiable papers, for sale for varying amounts. Some young men, eager to emigrate to the United States, entered as "paper sons." They changed their family names, memorized details about the family and village histories of their "paper fathers," and attempted to enter after passing through gruelling sessions of detailed questioning by American immigration officials.[53] There is no way to calculate how many persons entered the United States during the decades of exclusion as "paper sons." All we know is that in the 1960s, when the Immigration and Naturalization Service instituted a confession program whereby "paper sons" could adjust their status, approximately 8,000 confessions were made.

It is even more difficult to calculate how many Chinese entered illegally by jumping ship, slipping across the Canadian and Mexican borders, or simply disappearing after entering as temporary tourists. Immigration Service officials and Congressional committees made much ado about the smuggling of Chinese into the country.[54] The accusation of fraud gave impetus to the enactment of ever more repressive laws. In 1888 Congress passed the Scott Act, which prohibited the return of any Chinese laborers who had departed from the United States. Approximately 20,000 Chinese who had been issued certificates for temporary visits abroad under the terms of the 1882 act were out of the country when the Scott Act was passed. They were denied reentry. Over six hundred persons with legitimate certificates permitting their reentry were actually on board ship en route to the United States. Upon arrival, they were not permitted to land and were returned to China.[55] In 1892, the Geary Act was passed. It required all Chinese laborers residing in the United States to register. Those who were admitted legally had to carry on their person at all times certificates of residence.[56] The Chinese Six Companies, after seeking legal counsel, advised Chinese residents not to register. This unexpected act of civil disobedience created problems for the U.S. government. It would have been prohibitively expensive to arrest and jail all the Chinese who did not register. The 1893 McCreary Amendment to the Geary Act sought to ameliorate the situation by extending the registration period for six months.[57]

The Geary Act had extended Chinese exclusion for another ten years. In 1898, a Congressional Joint Resolution prohibited the further immigration of Chinese into Hawaii and prohibited the immigration of Chinese from Hawaii to the continental United States.[58] A 1900 act required Chinese in Hawaii to register also. Chinese exclusion was also extended to the Philippines after the United States colonized the country. The Act of April 29, 1902, extended Chinese exclusion laws indefinitely, and required the registration and certification of Chinese in the "insular possessions" of the United States.[59]

Meanwhile, in 1894, China and the United States had signed another treaty. When this treaty was about to expire in 1904, the Chinese Minister in Washington, D.C. denounced the 1894 treaty and announced that the Chinese government would not sign a new discriminatory treaty. In reaction, Congress passed the Act of April 27, 1904, which extended all Chinese exclusion laws without any limitation in time.

During this period, the Bureau of Immigration, established as a Treasury Department unit in 1891, under the zealous leadership of President Theodore Roosevelt's Commissioner General of Immigration, Terence Powderly (a former official in the Knights of Labor), began to carry out its work in an especially harsh way with respect to Chinese immigrants. The collectors of customs stationed at the ports of entry had the authority to examine and accept or reject Chinese persons entering under the "exempt classes" categories. In an opinion issued in 1898, Attorney General John Griggs had ruled that the word "merchant" was different from the word "trader." A merchant must conduct business under his own name, at a fixed place of business. Salesmen, buyers, and clerks, on the other hand, though engaged in trading, were not merchants. Griggs's opinion enabled immigration officials to restrict greatly the number of merchants who could enter. The meaning of "student" was also further restricted. A Chinese person could enter as a student only if he or she came for higher education in some branch of knowledge for which academic facilities were not available in China. To qualify for entry, moreover, the students' support and maintenance while in residence in the United States must have been provided for, and they had to return to China after the completion of their studies.[60] Under these narrower definitions, a larger proportion of potential immigrants were rejected upon arrival. Attempts at deportation were also stepped up. Even merchants who had been specifically invited to exhibit at the St. Louis Exposition were badly maltreated upon arrival. Powderly's successor, Frank P. Sargent, Commissioner General of Immigration from 1902 to 1908, was equally zealous. He used his annual reports as forums for publicizing alleged widespread fraud committed by the Chinese. In 1903, members of the Immigration Bureau aided the Boston Police Department in carrying out a raid on Boston's Chinatown, resulting in the arrest of over two hundred persons.[61]

The consequences of the public policies of this period on the social structure of the shrinking Chinese-American communities are not easily documented.[62] The Chinese-American population lived in constant fear of harrassment, investigation, or deportation. They learned to adopt a posture of lying low and coping with their situation through evasion rather than confrontation.

Only once during this period did Chinese anger erupt into a mass movement. This occurred in 1905. Chinese merchants, students, and even some members of the gentry participated in a mass economic boycott of American products sold in China. Although the locus of this protest movement was in China, recent research has shown that a great deal of the impetus and financial support came from Chinese living in the United States. Specifically, according to Delber McKee, Chinese-American members of the Chinese Empire Reform Association were especially active in collecting money to send back to China in support of boycott activities. A General Society of Chinese Residing in the United States for the Opposing of the Exclusion Treaty was formed. The San Francisco branch drew its support from a wide assortment of Chinese-American community groups, among them the Chinese Mercantile Associations, the Chinese Christian Societies, the Chee Kung Tong, the Chinese Empire Reform Association, and the publishers of the *Chung Sai Yat Bo*, the *Man Hing*, and the *Wah Kee* newspapers. In China itself, the boycott erupted in July, 1905 and continued in certain port cities well into the spring of the following year.[63] American diplomats in China put tremendous pressure on the central Chinese government to stop the boycott. Although the imperial government issued an edict on August 31, 1905, to end the boycott, few heeded it. The fact that the Chinese and Chinese Americans chose an economic boycott to protest the exclusion of Chinese immigrants indicates that the Chinese understood very well what America's major interest in China was—trade. In the long run, the boycott did little to harm America's China trade, but it was an outpouring of nationalism of more than symbolic significance. The Chinese understood that although Chinese exclusion started as a class-based policy (to which the Chinese officials, in their own upper-class elitism, had acquiesced) it had, by 1905, been extended to a racially-based policy directed against the people of a whole nation.

Having learned the bitter lesson that even a protest of national proportion did nothing to cause the United States to reverse its policy of exclusion, the Chinese-American communities turned inward to build what life they could for themselves. The population was now more sedentary, having been driven into the ghettos of Chinatowns. Chinese immigrant pioneers no longer roamed the west for work. They eked out a living by working in laundries, restaurants, and small stores. The two main occupations open to them outside of the confines of Chinatown were working as domestic servants and cooks.[64] In California, a number of Chinese continued in farm work. Since Chinese immigrants were no longer contracted in large gangs to work on railroad construction and maintenance or in swamp land reclamation, labor contractors probably declined in importance. Merchants and literate men able to deal with the outside world consolidated their leadership.

America's concern with trade and her immigration policies, which favored the merchant class, were responsible for institutionalizing a pattern of social stratification in Chinese-American communities which differs from the pattern found in traditional China. There, men with "new learning" (Western-educated) and merchants acting as compradors formed two newly-emerging elites in society, but the traditional ruling class of scholar-gentry continued to retain positions of power (albeit sometimes under new guises) even after the 1911 revolution and well into the twentieth century.[65] In Chinese-American communities, however, though diplomats sent from China sometimes acted as spokespersons for the Chinese-American population, especially in matters of international import such as the signing of new treaties and immigration laws, in the day-to-day lives of the communities, the merchant elite held sway. In the early decades of the twentieth century, their elite status derived from their wealth, their ability to provide employment, their control over community organizations, their connections with forces of coercion affiliated with the underworld, and their aboveground connections with American branches of political parties established in China. The shortage of women throughout the first century of Chinese-American history and the consequent delayed appearance of a second generation meant that the elite established in the very first years of Chinese immigration continued to hold power for a century. Only in the late 1920s and early 1930s did organizations formed by second-generation Chinese Americans begin to find some voice in community affairs.[66]

In terms of U.S.-China relations, the early American attempts to secure a "fair share" of trade and political concessions became formally institutionalized in the famous Open Door policy. Although the policy of Chinese exclusion threatened to close the open door, once again China's military and political weakness made it possible for the door to remain open to American activities in China but closed to Chinese immigration into the United States. As one writer has said, "China's reactions were not of prime importance to American policy makers."[67] Unless we understand the highly unequal balance of power between China and the United States during this entire period, it is difficult to understand how the American labor movement could so outmaneuver opposing forces which were economically or morally more powerful. The American Asiatic Association, a group of powerful business interests opposed to Chinese exclusion, surely would have been able to exert enough political influence to counter labor's political power. Or, forces such as the many Protestant missionary boards with active interest in China surely could have summoned sufficient moral authority to counter Samuel Gompers of the American Federation of Labor or an assortment of senators and congressmen from the Pacific coast. In the end, however, the United States's international position made it possible for her to pose as a "friend to China" on the one hand, and to justify the discriminatory treatment of Chinese in America on the other hand, for *we* knew that China realized that unless she "cooperated," a worse fate might have befallen her as the European powers, Russia and Japan all eagerly clamored for a slice of the "Chinese melon."[68] The fate of Chinese Americans was only a very minor worry to the beleaguered Chinese government, and Chinese Americans themselves, attempting to survive in a repressive environment, could do little during this period to assert their rights. Public policy had so completely circumscribed so many facets of their lives that there was almost no leeway for action. The fact that this repressed minority survived at all during this period is testament enough to their strength-that very ability to endure which has cast such dark fears into the hearts of the exclusionists.

1943-1968: The Entry of Expatriate Intellectuals and Political Refugees

The Chinese exclusion laws were repealed by Congress in 1943. This action had nothing to do with what was happening in Chinese-American communities. Rather, once again, international relations dictated public policy. Japan had encroached bit by bit into Chinese territory until, in 1937, formal war between China and Japan broke out. The Chinese people rose up to fight a war of resistance and national salvation. Meanwhile, in Europe, Hitler and Mussolini rose to power. The Allies fought to defend "democracy" against "fascism." In the eyes of the American public, the Chinese people, who were fighting against the Japanese militarists allied with the Nazis and the Italian Fascists, all of a sudden assumed heroic proportions. When Madame Chiang Kai-shek visited the United States, she was welcomed as a heroine and given the honor of addressing Congress. Her eloquence and charm captured the American public's imagination. When the United States entered the war after the bombing of Pearl Harbor, China and the United States became allies. The United States sent military aid to the Chinese Nationalists, but all did not go well.[69] By 1943, the United States was gravely concerned about "keeping China in the war." Congress repealed the Chinese exclusion acts-a sore point between the two nations for some sixty years-as a gesture of goodwill.

The repeal of Chinese exclusion did not greatly affect Chinese immigration, for only 105 persons were permitted to enter per year. Moreover, anyone with even half Chinese blood, regardless of citizenship or place of residence, would be chargeable to the Chinese quota. Perhaps more important was the clause which permitted Chinese immigrants to become citizens through naturalization. Naturalization lessened the threat of deportation, and enabled the new citizens to gain the right to vote.

The first law which enabled the entry of more than a token number of Chinese immigrants was the War Brides Act of 1945 and its 1947 amendment. Six thousand Chinese war brides (out of a total of 100,000 war brides and war grooms so admitted) entered over a three-year period. This represented the first large-scale entry of Chinese women in Chinese-American history. In the ensuing years, some Chinese immigrants entered as refugees. Under the 1948 Displaced Persons Act, 3,500 Chinese who claimed they were unable to return to China "because of fear of persecution on account of race, religion, or political opinion" were allowed to adjust their status. They were given permanent residence status. In 1953, a Refugee Act enabled some 2,000 Chinese, whose passports had been endorsed by the Nationalist government in Taiwan, to be admitted. The Refugee Escape Act of 1957 and the Act of September 22, 1959, permitted the entry of another 1,000 Chinese refugees. The largest group of refugees entered under the provisions of the Presidential Directive signed by President Kennedy in 1962. By 1967, over 15,000 persons had entered under its provisions.[70]

The Chinese immigrants entering under the above acts differ from the first two waves of immigrants in several ways. Among the students who had their status adjusted were many highly educated intellectuals. They were in the United States to receive advanced training. During the war, some defense industries, in need of skilled manpower, had begun to open their doors to minorities previously barred from employment. This trend continued in the post-war period. For the first time in Chinese-American history, Chinese engineers and scientists found jobs in the fields in which they had been trained. Many of these expatriate intellectuals provided, in time, the basis for the 1960s stereotype of the successful Asian minority. Coming from privileged, upper-class backgrounds, they were able to gain acceptance in certain circles of American society more readily than any of their predecessors, even though some of them suffered from subtle forms of discrimination and some language disability.

Those who came as refugees, on the other hand, brought with them the asset of being refugees from communism. With the liberation of China—interpreted by some Americans as a "loss"—and then the outbreak of the Korean War and the advent of McCarthyism in American national life, anti-communist refugees bore silent testimony to the evils of communism and the attraction and moral superiority of free-world democracy. Among the refugees, priority was given to persons with technical skills needed by the United

States. After the Soviet Union launched Sputnik into orbit, Chinese refugee engineers and scientists were quite welcome as employees.

In terms of geographic and linguistic background, the immigrants of this period came mostly from north and central China and were Mandarin speakers. They did not identify themselves with the original Cantonese-speaking laborers from Kwangtung province. Residential segregation was declining, and many of the new immigrants found homes in the growing suburbs around the large metropolitan areas. If they ventured into Chinatown, it was mainly to eat a meal or buy some groceries. Their children became Americanized more rapidly and more completely than he second- and third-generation "true" Asian Americans. Although the Cold War mentality cast China in the role of an implacable enemy, the expatriate scholars who taught in the universities interpreting Chinese culture to Americans, the engineers who worked in defense industries, and the less privileged workers who ended up in the service sector were nonetheless the "good guys." They were the ones who had opposed communism and who had sought sanctuary in America.

This is not to say that security agencies such as the FBI were sanguine about the presence of so many more Chinese in the United States. Elaborate files were kept on persons with any sign of leftist leanings. A little-known history of political harrassment during this period is only slowly coming to light. Within the Chinatowns themselves, the American branches of the Kuomintang, in cooperation with Chinatowns' power elites, kept a tight watch over the residents. The grip of the KMT and the Chinese Six Companies did not begin to decline until the early 1970s.

Public policy towards Chinese Americans during this period was directed at alleviating some of the disabilities caused by former discriminatory laws. Some laws, such as those against miscegenation (originally enacted against Blacks, but later made applicable to "Mongolians"), were quietly removed from the statute books. Others became inactive through nonenforcement. While much of the impetus for the improved treatment of Chinese Americans came from a genuine desire to make up for past injustice, some recognition must also be given to the international context in which the United States found itself in the 1950s and early 1960s. During the Cold War, the United States was busy around the world trying to "win the minds and hearts of men." Third World countries looking at the history of racism in the United States found it easy to be skeptical. Domestically, the United States had to "clean up its image." The move in this direction was greatly hastened by the rise of the Civil Rights Movement. Black youth, white youth and eventually Asian American and Chicano/Latino youth demanded an end to centuries of racial discrimination.

In this atmosphere of militance, the cultivation of an image of a minority who had "made it" by dint of its own hard work and nonmilitant acceptance of the status quo was a useful—indeed, necessary—political expedient. Asians in America seemed to fit the bill. The image of a "successful minority" was so alluring that some Asian Americans came to promote it themselves. Asian-Americans seemed proud to be held up as a counterexample to Blacks and other minorities. But not all Asian Americans felt this way. Some joined the Movement themselves. Some who became concerned with domestic issues were first made aware of the history of anti-Asian racism by the nature of the Vietnam War. Asian American antiwar activists saw the Vietnam War as a racist war against an Asian country. They began to realize that it was impor-tant to join in the fight against racism at home in America. International and domestic politics once again were intertwined.

1968–Present: The New Immigration

In October, 1965, President Johnson signed an act to abolish the national ori-gins immigration quota system as of July 1, 1968. In the interim period, some 6,000 Chinese immigrants were admitted into the United States. Thereafter, in addition to a quota of 20,000 persons per year, some Chinese could be ad-mitted on a nonquota status. Moreover, persons from Hong Kong were charge-able to Great Britain's quota. It is estimated that some 25,000 to 30,000 persons of Chinese ancestry immigrate into the United States per year.

The new immigrants have profoundly changed the demographic charac-teristics of the Chinese American population. The historically imbalanced sex ratio is finally equalizing. In contrast to the immigrants who came in during the 1943–1965 period, more of the new immigrants are of working-class status. Many are relatives of persons already here. Long-separated families have been reunited. The majority of the new immigrants now come as family units.

The new arrivals have faced many problems. One set of problems is due to conflicts among different segments within the Chinese-American communities themselves. Among the youth, there is antagonism between the American-born and the foreign-born. Usually, this antagonism is submerged and expresses itself only in the form of social separation. On the campus of the University of California at Berkeley, for example, where there are almost 5,000 students of Asian ancestry, the American-born tend to avoid mixing with the foreign-born, claiming that the latter are different and that they cannot communicate. The foreign-born, on the other hand, deal with this rejection by saying derogatory things about the moral conduct of the second-, third- or fourth-generation Asian Americans. According to some commenta-tors, the antagonism between the two groups of youth also finds expression in more violent means. Some of Chinatown's much-publicized gang warfare is said to be due to the hostility between the two groups.

Intergenerational conflict is also becoming a serious problem. Many of the immigrant families manage to make ends meet only when several family members work. (The census data on the relatively high *family* income among Chinese Americans is deceptive: family income is high only because more Chinese-American families have multiple wage earners than the general population.) When both parents work, and there is no money to hire baby-sitters, children, including very young ones, are sometimes left on their own. Some of these children run around the streets, drop out of school, and engage in crime.[71] The long-standing stereotype that juvenile delinquency does not exist among Chinese Americans has now been shattered. Many parents are disappointed and disillusioned. Some had come to the United States motivated by the availability of free public education for their children. They were willing to suffer downward social mobility themselves in order to afford their children a better opportunity to have bright futures as professionals. But their children do not appreciate their sacrifice; in fact, they resent hearing about it. They are contemptuous of their parents' intense preoccupation with earning money, and they resent the pressure their parents put on them to become professionals in order to enhance the family's social standing.

Other intracommunity conflicts arise out of different political beliefs. The leftists, the liberals, and the conservatives among the Chinese Americans naturally do not see eye to eye on many political issues. Even among people with the same general political philosophy, sectarian disputes are quite frequent. Beyond the sectarianism, however, the commitment to social change on the part of a sizeable number of activists is genuine.

A different set of problems arises out of the new immigrants' relationship to the wider society. Those with little knowledge of English suffer the most. They are virtually condemned to live and work in overcrowded Chinatowns, where a shockingly large proportion of the housing is rated as substandard by the Census Bureau,[72] and where wages are often below the legal minimum.[73] Bilingual social services are inadequate. Job training or retraining opportunities are limited. Today, it appears that discrimination is based on linguistic ability. In the past, public policy discriminated on the basis of class or race, while today one's knowledge of English or lack of it plays a key role in determining whether one has access to equal opportunities in education, employment, housing, and social and political participation.

Public policy today appears to be ambiguous. While much lip service is paid to promoting affirmative action and other avenues to the achievement of a truly egalitarian and pluralistic society, there has, in fact, been a retrenchment of gains made in the 1960s and early 1970s. It seems that those who make policies will act in a minority group's interest only when the minority group demands its rights. Economic recession is used as an excuse to curtail the development of means to rectify the past history of discrimination.

The present phase of Chinese immigration began during the same year that the Nixon-Kissinger doctrine was introduced. The United States had learned by then that communism was not a monolith. We had even learned to coexist with communist nations, including the People's Republic of China. But it took six years after the issuance of the Shanghai Communiqué before full normalization between the United States and China took place. Corporations and tourists are flocking to China. The lure of the China market once again beckons. Meanwhile, how will Chinese Americans fare? Will they continue to be pawns in an international game of power politics? Or will they be treated as equal human beings in a democratic, pluralistic society? To a large extent, I believe the future of Chinese Americans lies in our own hands. We Chinese Americans must stand up for our rights, we must organize ourselves to affect public policy, and we must participate fully in all walks of public life. If there is one lesson we can learn from our history, it is that we must fight for whatever human rights we hope to enjoy.

Notes

1. Blacks, Chicanos and Native Americans have been affected even more adversely by public policy. None of the nonwhite minorities was a true immigrant group, however. The Chinese Americans are here compared to other *immigrant* groups.

2. The most important arrangement adopted by Chinese immigrants to the United States from the prior experience of migration to Southeast Asia was the credit-ticket system. Emigrants who could not afford to pay for their passage would sign up with a labor recruiter who advanced them the fares. After the immigrants arrived at their destinations, employers interested in hiring them paid off the labor recruiter, and then the immigrants repaid their employers by having a portion of their wages deducted each month. Interest was usually charged. See Ta Chen, "Chinese Migrations, with Special Reference to Labor Conditions," *Bulletin of the United States Bureau of Labor Statistics*, no. 340 (Washington, D.C.: U.S. Government Printing Office, 1923), pp. 13–14; and T. W. Chin, H. M. Lai and P. P. Choy, eds., *A History of the Chinese in California* (San Francisco, Ca.: Chinese Historial Society of America, 1969), p. 15.

3. H. M. Lai and P. P. Choy, *Outlines: History of the Chinese in America* (San Francisco, Ca.: Chinese American Studies Planning Group, 1973), p. 40.

4. Ta Chen, "Chinese Migrations," p. 17.

5. Ibid.

6. Ibid.

7. The "coolie trade" to Peru has been studied in Stewart Watt, *Chinese Bondage in Peru: A History of the Chinese Coolie in Peru, 1849-1874*

(Westport, Conn.: Greenwood Press, 1970). The immigration of Chinese contract laborers to Cuba and Jamaica has been treated in Ching Chieh Chang, "The Chinese in Latin America: A Preliminary Geographical Survey with Special Reference to Cuba and Jamaica," (Ph.D. Diss., University of Maryland, 1956), pp. 1–21., and in D. C. Corbitt, *A Study of the Chinese in Cuba, 1847–1947* (Wilmurs, Ky.: Ashbury College, 1971), pp. 1–86. Chinese contract laborer migration to other parts of the world is treated in P. C. Campbell, *Chinese Coolie Emigration to Countries within the British Empire* (London: P. S. King & Son, 1923).

8. Mary R. Coolidge, *Chinese Immigration* (New York: Henry Holt & Co., 1909), pp. 41–54.

9. Gunther Barth, *Bitter Strength: A History of the Chinese in the United States, 1850–1870* (Cambridge, Mass.: Harvard University Press, 1964); Stanford Lyman, "The Chinese Diaspora in America, 1850-1943," in *The Life, Influence, and the Role of the Chinese in the United States, 1776–1960*, Proceedings/Papers of the National Conference, Chinese Historical Society of America, San Francisco, Ca.: 1975, pp. 128–146.

10. Brinley Thomas, *Migration and Economic Growth: A Study of Great Britain and the Atlantic Economy* (Cambridge: Cambridge University Press, 1954).

11. Caroline Golab, *Immigrant Destination* (Philadelphia, Pa.: Temple University Press, 1977).

12. For the first decade after the completion of the transcontinental railroad, the Central Pacific and Union Pacific lines had no competition, so railroad fares and freight rates were high. Only with the completion of a second, and then a third transcontinental line did rate competition bring fares and freight rates down. It was only in the 1880s that the railroads played an active role in promoting immigration to California.

13. The best known example of Chinese immigrants performing labor which was unfamiliar to them is railroad building. While the popular accounts frequently depict the Chinese as only unskilled laborers, in fact they constituted the bulk of the skilled labor as well.

14. One example is Chinese involvement in agriculture in California. While most of the immigrants came from peasant backgrounds, the crops they cultivated in California were different from those grown in China. Soil and climatic conditions also differed, which meant that different cultivation methods had to be used.

15. Chinn, Lai and Choy, *A History of Chinese in California,* pp. 30–64, and George F. Seward, *Chinese Immigration: Its Social and Economic Aspects* (1881; reprinted New York: Arno Press, 1970), pp. 30–135, describe the many different kinds of work and entrepreneurial activities Chinese immigrants engaged in.

16. Rose Hum Lee, *The Chinese in the U.S.A.* (Hong Kong: Hong Kong University Press, 1960), pp. 142–184, and S. W. Kung, *Chinese in American Life* (Seattle, Wash.: University of Washington Press, 1962),

pp. 197–227, are two examples of how the structure of Chinese American communities has been described in organizational terms.

17. The fact that, historically, certain underworld figures and organizations controlled some of the most lucrative businesses in Chinatown (gambling, prostitution, narcotics) and wielded a great deal of coercive power through their employment of "highbinders" (gangsters) makes it very difficult to do a definitive study of the power structure and class structure of Chinese-American communities.

18. William Hoy, *The Chinese Six Companies* (San Francisco, Ca.: Lawton R. Kennedy, 1942), gives a brief official history of the Chinese Six Companies. The real name of the association is the Chinese Consolidated Benevolent Association. It was formed by the merger of six (and at times seven or eight) district associations. The Chinese Six Companies mediated disputes, acted as community spokesman, organized mutual aid efforts, and hired legal counsel to fight all anti-Chinese legislation.

19. There have been numerous studies of village China. One which deals specifically with a village in Kwangtung is Daniel H. Kulp, *Country Life in South China* (New York: Columbia University Press, 1925). For an interesting discussion of the relationship between class and clan in Kwangtung province see Frederick Wakeman, Jr., *Strangers at the Gate* (Berkeley, Ca.: University of California Press, 1966), pp. 109–116.

20. Alexander Saxton, *The Indispensable Enemy: Labor and the Anti-Chinese Movement in California* (Berkeley, Ca.: University of California Press, 1971), p. 52.

21. Ibid.

22. California Statutes, 1880: 123; 1893: 215; 1901: 56; 1915: 57; and 1917: 668.

23. For brief dicussions of Chinese-owned manufacturing companies, see Ping Chiu, *Chinese Labor in California, 1850–1880: An Economic Study* (Madison, Wisc.: State Historical Society of Wisconsin, 1967), pp. 89–128, and Chinn, Lai and Choy, *A History of Chinese in California*, pp. 49–56.

24. California Statutes, 1880: 39.

25. Ibid., 1913: 206. In addition to California, ten other states passed Alien Land Laws: Arizona (1917), Louisiana (1921), New Mexico (1922), Idaho (1923), Montana (1923), Oregon (1923), Kansas (1925), Utah (1943), Wyoming (1943) and Arkansas (1943).

26. While Chinese workers were paid lower wages than white workers, it should be remembered that the Chinese immigrants did not necessarily think of themselves as "cheap labor." California had higher wages than the eastern states. Chinese laborers in California often earned higher wages than white workers in other parts of the country, and, of course, they earned higher wages than their compatriots in China.

27. Examples of California state legislation which attempted to control Chinese immigration (a *national* matter) were: California Statutes,

1858: 295; 1872: 970; 1874: 979; 1877: 1056; 1884: 6; 1885: 232; 1889: 572; 1891: 185; 1893: 144; and 1901: 940. After 1905, state legislation and resolutions were directed at Japanese immigration.

28. Ibid., 1880: 22.

29. Ibid., 1885: 99; 1891: 160; 1893: 253; 1903: 86; 1909: 903; 1917: 667; 1921: 1161; and 1927: 308. For an excellent study of school segregation in California, see Charles Wollenberg, *All Deliberate Speed: Segregation and Exclusion in California Schools, 1855-1975* (Berkeley, Ca.: University of California Press, 1976).

30. Local municipal ordinances were the most common form of legal harrassment. For a study of anti-Chinese ordinances in San Francisco, see William J. Courtney, *San Francisco Anti-Chinese Ordinances, 1850-1900* (San Francisco, Ca.: R & E Research Associates, 1974).

31. California Statutes, 1855: 194.

32. Chinn, Lai and Choy, *A History of Chinese in California*, p. 24.

33. European immigrants living in the large urban centers secured some rights for themselves through the casting of bloc votes. Ward bosses controlled and were able to deliver bloc votes to politicians, many of whom were associated with city political machines. Since Chinese immigrants did not have the franchise, politicians ignored them and even found them to be easy scapegoats.

34. Charles I. Bevans, "Treaties and Other International Agreements of the United States of America, 1776-1949," *Department of State Publications*, vol. 6 (Washington, D.C., 1970), p. 683. (Article VI, Treaty of Peace, Amity, and Commerce, signed at Washington, July 28, 1868, supplements treaty of June 18, 1858.)

35. Chinn, Lai and Choy, *A History of Chinese in California*, p. 25.

36. U. S., Congress, Act of May 6, 1882 (22 Stat. 58).

37. Stuart C. Miller, *The Unwelcome Immigrant: The American Image of the Chinese, 1785-1882* (Berkeley, Ca.: University of California Press, 1965).

38. Coolidge, *Chinese Immigration*.

39. Saxton, *Indispensible Enemy*, p. 52.

40. Michael Reich, "The Evolution of the United States Labor Force," in *The Capitalist System: A Radical Analysis of American Society*, ed. R. C. Edwards and M. Reich (New York: Prentice-Hall, 1972), p. 175. (Table 4-J).

41. U. S., Congress, Senate, *Congressional Record*, 47th Congress, 1st sess., 1882, p. 1487.

42. Ibid., p. 1546.

43. The first American ship to sail directly from New York to China was the *Empress of China*. She set sail in 1784 with a cargo of ginseng, and returned fifteen months later, making a profit of over $30,000. Her supercargo, Major Samuel Shaw, was appointed in 1786 as the first American merchant-consul in China. There were two "streams" in the American China trade: one originating on the East coast, with New York, Philadelphia and Salem dominating the trade (Boston lagged

behind in developing the China trade), and one originating on the northwest Pacific coast. The latter trade carried furs supplied by trappers in the northwestern territories, and sandalwood obtained in Hawaii. It is interesting to note that the War of 1812 gave the China trade a boost. After the war, Great Britain kept American vessels out of the West Indies. Thus, American merchants showed an escalated interest in seeking new areas of trade, and the China trade proved to be the most lucrative. American military presence in China first appeared in the form of a naval vessel in Chinese waters in 1819. For studies of the early period of the China trade, see Part I of Tyler Dennett, *Americans in Eastern Asia* (New York: Macmillan Co., 1922), and Foster R. Dulles, *The Old China Trade* (Boston, Mass.: Houghton Mifflin Co., 1930). The latter has been criticized for being a popularized, romanticized work. The opium trade, as part of the American China trade, has been described in Charles C. Stelle, "American Trade in Opium to China Prior to 1820," *Pacific Historical Review* 9, no. 4 (December 1940): 425–444; Charles C. Stelle, "American Opium Trade to China, 1821–1839," *Pacific Historical Review* 10, no. 7 (March 1941): 47–74; and Jacques M. Downs. "American Merchants and the China Opium Trade, 1800–1840," *Business History Review* 42, no. 4 (Winter 1968): 418–442. For the role played by American consuls in promoting American commerce in China, see Eldon Griffin, *Clippers and Consuls: American Consular and Commercial Relations with Eastern Asia, 1845–1860* (Ann Arbor, Mich.: Edwards Brothers, 1938). The role of Chinese compradores has been analyzed in Yen-ping Hao, *The Comprador in Nineteenth-Century China: Bridge Between East and West* (Cambridge, Mass.: Harvard University Press, 1970). China's trade statistics may be found in Liang-lin Hsiao, *China's Foreign Trade Statistics, 1864–1949* (Cambridge, Mass.: Harvard University Press, 1974). The writings of John King Fairbank are especially sensitive to the subordinate role played by the United States vis-a-vis Great Britain in China. See John K. Fairbank, *Trade and Diplomacy on the China Coast: The Opening of the Treaty Ports, 1842–1854* (Cambridge, Mass.: Harvard University Press, 1953), and his bibliographical essay, "America and China, 1840–1860," in *American-East Asian Relations: A Survey*, ed. Ernest R. May and James C. Thomson, Jr. (Cambridge, Mass.: Harvard University Press, 1972), pp. 19–33.

44. Bevans, *Treaties*, pp. 647–658, gives the text of the 1844 Treaty. For an analysis of the background to the signing of the treaty, see Te-Kong Tong, *United States Diplomacy in China, 1844–60* (Seattle, Wash.: University of Washington Press, 1964). See also Tyler Dennett, *Americans in Eastern Asia: A Critical Study of United States' Policy in the Far East in the Nineteenth Century* (New York: Macmillan Co., 1922), pp. 128–174.

45. Bevans, *Treaties*, pp. 659–670. Articles V, XIV and XXIV refer specifically to these three new privileges.

46. Ibid., p. 682. The right to emigrate and expatriate is contained in Article V.

47. Frederick W. Williams, *Anson Burlingame and the First Chinese Mission to Foreign Powers* (New York: Russell & Russell, 1912), presents a strong defense of Burlingame, and emphasizes that Burlingame undertook the mission at the request of the Chinese government because he was a humanitarian devoted to the promotion of international peace. Williams also points out that prior to his diplomatic career, Burlingame had been a strong critic of slavery while he served for three terms in the U. S. House of Representatives.

48. Bevans, *Treaties*, p. 686 (Article 1).

49. U. S., Congress, Senate, *Congressional Record*, 47th Congress, 1st. sess., 1882, pp. 1585, 1636.

50. Coolidge, *Chinese Immigration*, pp. 151–167, gives a detailed discussion of how the 1880 treaty was negotiated.

51. Tien-yi-Li, *Woodrow Wilson's China Policy, 1913–1917* (New York: Octagon Books, [1952] 1969), pp. 23–89, provides some general background to American policy in China during the 1911 Revolution period. American policy in China in the 1926–28 period is analyzed in Dorothy Borg, *American Policy and the Chinese Revolution, 1925–1928* (New York: Octagon Books, [1947] 1968), and Russell D. Buhite, *Nelson T. Johnson and American Policy toward China, 1925–1941* (East Lansing, Mich.: Michigan State University Press, 1969), pp. 38–60.

52. Charles Chan, "Chronology of Treaties and Major Federal Laws Affecting Chinese Immigration to the United States," in *The Life, Influence, and the Role of the Chinese in the United States, 1776–1960*, p. 20.

53. For an illustration of one such questioning session, see Tseng-Tsu Wu, ed., *"Chink!" A Documentary History of Anti-Chinese Prejudice in America* (New York: World Publishing Co., 1972), pp. 97–102. [This document was quoted by R. D. McKenzie, *Oriental Exclusion* (Chicago, Ill.: University of Chicago Press, 1928), pp. 53–57, and was taken out of a brief submitted as part of a writ of habeas corpus case, Case No. 6436.]

54. U. S., Congress, Senate, Commission on Industrial Relations, "Smuggling of Asiatics," *Final Report and Testimony Submitted to Congress by the Commission on Industrial Relations*, vol. VII, 64th Congress, 1st sess., 1916, Senate Document no. 415, contains the testimony of many officials of the immigration service. These hearings reveal the attitudes and perceptions of these officials. The Scott Act, Geary Act and McCreary Amendment were passed *prior* to these hearings, of course.

55. Chan, "Chronology of Treaties," p. 18; Chinn, Lai and Choy, *Chinese in California*, p. 27, and Coolidge, *Chinese Immigration*, p. 203.

56. For a discussion of the difficulties created by this regulation, see Coolidge, pp. 302–334, and Delber McKee, *Chinese Exclusion Versus the Open Door Policy, 1900–1906: Clashes Over China Policy in the*

Roosevelt Era (Detroit, Mich.: Wayne State University Press, 1977), pp. 28-36.

57. Coolidge, *Chinese Immigration*, pp. 226-233.

58. Act of July 7, 1898 (30 Stat. 750).

59. Chinese exclusion was applicable also in Puerto Rica and other U. S. possessions in the Caribbean. In the case of Cuba, the United States put exclusion into effect a few days prior to turning Cuba back to Cuban control, and the Cuban government, mindful of the power of intervention which the United States possessed, allowed the law to remain in effect.

60. McKee, *Chinese Exclusion*, pp. 31-32.

61. Ibid., pp. 68-69, and John W. Foster, "The Chinese Boycott," *Atlantic Monthly* 97, no. 1 (1906): 122-124.

62. Ben R. Tong, "The Ghetto of the Mind: Notes on the Historical Psychology of Chinese America," *Amerasia Journal* 1, no. 3 (1971): 1-31, represents a seminal attempt to deal with this question in a historical-psychological manner.

63. The anti-American Chinese boycott of 1905 has been analyzed in McKee, *Chinese Exclusion*; C. F. Remer, *A Study of Chinese Boycotts with Special Reference to Their Economic Effectiveness* (Baltimore, Md.: John Hopkins Press, 1933); Anthony Milnar, "Chinese-American Relations with Especial [*sic*] Reference to the Imposition of the Boycott, 1905-1906," (Ph.D. diss., Georgetown University, 1948); Margaret Field, "The Chinese Boycott of 1905," in *Papers on China*, vol. 9, East Asia Regional Studies Seminar (Cambridge, Mass.: Harvard University Press, 1955); Edward J. M. Rhoads, "Nationalism and Xenophobia in Kwangtung (1905-1906): The Canton Anti-American Boycott and the Lienchow Anti-Missionary Uprising," in *Papers on China*, vol. 15, East Asia Regional Seminar (Cambridge, Mass., 1961); and Shih-shan H. Ts'ai, "Reaction to Exclusion: The Boycott of 1905 and Chinese National Awakening," *The Historian* 39, no. 1 (1976): 95-110.

64. U. S., Department of Commerce, Bureau of the Census, "Chinese and Japanese in the United States, 1910," Bulletin 127 (Washington, D.C., 1914), Table 55, p. 30.

65. For a detailed analysis of the socioeconomic backgrounds of those persons in Kwangtung province who participated in the 1911 Revolution, see Edward Rhoads, *China's Republican Revolution: The Case of Kwangtung, 1895-1913* (Cambridge, Mass.: Harvard University Press, 1975). Rhoads shows that many members of the lower gentry remained in power after 1911.

66. The most prominent second generation Chinese-American organization is the Chinese-American Citizens Alliance (CACA; originally named Native Sons of the Golden State—an obvious attempt to counteract the racist activities of the Native Sons of the Golden West), which has fought consistently for the civil rights of Chinese Americans. Among other issues, CACA opposed the attempts to disenfranchise American-born Chinese Americans, and successfully brought about the repeal of

the Cable Act. The Cable Act provided that any female U. S. citizen, regardless of racial origin, who married an alien ineligible for citizenship (Asians) would lose her own citizenship. Second generation Chinese Americans also formed numerous recreational and sports clubs, including Chinese-American branches of national organizations such as the YMCA, YWCA, the Lions, and the American Legion. (The affiliation with the American Legion is ironic: the American Legion was in the forefront of the anti-Asian movement.)

67. McKee, *Chinese Exclusion*, p. 215.

68. Although China as a nation was not formally colonized by the European powers, China lost control over parts of her territory through the granting of concessions, foreign settlements, leased territories, special railway zones, and special status areas to the various foreign powers. Foreigners enjoyed extraterritoriality in these areas, organized their own police forces, administered justice, levied taxes and carried on business in the areas under their control. The International Settlement in Shanghai was administered jointly by several of the powers; within its borders, only non-Chinese "ratepayers" could vote. There were only a few thousand "ratepayers," and their decisions controlled the lives of nearly 700,000 people. Great Britain had six concessions (in Canton, Hankow, Chinkiang, Kiukiang, Tientsin and Newchwang), France had four concessions, as did Japan. Italy, Belgium, Germany, Austria-Hungary, Japan, and Russia also had concessions. In addition to the concessions, the foreign powers had leased territories on which they established military bases. Foreign railway companies (such as the Sino-Russian North Manchuria Railway Company, the Japanese South Manchuria Railway Company, and the French Yunnan Railway Company) exercised control over the territory on each side of their railway lines. The companies collected taxes and had their own postal communications and armed patrol. In the Foreign Legation Quarter in Peking, the foreign powers had set up garrisons. Moreover, the Chinese were not allowed to erect buildings in the zone surrounding the Legation Quarter. At the turn of the century, it appeared that the dismemberment of China was imminent. That was why China could not afford to antagonize the United States.

69. In particular, General Joseph W. Stilwell, commander of the China-Burma-India theater during World War II, had problems with Chiang Kai-shek. For some intimate glimpses of Stilwell's experience in China, see Theodore H. White, ed., *The Stilwell Papers: General Joseph W. Stilwell's Iconoclastic Account of America's Adventures in China* (New York: Schocken Books, 1972); Barbara W. Tuchman, *Stilwell and the American Experience in China, 1911–1945* (New York, 1972); and John F. Melby, *The Mandate of Heaven: Record of a Civil War, China, 1945–1949* (Toronto: University of Toronto Press, 1968).

70. Chan, "Chronology of Treaties," p. 22.

71. For an analysis of crime in Chinatown in historical and political perspective, see Paul Takagi and Tony Platt, "Behind the Gilded

Ghetto: An Analysis of Race, Class and Crime in Chinatown," *Crime and Social Justice* (Spring-Summer, 1978): 2-25.

72. U. S., Department of Health, Education and Welfare, Office of Special Concerns, "Asian Americans," *A Study of Selected Socio-Economic Characteristics of Ethnic Minorities Based on the 1970 Census,* vol. II (Washington, D.C., 1974), Table G-5, p. 130, shows that in the U.S. as a whole, 8 percent of the population live in substandard housing, whereas 20 percent of the Chinese-American population live in substandard housing. 4 percent of the total population live in houses without complete plumbing, while 10 percent of the Chinese-American population live in houses without complete plumbing. In San Francisco, fully 24 percent of the Chinese-American population live in substandard housing, compared to a figure of 6 percent for the San Francisco general population. In New York, 30 percent of the Chinese-American population live in substandard housing, compared with 10 percent of the general population. Due to the poor housing conditions, the rate of tuberculosis among Chinese-Americans living below poverty levels is extremely high.

73. For two analyses of the factors contributing to low wages among Chinese-American workers, see Dean Lan, "Chinatown Sweatshops," in *Counterpoint: Perspectives on Asian America*, ed. Emma Gee (Los Angeles, Ca.: University of California Press, 1976), pp. 347-358; and Ivan Light and Charles C. Wong, "Protest or Work: Dilemmas of the Tourist Industry in American Chinatowns," *American Journal of Sociology* 80, no. 6 (1975): 1342-1368.

Edwin Clausen

Pluralism or Class: "Success" and Former American-Educated Students in the United States

Two recent studies funded by the Carnegie Council on Children give new life to the controversy over what determines a person's social, economic, and political position in American society.[1] These works investigate the importance of the environment in which a person lives in determining that person's future. The authors conclude that minorities are often condemned to a continued life of poverty, unemployment, and political impotency because that is the environment which America forces upon them by virtue of its institutional and structural design. Such has been the case for many Chinese Americans and Chinese immigrants.

Chinese immigrants and Chinese Americans have historically suffered greatly in the United States and, despite some recent statements to the contrary,[2] they generally continue to bear the burdens of social, economic, and political oppression. Yet there is a group of Chinese who have achieved prominence and professional standing in America. Many of these people came to the United States immediately after the liberation of China in 1949. Most of the studies that focus on these people are superficial, presenting "success" stories of little analytical insight. These studies fail to investigate in any depth the relationship of the immigrants' background to their "success" in this society. This article attempts to do just that: to study their social and economic background in an attempt to determine if there is a correlation between their life in China and their life in the United States. In determining if there is such a correlation, the article questions whether cultural pluralism exists in the United States.

Prelude to Exclusion: Chinese Students and
America, 1900–1920

Perhaps the most famous Chinese to study in the United States prior to 1949 was Hu Shih. As Hu prepared to leave the United States in 1917 there was little doubt in his mind that his American education would enable him to play a significant role in China's future: "You shall know the difference now that we are back again."[3] This optimism was characteristic of students who came to the United States for education. These students expected to assist the nation in solving what they considered its fundamental problem: saving China (*chiu-kuo*) from national extinction (*wang-kuo*).[4] By 1917 over half a century of imperialist challenge had forced many Chinese intellectuals and students to look to the West in search of a solution to imperialism. Many found in the United States what they thought was the answer.[5]

Paradoxically, residence and education in the United States heightened their sense of purpose but also produced a sense of ambivalence. Hu Shih expressed this uncertainty most succinctly. He had become attached to his American friends and life; he was joyous to return to China but unhappy to leave the United States.[6] Like Hu Shih, many of the students were attracted to life in America. They remembered such things as the "performance of *A Midsummer Night's Dream* among the oak groves on campus [that] was really a masterpiece of beauty. Youth, love, beauty, and joy of life were all vividly portrayed in the pleasant masquerade."[7] They were awed and inspired by the material achievements they witnessed in such cities as New York. The magnitude of the city and its diversity stirred feelings of admiration and respect. The skyscrapers, the rapid circulation of subways and elevated trains, the "dazzling lights of moving advertisements on the tops of tall buildings; the theatres, night clubs, hotels, and restaurants," all contributed to the effect of the city upon the young students.[8]

While the physical environment of the country affected the students, the intellectual climate had even more impact. This intellectual atmosphere—sometimes inseparable from the general surroundings, as in the case of one student—created a "new mood of vibrant and unshakable optimism."[9] Americans, this student believed, manifested a "naive optimism and cheerfulness" that led him to believe that "in this land there seemed to be nothing which human intelligence and effort could not achieve."[10] The experience of these students was often deepened because they became engrossed in much of American life and culture. They participated in sports, debated, gave public lectures, participated in political debates, won coveted scholastic awards, mingled with community members, and interacted with inspiring mentors who seemed to represent the essence of their college experience: "The spirit of self-reliance prevailed in the college and other schools of the university. . . . There was total academic freedom in Columbia at that time. The professors prized independent thinking and often criticized current abuses and corruptions in society and politics."[11]

In the first twenty years of the twentieth century students developed a cosmopolitan attitude towards life and other people.[12] This worldliness and what many perceived to be an environment of individual freedom within an ordered and legal society were to be crucial ingredients in their proposals for China's future. America provided an example of "liberty within the orbit of the law and freedom of thought and speech within the domain of reason. . . . Great industries, international banking and big business, and the utilization of invention, engineering, and material resources to the fullest extent, all showed the spirit and application of Americanism."[13] Although certainly not desiring a transplanted America, many of these early twentieth-century students drew upon their American experiences for examples of how to "save China."

Many of these students preached that China needed a "transvaluation" before it could become an equal of the other nations of the world. Many also believed the success or failure of this transformation of China hinged on education, for only through the development of a proper education system could China alter its traditional patterns and solve what they believed to be its central problem: "China is more than two thousand years old. It is a society that does not meet modern needs."[14] Although the cataclysmic events of the May Fourth Movement introduced political confrontation and activism into China's search for parity with the West, most of these students trained in the United States continued avoiding political questions[15] and especially political confrontation, while advocating a cultural transformation with "education . . . as . . . the foundation of the era."[16]

Many of the students trained in the United States during the years 1916–23 and later in the 1930s and 1940s argued for a democratic, liberal, and scientific China. American-trained students of these periods stressed the liberation of the individual from the burdens of the past. Many of them hoped their ideas for China's future would become reality through education. But their experiences in the United States and the influence of their American professors taught them that this education should be politically neutral.[17] While some students who studied in the United States later became vocal and scathing critics of democracy and individualism, most maintained a commitment to these goals.[18] Most believed that individualism was the source of the West's strength and that it was the means by which Chinese could escape being "trapped by history."[19] The opening issue of New Tide (Hsin ch'ao), an important source for debate on how to make China "progressive," proclaimed this spirit: "Real learning produces individuality and independence. . . . Through this magazine we hope to fight for spiritual emancipation."[20]

Although many of these intellectuals warned against blind imitation of the West and of the United States in particular,[21] they did counsel that for "spiritual emancipation" it was necessary for China to develop an environment in which individualism flourished as a means of freeing people and of forming a strong and democratic nation.[22] Frequently citing John Dewey, under whom many of the most influential had studied, they proclaimed that for China to become a "modern" society, the individual, not military power, had to be the source of the society's puissance.[23] The individual was exalted as the wellspring of a democratic society and hence of national strength and unity. The development of a sense of individualism and democracy, in turn, had to come through education. Education was presented as the means of achieving a "thought" revolution. This "thought" revolution was at the essence of these intellectuals' solution to China's impotency in face of imperialism. They believed that only through education and the complete transformation of people's thoughts could China undergo the necessary cultural change that would eventually take China out of the past and into contemporary life.[24]

In 1919, at the Versailles Conference, Japan's territorial designs on China became clear. Nationalistic sentiment poured forth in China, and politics and activism dominated student activity. Many of the American-trained intellectuals eschewed political activism, maintaining that China must continue to undergo a cultural revolution, which was crucial to its eventual transformation and salvation.[25] Some of these people even maintained that the May Fourth Movement constituted a "setback" to the New Cultural Movement.[26]

These intellectuals considered the intrusion of politics into education inimical to the cultural transformation necessary for political and social transformations. They believed that culture gave rise to politics, not vice versa.[27] A cultural transformation had to precede other changes if China was to become a truly reformed society. The transformation had to be slow and gradual, based on an education system that was problem oriented, "practical," and nonideological. From the period of the May Fourth Incident in 1919 to the culmination of the Communist liberation in 1949, these people remained convinced that political activism and political control over education put the cart before the horse. Outbursts of nationalistic sentiment expressed through demonstrations and student activism were branded as excessive and ultimately harmful to the proper approach to China's development and transformation.

The May Fourth Movement heralded a new divergence of opinion among the intellectuals and students as to China's future. The disagreement was most pronounced between those who advocated a cultural transformation through nonideological, apolitical education and those who advocated the transformation of China through revolution. Later the American-trained students became alienated from the two major solutions to China's predicament: the revolution from the countryside and the counterrevolutionary reaction of the Nationalist government. Despite this division and alienation, the education system after 1920 was dominated by students who returned from the United States.[28] This control of the education system by American-trained students not only reflects the one area in which the United States exercised predominant influence in a brutalized China; it also fostered an environment in which many students continued to accept America as the source of inspiration for China's future. In the 1930s and 1940s these students were to develop values and attitudes which, when coupled with their class standing, alienated them from much of Chinese society and prepared them for life in the United States. As one such former student remarked,

> "I think my education, and especially my religion, alienated me from the Communists. My liberal democratic political beliefs and education set me apart from the Kuomintang. . . . I think that overall—a friend once commented to me upon this situation—that I am more apt to live in the United States than in China. In retrospect, I agree with him. It is not easy to say, but I would have had greater difficulty living in China under those two groups."[29]

Profiles in Alienation: The End of an Era

Research has suggested that many American-trained students were estranged in the 1930s and 1940s from the two parties that sought to reflect and direct China's future. Their backgrounds, education, fervent belief in "American-style" democracy and individualism, and desire to see professionalism divorced from politics combined to create a conflicting sense of hope and frustration. As one of them concluded, "we knew, or at least I knew, that we opposed both the Communists and the Nationalists. I only hoped that somehow my training would let me be of service. I had gone to America with self-confidence. I don't know—maybe I was overestimating what I would do. When I returned and worked for a little bit, I was really unhappy. What could I then do?"[30] Such comments reflect the end of an era in China's quest to regain its independence from foreign encroachment and to solve domestic problems that wracked China for close to a century. In many ways, both imperialism and China's response to that encroachment suggest a cruel irony. In the nineteenth century, students began to travel to the United States to acquire the training and knowledge to "save the nation." This education, combined with a particular social and economic background, ultimately alienated many of them from the two political groups that sought to direct China's destiny and from the peasant who was finally to determine that destiny. Subsequently, these students found that their American-influenced values and political beliefs were unacceptable in China. Many of them consequently immigrated to the United States, and their "success" in American society correlates with their backgrounds and beliefs.

In general, the social background of the students who studied in the United States is indicated by the fact that in the 1930s over 80 percent of the college students came from families of businessmen, officials, teachers, and other professionals.[31] Numerically, these university and college students constituted only .01 percent of the population. The annual cost of the education, even in the comparatively inexpensive government institutions, was equivalent to approximately five months' wages for a Shanghai textile worker. It was even further beyond reach of the average Chinese peasant. It would have cost the income from five and a half years of labor for the textile worker to put his child through a four-year missionary school.[32] The cost of education at the prestigious Christian schools was reflected in the taunts that they were "schools for the aristocracy" (*kuei-tzu hsueh-hsiao*) and that their converts "ate religion" (*chih-chiao*).[33]

This elitism was confirmed by a study of family life in Peking. The investigator reported that, in general, college professors' income was the highest of 283 families surveyed and that "the amount spent by these families for education of the children ... was proportionately commensurate with their higher incomes."[34] This type of background also characterized students who attended Tsinghua College (later Tsinghua University), one of China's most prestigious institutions prior to liberation. The college was the result of the return of the remainder of the indemnity paid to the United States as punishment for the Boxer Rebellion. A little song suggests the desirability of Tsinghua and the distance that was perceived by many to exist between the students of Tsinghua and those of other colleges. The song goes: "Peita boys are old; Shih-ta boys are poor; only Tsinghua boys are eligible suitors."[35]

The college was established as a two-year preparatory institution and was basically an American transplant to Chinese soil. Its students received grants to study in the United States. Few of the students that attended the college came from peasant families or those of urban workers. In a 1924 survey of the family heads of Tsinghau students, over 32 percent were government employees, almost 31 percent were educators, 13 percent were industrialists, and only 3.7 percent were farmers.[36]

Of the former American-trained students I polled, the vast majority attested to this elitism. The large majority of those who responded to my questionnaire characterized themselves as being either "atypical" or "somewhere in between" when compared with most Chinese in China prior to their immigration to the United States.[37] This information correlates with the fact that most people questioned indicated that they were from urban backgrounds.[38] Additionally, most respondents' families were financially more secure than the vast majority of Chinese. The great majority of respondents indicated that by Chinese standards their families were in the middle or upper classes.[39] Most indicated that their fathers were either employed in education, government, private business, or some combination of these three professions.[40]

As noted, students in general constituted an elite in China. Those who traveled to the United States for advanced education were an elite within that already select group. Their status tended to separate them from China's rural and urban working populations. This tendency was reinforced by their development of an essentially bourgeois attitude and, particularly, a belief in

American-style democracy and individualism. This development of a particular outlook and value system became especially pronounced in the 1930s and 1940s. Their attitudes and beliefs resulted in a lack of knowledge about peasants' lives and the issues that affected them. A heightened sense of individualism fostered overt and covert hostility toward the interests of the group that was to carry China's revolution. Although there were notable exceptions, such as James Yen, T'ao Hsing-chih, and Chang Fu-ling, many of these intellectuals manifested an attitude similar to that of Lin Yutang.[41] For Lin there was no quick, comprehensive solution to China's difficulties because each individual must find his own outlook on life and deal with his own particular problems: "What, then, is the human ideal? Can there be a universal human ideal? The answer is probably no. Every man must find his own philosophy. Every man has, in fact, his own philosophy, his attitude toward life. At least, every taxicab driver I know is a philosopher. . . . Each one has found life as he makes it."[42] Lin carried this individualist perspective further by concluding that life consists mainly of the enjoyment of oneself, of "having a haircut once in two weeks, or watering a potted flower, or watching a neighbor falling off his roof."[43]

Other intellectuals expressed similar beliefs, though not in such absolute terms. Hsu Chih-mo concluded that "I only know and believe in myself. In my mind, democracy is the universalization of individualism. The essence of real democracy is an individual's self-awareness and self-improvement."[44] Like Lin Yutang, he concluded from this belief in individualism that "the memory of beauty is the most precious possession of man and the instinct to appreciate beauty is the key to heaven."[45]

Students trained in the United States also had a penchant for urban living. The tendency to gravitate towards cities is now well documented, and those individuals that I surveyed reflected this pattern.[46] Over 80 percent of them indicated that when they were living in China they preferred living in large cities.[47] Their urban background at home, their city life-styles in the United States, the fact that most major colleges and universities were located in large cities, especially Shanghai and Peking, their attraction to a cosmopolitan environment and life-style, and their belief that "progressive trends" developed most clearly and rapidly in the cities where intellectual and social diversity "flourished," made life in other environments less desirable, if not unbearable.[48] One former student I interviewed summed up why he considers himself to be atypical of most Chinese and why he prefers living in the city:

> I was sort of a middle-class boy. I went to high school and it was
> private. . . . I did this as most of the young Chinese men and women
> would like to have done. Of course, most of them were not able
> to go to school and that is why, if you consider the whole popula-

tion, I belong to the minority group. The majority did not have the chance to go to school. So when I said typical, I was referring to a very small circle of peers who basically followed a similar pattern. And perhaps equally important I lived in Nanking which was the capital and it was full of highly educated and select people. . . . I wanted to live there because it was exciting and offered the opportunities.[49]

Most people I surveyed were from families with additional members competent in English and educated in "foreign-sponsored or foreign-located institutions." Most of those institutions were American-oriented or located in the United States. The families expressed some or much dissatisfaction with their life in China, felt less sophisticated than Westerners or Western nations, held positive attitudes toward Americans, and believed that Americans perceived Chinese in a positive fashion.[50]

The backgrounds of the students I sampled and interviewed reflected not only common values and hopes for China's future but also a disillusionment that gradually developed as they experienced life in the United States or attempted to implement their beliefs in China. For these people, values, hopes for China's future, and disillusionment were interrelated. The majority of the people I questioned responded that they were either "somewhat dissatisfied" or "definitely dissatisfied" with their life in China.[51] During interviews with many of those who filled out my questionnaire, I received a variety of answers as to why this discontent developed. Perhaps one person expressed most clearly a consensus of opinion when he concluded: "How could I feel satisfied? Sure I was comfortable and was having a first-class education, but look at the political situation and the war. The Japanese had almost destroyed China and the two parties fought each other. I was more of a liberal democrat—what future was there for me? And I realized at that time that my hope for China's future was dim."[52]

Much of the discontent arose over the issue of whether politics should influence education. Most of the people I surveyed believed that education was the cure for China's ills.[53] This education, they believed at the time, had to be apolitical and should determine China's future. China should not change through "political revolution."[54] They also believed that "the purpose of education was to create highly trained people responsible to the integrity of their profession and as free from political debates and government regulation as possible."[55]

This desire for the separation of politics and education was also indicated by the fact that the majority questioned said that they felt that educators should "rarely" or "never" be active in political matters. With regard to political discussions, an even larger majority indicated that they believed that educators should be actively involved at least occasionally. Yet a large percentage felt that even political discussion should be entered into "rarely" or "never."[56]

Many of the questions I asked during my interviews with these former students concerned their reflections upon their life in China prior to taking up residence in the United States. We spent much time discussing whether at the time they considered themselves to "have been uneasy with the Nationalist Party and the Chinese Communist Party and their plans, as [the interviewees] perceived them, for China's future." Although there were some reservations, most responded that indeed the parties were distinct and that they, the interviewees, were not very happy with either party or their plans for China.

This estrangement was often subtle and complex. As one person explained, his discontent developed slowly, out of a concern for China and the failure of the Kuomintang to put promises into practice:

> But at that time—the Sino-Japanese War—there was cooperation
> between the Nationalists and the Communists, and I did not feel
> that it was wrong to join the Communist party, although I did not
> agree with it. Yet, I told you that even I intended to go to Yenan.
> So at that time I did not have the feeling that the Communists were
> enemies. . . . Yet quite frankly at that time we did not have great
> faith in the Nationalists because they did not solve many of the
> problems that we worried about. And they tended to interfere in
> things and to exercise control and allow no freedoms.[57]

The complexity of the situation and the impact of Western encroachment in China on these intellectuals' position was outlined by another former student. He believed that liberals, like himself, were caught in the middle and that no matter which side was victorious, their desires for China would never be satisfied. In the late 1930s this student had professors who attempted to conduct "liberal discussions criticizing certain ways of the government— what the government was doing. I recall one of them was jailed and I never saw him again. This impressed me very much."[58] This interviewee related that these intellectuals were

> not Communists. But like me, eventually they desired educational
> freedom and felt that a democratic situation should exist. But we
> also realized that the nation had serious problems that were not
> being solved and therefore we liked to make criticisms. . . . But to
> do that was labeled rebellious and could get a person into serious
> personal trouble. We did not like the Communists either. . . . Per
> haps it was because of the impact of our American-like education
> and we favored education and liberal reform."[59]

Another person reflected this sense of alienation clearly when he concluded that

> the failure to introduce democracy during the Sun-Chiang periods
> was the tragedy of China. And people like me are partly to blame
> because we were apart from many Chinese and we did not under-
> stand that politics were necessary. We believed in education and in
> democracy, but these were empty ideas because education was
> political and democracy for us did not always mean democracy
> for many Chinese.[60]

For many such alienated students and former students, the final solution to their dilemma was to immigrate to the United States. Rejecting the revolutionary transformation of China that surged forth from the countryside, as well as an exiled life on Taiwan under the Nationalists, these people believed that the United States offered a climate conducive to their political and social beliefs and a place where they would be able to work in professions commensurate with their education and skills. Imperialism turned paradoxically upon itself. The "Americanization" of China's education system did not result in a liberal and capitalist China, but rather produced an elite that no longer fit the new social and political context. Their values and beliefs, which rendered them ineffectual in China, enabled them to function quite well in the United States.

Reflections on "Success": Life in the United States

Almost all of the former students I surveyed are content with their lives in the United States. For instance, over 94 percent of the people who responded to the questionnaire indicated that they are "at home in the United States."[61] This feeling of attachment was bolstered by their overwhelming belief that their life in the United States is happier than it was in China.[62] Similarly, 95.4 percent signified that they are materially and economically content,[63] while 90.6 percent felt that they are either "totally acculturated and partici-patory" or "generally acculturated and participatory."[64] These same people also feel that the United States is the "most politically, socially, and economi-cally egalitarian nation in the world"[65] and that it is a "culturally pluralistic" nation.[66]

While many of these former American-trained students expressed discontent with their life in China, the statistics above make it clear that such was not the case for life in the United States. Much of their satisfaction with American life may be attributed to the influence of their specific social backgrounds. In other words, their training and social status make mobility in America more probable, compared with other Chinese of different experiences. All the people I questioned received advanced education, and most came from upper-middle- to upper-class families. Although their class and educational background may not have prepared them for participation either in a transforming or reactionary China, it certainly seems to have assisted them in America. For instance, 95.6 percent of the people questioned indicated that at the time they decided to live in the United States, their employment coincided with their education training.[67] Further, 96.7 percent indicated that they are now employed in the profession for which they were trained.[68] Almost all of them are satisfied with their current employment.[69]

The influence of background upon their ability to enter professional circles in the United States was reflected in their comments in response to my questioning about why they believed they "are successful in the United States." One person emphasized the type of education he received prior to taking up permanent residence:

> The reason for my 'successfulness' is that I not only had a better
> education but one that cultivated values like Americans. I learned
> to believe that the individual was important and that it takes a
> certain system of politics for individualism. This is American
> democracy. This thought system may not have been completely
> conscious to me in China but it was there.[70]

Another person stressed socioeconomic conditions as the important reason for mobility in this society. He was careful to distinguish between his own background and that of those who came earlier or who now reside in Chinatown: "Well, for one thing I think it is because I belong to the new type of Chinese who are not in Chinatown, but rather who have come at a different level of society. . . . They came at a very low social and economic level and I think that has something to do with it."[71] This sense of being part of an elite was reiterated by others. Another individual concluded that by virtue of an advanced education, he was among a tiny minority in China and that the particular education not only made him part of an elite but made him more flexible in America. He stressed the differences between his experiences and those of past Chinese:

> Back in the 1870s very few Chinese who came to the United States
> had any skill at all. They did contribute to this country but as
> manual workers. There were some others like Yung Wing who came
> but they were a small number. . . . I came as a university graduate
> from a college with an American curriculum and ideas. We knew
> [American] traditions, the history, the geography, the government,
> and the legal system. . . . And because of this education we were one
> of millions and I was the only one from my town of 14,000 people
> to be able to complete a college education. And it was a special

education—very American. . . . This special education also fit with some changes in this country after 1943. Immigration laws changed and Americans became scared of the Communists. This really helped.[72]

While these former American-trained students are now quite happy with their life in the United States, they stressed that their perception of the United States did not always match reality. All had a certain view of America prior to coming here, either for study or for permanent residence. As one person explained, "it was a bit idealized, but this is quite true for all similar circumstances. People often have the oversimplified conception of a foreign system until they live under it."[73]

Another interviewee was much more specific in detailing her idealized view of the United States prior to her entrance into Vassar. The most serious discrepancy between what she believed and what she experienced involved white attitudes toward Black Americans. Her experience was made even more disturbing because of a conversation she had at the time with another Chinese student:

> Well, my parents had given me a rather idealized version of American democracy. Again, I had to find out it wasn't all that perfect as they had pictured it to be. When I arrived at Vassar, there were only two what at that time were called "Negro" students. One was very black. They both lived in my dormitory. Well, anyway, so they were very friendly and very nice people, and I became quite friendly, and we did things together and were seen very much in each other's rooms. And Vassar at that time, of course, was one of the very progressive colleges, and, in fact, I think that it shocked a lot of people that Vassar should admit black students at that time. And then nobody said anything to me about consorting with Blacks, until one day a Chinese girl who had graduated from Vassar the year before came back to visit, and so somebody said, "Here is the new Chinese student." So she came to my room, and I brought in my friends to meet her. Among them was one of the Black students. And so she sort of froze a bit. Then, after everyone left, she said "Let me tell you something. Don't consort with Negroes." I said, "What is wrong with Negroes?" She warned me that she might be accepted in the college, but when she leaves college she will be nowhere, and you don't want to be seen with her. Again, this was a great shock. I didn't listen to her. I thought, well of all things to learn from Americans, she learns this.[74]

Another person already knew of the plight of Black Americans, but believed Americans to be "happy and naive people." When he arrived he was pleasantly surprised to discover that the happy and naive view was an incorrect stereotype:

> Then when I came I realized that there were a lot of serious and
> capable people. If the country was full of naive people it would have
> been falling apart. Instead, it has become a great country. There are
> a lot of serious people, and people who are more moral than the
> Chinese. I think there is a moral force more powerful than that
> which is talked about by people with regard to China.[75]

Just as the people I questioned discussed disparities between their perceptions of the United States and the reality they experienced when first arriving in the country, all believed that life in America has changed them. As already noted, these people were prepared, psychologically and educationally, for life in the United States. Much of this preparation, often unconscious, centered around the maturation of their political beliefs and their hope that China would develop into a liberal democratic state with a capitalist economy. For one interviewee, life in America has strengthened this belief:

> I wanted China to be liberal and democratic. I felt that this was
> necessary for political freedoms. Now that I have been here for
> twenty years, I feel this even more. What I value most here is my
> political freedom. This is a change. In many ways I was not right
> in my hope for China, and I was abstract about what that freedom
> meant. Now I value it for personal and practical reasons.[76]

Another person felt that he was correct about the political system in the United States and his affinity with it prior to coming to the United States to live. For him the biggest change was an understanding of this country's religious diversity and richness—something he felt was lacking in his experience with Americans in China.

> I had many American teachers in China, but usually these teachers
> were missionaries. They always tried to inject the Bible and religious
> teachings into education. They were honest and good men but I dis-
> liked them because they tried to use teaching to introduce religion
> through the back door, so to speak. I was very uneasy about this.
> But when I came here to live I learned that although there is some
> religious prejudice, people do have the right to practice their own
> religion or even not to practice any. This changed my life, and I
> now am more tolerant of religion and religious beliefs.[77]

For another former American-trained student, the changes have been deep. He felt, in retrospect, that he was more prepared to live in the United States than in China under the Nationalists or the Communists, but his life

in this country has changed him in ways that were not even perceptible to
him until a recent trip to Taiwan and Singapore:

> I would like to mention a couple of things. I went back to Taiwan
> and Singapore to be among Chinese, and I found that my perception
> of life, my comments on person-to-person relations were so out-
> rageous as viewed by my relatives. Therefore my behavior in life, in
> human relations, must have changed to a substantial degree, without
> much self-knowledge of this change. Number two, I believe, for
> example, in a small family as opposed to the old Chinese concept of
> the extended family. I believe in educating the children to be on
> their own as opposed to the Chinese approach: taking the children
> under your own household and preserving the family name. I do not
> believe that can be arranged in a fast-moving society. I now also
> believe in giving consultation to your kids as a means of education,
> as opposed to disciplining them through the imposition of parental
> authority. . . . All of these perceptions and beliefs are changes. . . .
> Life as we live it here in America allows for so much individualism,
> self-perception, and self-management of your life. This is not
> possible in Taiwan or in the Chinese communities in Southeast
> Asia or in China. I feel that a person simply is not fulfilled in those
> places.[78]

As I have noted, most of these people consider themselves well adjusted
to American life and generally "acculturated and participatory." They also
feel that the United States is a culturally pluralistic society—a feeling reinforced by the fact that most identify themselves as Chinese Americans.[79]
Such identification is important for these people, for as one interviewee
expressed it: "I consider myself Chinese American because I am an American
citizen and believe in the way of life in the country. I owe this country a lot.
But my origin is Chinese. I consider the United States a miniature of the
United Nations. And I am one of the representatives here—from China."[80]

The fact that the United States is a nation of many cultural groups does
not lessen the concern felt by many of these people that they and their
children may lose much of their cultural heritage. Of those surveyed, 89.9
percent were either "somewhat" or "very" concerned that their family retain
ties to Chinese culture.[81] These people were at least moderately concerned
that their children would lose contact with Chinese culture and history.[82]
Additionally, a great percentage indicated that they either moderately or
greatly encourage their children to learn Chinese history and culture, while
an even greater percentage indicated that their children have studied or will
study Chinese language.[83]

Their concern that their families and children keep at least vestiges of their
heritage does not in any way give rise to ethnocentricity. In fact, the people I

surveyed seem to be much more tolerant, if not appreciative, of different ethnic and cultural groups than the society at large. The vast majority indicated that they would have no objection if their children had close friends of a variety of national, religious, or ethnic backgrounds.[84] They also indicated that they have no qualms about their children dating or marrying a non-Chinese person.[85] This lack of prejudice is given further statistical reinforcement in that a majority of the respondents indicated the following: three or more of their five closest friends are not Chinese; they feel equally comfortable with either Chinese or non-Chinese; their children's five closest friends are either all non-Chinese or Chinese and non-Chinese and the children are comfortable with both non-Chinese and Chinese children.[86]

The respondents feel that most Americans' attitude towards Chinese in the United States is either "very friendly" or "friendly."[87] This perception of the general attitude held by Americans towards Chinese seems to hold in specific situations. Over 95 percent of those who answered my questionnaire indicated that the attitude of fellow workers or those in their employ is "friendly" or "very friendly."[88] Of those who are not self-employed, the great majority believe that their employer, supervisor, department head, etc., treats them the same as other employees.[89]

Most surveyed believe in ethnic interaction and perceive Americans' attitudes toward them to be friendly. Yet there is a large discrepancy between how they feel Americans compare them to other Chinese in the United States and how they themselves see that comparison. Most indicated that Americans in general believe their families to be "typical" of most Chinese families in America, while the majority of those surveyed see themselves as different from most Chinese families.[90]

One interviewee believes that Americans consider his family to be different from most of the Chinese living in the United States. He explained his feelings, stressing the superficiality of the situation: "Only in a superficial way [do they see me as different], because generally they are not able to tell the important differences. However, most of the Chinese here tend to have a heavy accent. I do not. In fact, I hardly have one and they notice this. Also, since I was brought up among American missionaries, I think in some ways I am very much like Americans."[91] Most of the other people I talked with did not feel that Americans are even able to make such superficial distinctions. This position was clearly delineated by one man's explanation that

> most Americans do not make the distinction between two groups of Chinese. . . . The first have settled in this country for a long period of time, having come with a lower social, economic, and education background. That is the majority of the so-called overseas Chinese. Then you have group B with whom you are working. They repre-

sent, I would say, exactly the opposite in the Chinese social structure. Most of us came from the top because we were able to come as students to begin with, and that requires membership in a high social group in China.[92]

In an attempt to explain the difference between their views and those of Americans in general, one person stressed that Americans continue to see Chinese in terms of stereotypes. He feels that they are not yet sophisticated enough to recognize and understand the differences among Chinese in America. He explained that

> when I talk to most Americans their impression of Chinese is a group of laundry men, restaurateurs, and servants. Most of those people who came from Canton were poor peasants when they came here, and racism forced them to eventually accept and take jobs that helped worsen images. . . . Yet these people had great strength, as do many Chinese who now live in Chinatown. When I first came, as a person of education and higher status, I was a little snobbish and looked down upon these less educated people. I do not do this now, but most Americans do, and they don't know the differences between them and us and also how strong they are.[93]

Two of the above interviewees point to the differences in their background and current social standing as important for understanding the diversity of Chinese in the United States. Almost 100 percent of those surveyed indicated that they are different from the Chinese who live in Chinatowns.[94] Further, only 8.1 percent of those sampled feel that they are "very" aware of the problems facing Chinese who live in Chinatowns, while 47.7 percent indicated that they are "somewhat" aware. The remainder of the people signified that they are "barely" or "not at all" aware of the problems.[95] This sense of separation also is reflected in that 66.2 percent of the respondents either "rarely" or "never" spend time participating in the affairs of Chinatowns.[96] Additionally, they were asked to indicate if they could identify Dennis Kearney or the Rock Springs incident. 87.5 percent could not identify Kearney, while 79.5 percent were unable to identify the Rock Springs incident.[97]

This gulf between groups of Chinese was discussed during the interviews. Most interviewees believe that the chasm developed out of the different historical circumstances which shaped the two groups and their responses to American society. These forces were primarily social and educational in nature. After discussing regional differences, one person expressed his belief that many Chinese who came in the nineteenth century and who come from Hong Kong today are of much different social, economic, and educational backgrounds than people like myself. I came from a family that had some money, and our social position was better. We also had much more contact with Western and mostly American ideas through the education system. This was reinforced when I came to America. The same was true for some other members of my family. When I came to live in the United States, I was more prepared for life here than the person who is of a lower class and therefore has generally not had this type of education. There is discrimination here, at all levels, but the difference in whether you make it or not is due more to social and economic factors than to race—especially in the second half of this century. As a result of these differences in our experiences in China, we do not associate with each other very much here. The separation does exist and it is because of social positions that started in China and continue here. People need to understand this.[98]

These people's professional status in the United States makes it difficult for them to develop close ties with Chinese of much different backgrounds. One person recalled,

I attended several times a Chinese mass. There all Chinese attended, but they were of varied social and educational backgrounds. Among the various social groups there was very little in common. I left and thought that there simply was no common interest. I would rather be with someone with shared interests because we can talk and have things in common. With people of less education and not in professions, it is difficult to do anything. . . .[99]

The same sentiment was echoed by almost all the people I interviewed. I asked all the interviewees if they felt that Chinese in the United States share a common cultural and ethnic heritage and whether this in some way gives them a sense of common experience that makes it easy for them to identify with one another. One person agreed, maintaining that it is not easy for him to be in a situation in which most people are not Chinese: "When I go to a party with Anglo-Saxons I have to watch what they are interested in, what kind of conversations they would like to carry on, and I have to share their jokes which I may not really enjoy. They want to talk about cars, football, baseball, etc. I am not interested in them. When Chinese get together we have much more in common."[100] This type of observation was not the typical response. More common was the viewpoint expressed by another individual:

I feel that the important thing is common background and interest— at least for me. Most people think that just because two people are Chinese they automatically have something in common. Why? If a person is a prominent businessman or a university professor, what does he have in common with a plumber or a cook, even if all have the same cultural or ethnic heritage? People who say this about Chinese are making something that does not exist.[101]

Another person was even more explicit in his answer, concluding that common heritage is not significant because of class differences and differences in historical experiences:

Yes, we come from China or are of Chinese ancestry. But that is where the similarity ends. I am not looking down on Chinese of less fortunate backgrounds when I explain this. I want that to be understood. But I am from the basically upper-middle class in this society, and I was in relative terms in China. I have much education and have not faced the economic problems of many who live in Chinatown or in poor conditions in Hong Kong. Although I have encountered racism in the form of stupid stereotypes, I have not faced the kind like the others have. How can people say we are similar? Naturally I have sympathy for them and would do what I can, but we do not identify with each other—isn't that what you asked?[102]

Despite the fact that these former American-trained students noted the gap between their experiences in China and in America and those of Chinese who live in Chinatown, all feel that racism is readily apparent today in American society. Most see this racism, as it affects Chinese Americans, as in part perpetuated by television and movies. They believe that neither portrays Chinese correctly, and most cite the continual presentation of stereotypes as the reason.[103] At the same time, these people generally indicated that they have not had difficulty obtaining employment in the United States; for those who indicated that they had such difficulty, only 47.8 percent said that it was because of discrimination.[104] On the other hand, most indicated that at one time or another they had some difficulty buying or renting a place to live for reasons not related to finances.[105]

One interviewee agreed that there was racial prejudice in the United States, but in his opinion it is surmountable and much less serious than in some other countries. He believes that

prejudice is inevitable—everybody has it. But the important thing is not racial background, but understanding and environment. Many Chinese have trouble communicating. Their English is not adequate, therefore there are bound to be misunderstandings. They need to improve that. Second, your social, economic, and educational background is important. I am a heck of a lot better off than many white people—many of them are tied by poverty. The same is true for minorities. This is difficult, because to overcome these obstacles is much harder than language. But it can be done.[106]

Most of the others I talked with agree that racism and discrimination exist, but find its roots to be deeper. For instance, another former student concluded that

> whenever you come to ethnic issues, you will take a long, long time
> for people to understand and tolerate. . . . One day for people to
> feel no difference—the idea of brothers and sisters and yet still
> retain cultural backgrounds—that is a long way off. Before that day
> we will continue to have social injustice, strife, discrimination.[107]

Generally, the people I surveyed believe in liberal methods that attempt to eliminate discrimination and racism. They believe that the government should make sure that there is no discrimination in housing and that schools are integrated.[108] They also disagree that private clubs, associations, etc., have the right to exclude membership on the basis of national, religious or ethnic background.[109] These people do not agree with the statement that "if minorities fail to achieve and end discrimination by peaceful and 'rational' means, they have the right to demonstrate and perhaps to violent confrontation."[110]

One interviewee believes that to end discrimination and racism, a combination of actions must be taken. He tended to emphasize the importance of economic disparity and the need to reduce great differences in wealth:

> I should say that I think the United States has made strides towards
> eliminating discrimination and racism. There is of course the need
> for the legislature to at least provide the legal framework within
> which discrimination would be unacceptable. Education can be a
> powerful tool to fight racism, and some steps have been taken in
> that direction. . . . But in the final analysis minority groups can
> only change with improvement of their socioeconomic status. This
> has both an obvious material advantage for the minority—and that
> makes it hard to do because those that have it want to keep it—
> but also a psychological one too. Americans do not care so much
> about the source of wealth as they do about the volume of in-
> come. . . . They respect wealth. Now of course the situation is a kind
> of chicken or egg situation. Peoples' ideas about minorities and
> minorities' economic position are tied together.[111]

Education was by far the most frequently cited solution to the problem of discrimination and racism. Many of the American-trained students believed while in China that their American education would be the means by which they would "save" China. This education was to be apolitical and designed to produce a person bound to the idea of professionalism as free from politics. They believed that "the ills of China would be cured if everyone were educated."[112] Although their faith in education waned somewhat during their residence in the United States, many still believe that "most of the ills in the world would be eliminated if everyone were educated."[113] They specifically indicated that social improvement comes through either education alone or through education in conjunction with democratic processes.[114] One interviewee explained his view of the solution to racism and discrimination: "The whole matter is the education. This provides the tools necessary for minorities to advance and help themselves and maybe this would help society in general understand its problems."[115] Another person explained the situation this way: "Education helps break down stereotypes and changes the mental picture of minorities held by whites. This has to begin young and continue throughout the education process. Everything must be done to be sure that minorities are properly pictured in the classroom and in books."[116]

While the majority of people questioned and interviewed express faith in the ability of education to solve specific and general social problems, they do not believe politics has any place in education. They indicate that government should be able to prevent discrimination in the education system.[117] But their responses to other questions indicate an aversion to the idea that politics should be part of or influence either education or educators and teachers. Most believe that people in education should be "apolitical except for voting."[118] The majority surveyed also believe that a person in education should "never" or "only sometimes" interject his or her personal or political opinion into a classroom situation.[119]

The demand that education be apolitical does not mean that these people feel that minorities should or must be inactive in causes that seek redress of grievances. Their thoughts about such activity are complicated, reflecting a blend of their liberal and class influences and their concern for minority rights. As mentioned earlier, they do not think that minorities necessarily have a right to demonstration or violent confrontation if "rational" means do not achieve correction of injustices. Yet these people expressed their belief that "we must owe a debt of gratitude to the Black people because they fought and therefore we get things—kind of fringe benefits. The same that applies to Blacks must apply to Asians. We truly owe Black people a lot."[120]

These people also believe that their views on political activism might not be shared by other Chinese of different backgrounds and ages. During the interviews, I asked them to respond to a quotation by Anna Chennault: "Some minority groups prefer to demonstrate and protest, but we Chinese are a more peaceful people. We prefer to work quietly and wait for recognition."[121] All generally accept it as true for them and their group, but they stress that this certainly is not the case for younger generations of Chinese or Chinese Americans. One such person stated that Chennault was behind the times. It might be so for people like me, but I do not know how she can say that about others. Some young Chinese either born here or who have recently come from outside feel that the social and political process is against them. They say that they are kept from education and in poor condition. They feel that action is needed to correct this, and because they see and experience the social injustices, they become involved in such things as 'yellow power.' Anna Chennault's view will be revised as people realize that these people are not going to remain quiet.[122]

For another person, such criticism of the statement is taken to another level by concluding that

personally, it is perhaps an adequate characterization for the early part of my life. But I have not remained so. I think it has to do with the level of success and one's social and economic position. When you have reached a certain level of success, you do not risk what you have got so far, but I think that at this point in time I can afford it. Further, for many Chinese in this country, they have nothing to lose from the start, so they protest and try to change things. Her view is old-fashioned, and I wonder if it was ever true.[123]

The people surveyed are not opposed to government activity in the lives of the people. Their pattern of thinking on this matter is similar to that held in China prior to coming to the United States. Most of the people who completed the questionnaire stated that when they were living in China, they would have disagreed with the idea that the best government is one that governs the least.[124] Approximately the same number currently disagree with the statement.[125] Similarly, a large percentage indicated that while in China they would have disagreed with the statement that government planning "results in the loss of essential liberties and freedoms."[126] Today, an equal percentage still disagree.[127]

Much of this "liberal persuasion" manifested by the respondents is demonstrated by answers to other questions. These people indicate that when they lived in China they would have disagreed with the statement that "only informed people should have the right to vote."[128] Today, even a larger percentage disagree with this statement.[129] Most of the people who responded to the questionnaire take a liberal position with regard to male-female relationships in society. For instance, 89 percent indicated that in China they would have disagreed with the idea that the husband should be the dominant person in a marriage. The same percentage would have disagreed that married women should not work outside the home.[130] Today, the percentage not agreeing with the idea that the husband should be the dominant partner is even higher, as is the number who disagree that a married woman should not work outside the home.[131] This liberal trend is currently reinforced by the fact that 90.1 percent support the Equal Rights Amendment, while 89.4 percent disagree with the statement that "no decent person can respect a woman or a man who has had sex relations before marriage."[132]

This study attempts to show the importance of social, economic, and educational background as a force in the determination of whether a minority will indeed have an equal chance for "success" in American society. It also suggests something about how Americans define success. While many of the people I surveyed and interviewed retain at least psychological ties to their Chinese heritage, their position in American society has not been a function of cultural pluralism. Indeed, their class background and their accommodation to the values and political norms of the society have been the determining factors.

Imperialism in China produced a cruel irony: American-educated Chinese in the 1930s and 1940s became estranged from their society and politically impotent. The background, economic status, and education that alienated them from Chinese society in turn helped them adapt and adjust much more easily to American society than other Chinese of different backgrounds. America has accepted these people, for they do not threaten the basic institutional structures of the nation. This "non-challenging" attitude on the part of these people and the forces that circumvent true cultural pluralism were best summed up by one interviewee: "I definitely think it is better to learn as much as you can before you come here and hopefully you will hold essentially the same values and maybe be of a better economic position. . . . You must accept the American way of life if you want to stay here. Now if you cannot, you had better go back because you will not feel happy."[133] The United States does not accept and appreciate cultural diversity because to do so would necessitate real structural and institutional changes. People of the "right" background and of the "right" values can maintain their position in the society. For the poor and for those who adhere, if only unconsciously, to their own cultural and political values, the society remains harsh and intolerant.

Notes

1. Richard de Lone, *Small Futures: Children, Inequality, and the Limits of Liberal Reform* (New York: Harcourt Brace Jovanovich, 1979) and John Ogbu, *Minority Education and Caste: The American System in Cross-Cultural Perspective* (New York: Academic Press, 1978).
2. Warren Burger, Chief Justice of the Supreme Court of the United States, made the statement that Asians in the United States have now overcome the burdens of racism. For one criticism of such a perspec-

tive, see E. H. Kim, "The Myth of Asian-American Success," *Asian American Review* 5 (1975): 122–145.

3. Hu Shih, *Hu Shih liu-hsueh jir-chi* (Taipei: Commercial Press, 1959), p. 1106.

4. For a discussion of this, see Joseph Chen, *The May Fourth Movement in Shanghai* (Lieden: E. J. Brill, 1971), pp. 20–30.

5. For a discussion of this process beginning in the middle nineteenth century, see Edwin Clausen, "Profiles in Alienation: To 'Save' China and the American Experience," (Ph.D. diss., University of California, Santa Barbara, 1979).

6. Hu, *Hu Shih liu-hsueh jir-chi*, p. 1147.

7. Meng-lin Chiang, *Tides from the West* (New Haven, Conn.: Yale University Press, 1947), p. 77.

8. Ibid., p. 87.

9. Jerome Grieder, *Hu Shih and the Chinese Renaissance: Liberalism in the Chinese Revolution, 1917–1937* (Cambridge, Mass.: Harvard University Press, 1970), p. 45. Also see Hu Shih, *Hu Shih liu-hsueh jir-chi*, p. 175, for an indication of this wave of confidence and optimism.

10. Hu Shih, "My Credo and Its Evolution," *Living Philosophies* (New York: Simon & Schuster, 1931), p. 251.

11. Jun-ke Choy, *The Reminiscences of Choy Jun-ke* (The Chinese Oral History Project, Columbia University, 1971), pp. 57–58.

12. For a brief discussion of the development of this outlook, see Clausen, "Profiles in Alienation," pp. 157–162.

13. Chaing, *Tides from the West*, p. 88.

14. Fu Ssu-nien, "Hsin Ch'ao fa-k'an chih-ch'u shu," *Hsin Ch'ao* 1, no. 1 (January 1919): 1.

15. For a clear description of the differences between the New Cultural Movement and the May Fourth Movement and the impact the latter had on the former, see Chen, *The May Fourth Movement in Shanghai*, pp. 1–32. Also see Jerome Grieder, "The Question of Politics in the May Fourth Period," in *Reflections on the May Fourth Movement: A Symposium*, ed. Benjamin Schwartz (Cambridge, Mass.: Harvard University Press, 1972), pp. 95–101. For a warning about the "culturalists" versus the "political activists" during the May Fourth Period, see Charlotte Furth, "May Fourth in History," in Schwartz, p. 66.

16. *Hsin Chiao-yu*, 1, no. 1 (February 1919): 1.

17. For an elaboration, see Clausen, "Profiles in Alienation," pp. 165–177.

18. Examples of such were Ch'en Ch'i-t'ien, Ch'ien Tuan-shen, Chang Chin-chien, and Ch'en Chih-mai. Many such people eventually concluded that "China's current situation absolutely does not allow us time for old-fashioned Western thought. We should immediately abandon superstitions about democracy. . . . We need a government with centralized power that can produce the best talent that is efficient and competent." Quoted in Lloyd Eastman, *The Abortive Revolution: China*

Under Nationalist Rule, 1927–1937 (Cambridge, Mass.: Harvard University Press, 1974), p. 148.

19. Lin Yu-sheng maintains that the belief in individualism was not deep in philosophical content or in emotional attachment. Rather it was "used mainly because they could support and justify the iconoclastic movement," and that it "performed effective functions for the realization of nationalistic goals." Lin Yu-sheng, "Radical Iconoclasm in the May Fourth Period and the Future of Chinese Liberalism," in Schwartz, p. 25. This may have indeed been true of some intellectuals, but for many others, commitment to liberalism and individualism was deep and sophisticated. Naturally, the belief in individualism was bound to a particular intellectual's attachment to and interpretation of nationalism and his concern for the future of China. But this emerging nationalism did not obscure or lessen the desire to see individualism as a functional reality in China.

20. Fu Ssu-nien, "Hsin Ch'ao fa-k'an chih-ch'u shu," *Hsin Chiao-yu* (1 January 1919), pp. 2–3.

21. For such a warning see T'ao Hsing-chih, "Tui-yu ts'an yu kuo-chi chiao-yu yun-tung ti i-ch'ien," *Hsin chiao-yu* (March 1920), pp. 521–522.

22. Chiang Meng-lin, "Ko-jen chih chia-chih yu chiao-yu chih kuan-hsi," *Kuo-tu shih-tai chih ssu-hsiang yu chiao-yu* (Taipei: n. p. 1962), p. 53.

23. Chiang Meng-lin, "Shih-chieh ta chan hou wo kuo chiao-yu chih chu yao tien," *Chiao-yu tsa-chih* 10 (October 1918). Reprinted in Chiang, *Kuo-tu shih-tai chih ssu-hsiang*, pp. 143–145.

24. See Chen, *May Fourth Movement in Shanghai*, p. 16, for a discussion of the essence of the eventual cultural transformation of China.

25. Fu Ssu-nien, "Hsin ch'ao fa-kan chih-ch'u shu," *Hsin ch'ao* 2, no. 2 (December 1919): 370.

26. Hu Shih, "Wu-ssu ti ti-erh-shih-pa chou-nien," *Ta-kung pao* (4 May 1947), p. 1, and Hu Shih, *The Reminiscences of Dr. Hu Shih* (Chinese Oral History Project, Columbia University), p. 193.

27. Grieder, "The Question of Politics," in Schwartz, p. 98.

28. Clausen, "Profiles in Alienation," pp. 180–193.

29. Interview 2, Tape II, p. 38. This and all similar references pertain to seventy-five interviews that I conducted with Chinese who were educated at least in part in the United States in the 1930s and 1940s. Most of them live in the United States and a few in Hong Kong. The people who live in Hong Kong all resided for at least fifteen years in the United States and did not move to Hong Kong because of discontent with their life in the United States. The interviews were done from 1976–1978. A guarantee of anonymity was given to each interviewee, therefore citation will only carry an interview number, tape reference, and transcript page number.

30. Interview 18, Tape II, p. 41.

31. Wang Shih-chieh, "Education," in *The Chinese Yearbook, 1935–1936* (Shanghai: n.p. 1935–1936), p. 471.

32. John Israel, *Student Nationalism in China, 1927-1937* (Stanford, Conn.: Stanford University Press, 1966), p. 5.
33. Philip West, *Yenching University and Sino-Western Relations, 1916-1952* (Cambridge, Mass.: Harvard University Press, 1976), p. 137, and C. T. Hu, "On 'Tu' and 'Yang'," *Chinese Studies in History* (Summer 1974): 6-7. Also see West, pp. 138-140, for a clear description and cost breakdown for Yenching.
34. Sydney Gamble, *How Chinese Families Live in Peking* (New York: Funk & Wagnall, 1933), pp. 281-282.
35. Quoted from *T'ung-fang tsa-chih* 40, no. 11: 57, in Y. C. Wang, *Chinese Intellectuals and the West, 1872-1949* (Chapel Hill, N.C.: University of North Carolina Press, 1966), p. 114.
36. See Ts'ao Yung-hsiang, "The Way to Improve Tsinghua," in *Tsinghau hsueh-pao*, Tenth Anniversary Special Issue, 7. The figures came from Wang, *Chinese Intellectuals*, p. 154.
37. 75 percent so responded, with "atypical" accounting for 14.1 percent and "in between" for 60.9 percent.
38. 66.3 percent considered their families to be from urban backgrounds, while 4.3 percent indicated that their families were from both rural and urban backgrounds.
39. 91.3 percent indicated that their families were in the middle or upper classes. There were 23.9 percent who considered their families affluent. Figures adjusted for 1.1 percent missing cases.
40. Those who selected education did so 17.4 percent of the time, while 19.6 percent selected government. Business accounted for 10.9 percent. 19.6 percent indicated that their father was employed in more than one category, including government. Only 10.8 percent indicated that their fathers were connected in any fashion with agriculture. Of those, over 50 percent were large landowners. Figures adjusted for five missing cases.
41. Lin was educated both in the United States and in Germany.
42. Lin Yutang, *The Importance of Living* (New York, 1940), as quoted in Wang, *Chinese Intellectuals*, pp. 401-402.
43. Ibid.
44. From Wang Yao, *Chung-kuo hsin wen-hsueh shih-kao* (Peking: n.p., 1951), p. 74.
45. From Wang Che-fu, *Chung-kuo hsin wuen-hsuch yun-tung shih* (Peking: n.p., 1951), p. 109.
46. See Wang, *Chinese Intellectuals*, p. 163, and Jessie Lutz, "The Chinese Student Movement of 1945-1949," *Journal of Asian Studies*, 31, no. 1 (November 1971): 91.
47. 80.2 percent indicated they preferred living in cities.
48. For the college distribution, see Wang, *Chinese Intellectuals*, pp. 366-368, and Israel, *Student Nationalism*, p. 6.
49. Interview 30, Tape I, p. 6.
50. See Clausen, "Profiles in Alienation," for specific statistics and details, especially pp. 219-225. The students themselves also believed that

China was less sophisticated, had studied foreign languages, mostly English, and had teachers who were either foreign-trained or were foreigners (mostly American). Clausen, "Profiles in Alienation," pp. 230–237.

51. 53.3 percent of the respondents indicated that they were either "somewhat dissatisfied" or "definitely dissatisfied."

52. Interview 6, Tape I, p. 18.

53. 81.6 percent indicated that they would have agreed with the statement, "In my opinion, most of the ills of China would be cured if everyone were educated."

54. 89.9 percent believed so. Figure is adjusted for three missing cases.

55. 79.5 percent so indicated. Adjusted for four missing cases.

56. 52.3 percent so indicated for activity in political matters. For political discussions, 59.3 percent indicated "occasionally," while 40.7 percent indicated "rarely" or "never." Adjusted for six missing cases.

57. Interview 59, Tape II, p. 39.

58. Interview 38, Tape II, p. 40.

59. Ibid., p. 41.

60. Interview 32, Tape I, p. 14.

61. Adjusted for five missing cases.

62. Adjusted for six missing cases, with a percentage of 87.2.

63. Adjusted for five missing cases.

64. Adjusted for seven missing cases.

65. 82.1 percent indicated that they agreed with the statement. Adjusted for nine missing cases.

66. 71.6 percent so indicated. Adjusted for four missing cases.

67. Adjusted for two missing cases.

68. Adjusted for two missing cases.

69. Interview 53, Tape I, pp. 17–18.

70. Interview 71, Tape I, pp. 21–22.

71. Interview 10, Tape I, pp. 10–11.

72. Interview 53, Tape I, pp. 17–18.

73. Interview 1, Tape I, p. 32.

74. Interview 74, Tape II, pp. 35–36.

75. Interview 64, Tape I, p. 18.

76. Interview 44, Tape I, p. 3.

77. Interview 29, Tape I, pp. 8–9.

78. Interview 31, Tape I, pp. 25–26.

79. 89.9 percent as Chinese Americans, 9 percent as Chinese, and only 1.1 percent as American. Adjusted for three missing cases.

80. Interview 52, Tape I, pp. 38–39.

81. Adjusted for six missing cases.

82. 7.2 percent are very concerned, 66.3 percent are "somewhat" concerned, and 24.1 percent are moderately concerned. Adjusted for nine missing cases.

83. 89.2 percent are concerned about history and culture, and 92.8 percent are concerned about language. Adjusted for nine missing cases.

84. 94.1 percent. Adjusted for seven missing cases.
85. Dating is 91.5 percent and marriage is 85.4 percent. Adjusted for ten missing cases.
86. Respective percentages are: 67 percent, adjusted for four missing cases; 90 percent, adjusted for two missing cases; 42.7 percent and 50 percent, adjusted for ten missing cases; and 77.1 percent, with 21.7 being more comfortable with white children, adjusted for nine missing cases.
87. 22.1 percent for "very friendly" and 72.1 percent for "friendly." Adjusted for six missing cases.
88. Adjusted for two missing cases.
89. 96.2 percent. Adjusted for fourteen missing cases. The percentage is the same for social interaction.
90. 87.7 percent for "typical" and adjusted for eleven missing cases. 71.2 percent for "different" and adjusted for twelve missing cases.
91. Interview 40, Tape I, p. 5.
92. Interview 15, Tape I, p. 8.
93. Interview 7, Tape I, p. 18.
94. 98.8 percent. Adjusted for six missing cases.
95. 31.4 percent indicated "barely" and 12.8 percent indicated "not at all."
96. Figure adjusted for six missing cases. While geographical location may have been prohibitive for some, for most this was not the case, as a Chinatown was within reasonable distance from their residences.
97. Figures adjusted for four missing cases.
98. Interview 61, Tape I, p. 8.
99. Interview 26, Tape II, p. 31.
100. Interview 6, Tape I, p. 26.
101. Interview 18, Tape I, p. 25.
102. Interview 47, Tape II, p. 30.
103. 96.4 percent, adjusted for eight missing cases, and 66.7 percent, adjusted for twenty missing cases.
104. 69.3 percent indicated none, adjusted for four missing cases. 47.8 percent, adjusted for six missing cases.
105. 61.1 percent, adjusted for two missing cases.
106. Interview 19, Tape I, p. 27.
107. Interview 69, Tape I, p. 13.
108. For housing, 94.1 percent, adjusted for seven missing cases, and for schools, 76.8 percent, adjusted for ten missing cases.
109. 81 percent, adjusted for eight missing cases.
110. 74.1 percent, adjusted for eleven missing cases.
111. Interview 18, Tape 1, p. 31.
112. 81.6 percent, adjusted for five missing cases.
113. For a discussion of this, see de Lone, *Small Futures*.
114. 52.9 percent and 20 percent, adjusted for seven missing cases.
115. Interview 23, Tape I, p. 26.
116. Interview 70, Tape I, p. 18.

117. 86.4 percent, adjusted for four missing cases.
118. 69.9 percent, adjusted for nine missing cases.
119. 54 percent, adjusted for five missing cases.
120. Interview 28, Tape I, p. 13.
121. Anna Chennault, "Chinese Americans in Politics—Past, Present and Future," Chinese Historical Society of America, *The Life, Influence and the Role of Chinese in the United States, 1776–1960* (San Francisco, Ca.: Chinese Historical Society of America, 1976), p. 126.
122. Interview 12, Tape I, p. 21.
123. Interview 37, Tape I, p. 17.
124. 79.5 percent, adjusted for four missing cases.
125. 73.8 percent, adjusted for eight missing cases.
126. 83.7 percent, adjusted for six missing cases.
127. 83.3 percent, adjusted for eight missing cases.
128. 67.4 percent.
129. 75 percent, adjusted for eight missing cases.
130. No adjustment.
131. Both adjusted for five missing cases.
132. Adjusted for five and seven missing cases, respectively.
133. Interview 55, Tape I, p. 27.

Todd Carrel

Red Guards

For more than a century, Chinese immigrants have come to the United States. In the last decade, men and women who are the products of a new, radical Chinese culture have come here. They are Chinese who grew up in a revolutionary society. Many of them are retired Red Guards—veterans of China's tumultuous Cultural Revolution that began in 1966.[1]

Their upbringing and education in the People's Republic of China equipped them with the necesary skills to perform well in American society. They are aggressive, bold, direct, curious, and willing and anxious to find new ways to solve problems—all traits that ease their transition to a new culture. Unlike generations of Chinese who preceded them to the United States, they are not made passive by their newly adopted nation. Instead, many have become invigorated by the move.

They are young, most in their late twenties, many unmarried, and they are dedicated to self-improvement and quick integration into the mainstream of American society. Schooled in the revolutionary ways of a new China, they rejected their homeland's reliance on continuous political struggle as the key to building a modern, egalitarian nation. Transplanted to American cities, they are trying to establish themselves as good citizens by studying hard and working hard. They are enamored of the American concepts of rule by law and free education. Most are working hard to learn English and to assume American cultural values. They are "conservative"—totally uninterested in movements, reforms, or local politics.

Between 1970 and 1975, more than 7,000 such persons from China were admitted to the United States. These are the young men and women who swam from their homeland, the People's Republic of China, to the British colony of Hong Kong. They made elaborate preparations for the dangerous journey out of China.[2] Many said they memorized maps of the terrain and practiced swimming and other exercises before beginning their trek. They brought medicine, food, clothing, and compasses for the five- to fifteen-day hike over the mountains of Guangdong Province to the coast.[3] Some carried inner tubes and makeshift life jackets. Most made the two- or three-mile swim across the shark-infested waters of Mirs Bay in small groups at night during the "swimming season"—the months from May to November when the water is not prohibitively cold. Some of them made it to the colony's shores in three hours, while others swam for as long as twelve hours They tell how some companions died during the swim.

These new immigrants are called "political refugees" by the United States Immigration and Naturalization Service and are placed in its seventh and lowest category for admission to the United States. The first six categories give preference to visa applicants who are either relatives of American citizens or permanent residents or who have skills needed in this country. They are admitted as conditional entrants and become eligible for permanent residence status after living in the United States for two years. Immigration officials estimate that about 2,000 of these refugees settled in the San Francisco area between 1970 and 1975.

Most of these Chinese immigrants are former students and workers from the cities of Guangdong Province. Many of them left their country because they did not want to spend years working on agricultural communes or in factories. Such work, some said, did not properly utilize their skills, while some said their education was not being used in the best interests of national economic development.

One twenty-eight-year-old man who came to the United States this year said

> I left because I couldn't get what I wanted. I worked in the country-
> side for six years, first in a village clearing land for cultivation, and
> then as part of a production brigade. We worked with the peasants
> but they didn't like us. They're selfish. There were more than
> twenty young people in that village, so that meant more mouths to
> feed. They didn't like us just because it meant less for them to eat.
> They're uneducated and they don't have any culture. But that's
> not their fault. I don't look down on them.[4]

Many said they were fed up with the mass political movements they felt robbed their countrymen of a chance to build up the nation. They tell stories of acquaintances who were once in important positions—teachers and doctors —who were harshly criticized in the heat of political campaigns and forced from their jobs. Others said they left because there was no political freedom in China. A few said they left China in order to enjoy more material prosperity.

Like thirty-year-old Henry Lee, who has lived in San Francisco for almost three years, these veterans of China's Cultural Revolution consider themselves staunch Chinese patriots. "I'm patriotic," Lee said, "I know how to live China. I love China—the country and the people—but not the government."

Henry Lee is not his real name. Like most of his friends from China, he does not want his employer or the FBI to know about his background.

He said that many people have the wrong impression about people from China and fear that they are troublemakers. Many of these young immigrants tell stories of friends and acquaintances being interrogated by local FBI agents. They said the FBI wanted to know if they, or anyone they knew from China, were active in communist or other political activities. Somewhat terrorized by their tenuous status as conditional entrants, many of them are careful to avoid anything that may be construed as a political meeting. This harassment by the FBI, coupled with their antipathy for constant meetings that were once a way of life in China, has contributed to their often apolitical behavior in the United States. They said they were still visitors in the United States, at least for their first few years here. Most of them added they feel disenfranchised from most political processes and that their treatment by some government agencies also disgusts them: "Why did they let us in if they're so afraid of us?," confided one twenty-seven-year-old immigrant who works as a busboy.

Ironically, the invasive efforts of the FBI are causing the refugees to distrust the United States government. Unfortunately, American officials are largely unaware of the background of this new class of Chinese immigrants.

American misconceptions about these Chinese immigrants, as well as their own desire to avoid politics, in many ways resulted from their participation in China's Cultural Revolution. Henry Lee's experiences during the Revolution were typical of many of the young Chinese who recently settled in the United States. In 1966, Lee and his high school classmates from Guangzhou formed a Red Guard brigade and began a two-year trek that took them throughout the densely populated eastern provinces of China. They went as far north as Manchuria and Inner Mongolia. They were part of the "link-up"— a national movement that encouraged millions of Chinese youth to journey around the nation and experience the ways of the Chinese revolution.[5]

Many of the young rebels, said Henry Lee, fancied themselves to be the vanguard of China's continuing revolution. To save the fruits of the revolution, they attacked persons they deemed too bourgeois in thought and deed. Their targets were mostly middle-aged persons, teachers, and local party officials, and they subjected them to harsh criticism and physical abuse. Lee said he never hit any of these people, although he agreed with his young comrades that most of them deserved public exposure and ridicule.

For the first six months he participated in the movements instigated by young Red Guards. But after groups of young men began to pillage the homes of richer families, smashing mechanical devices, burning books, and sometimes beating people to death, he became an onlooker instead of an activist. For months on end, Lee's brigade roamed from city to city, sightseeing as much as seeking out counterrevolutionaries. The "link-up" was not only a valuable lesson in Chinese politics but also a chance for the young Chinese to discover how their countrymen lived.

In the fall of 1968, when they returned to Guangzhou, about half of the Red Guards were sent to work clearing rocks, hoeing fields, and installing irrigation pumps in Guangdong Province's communes. Lee was assigned to a city job and spent the next five years working as a clerk and buyer for the stationery section in a department store. During those years, he said, he was compelled to attend almost daily political meetings with his coworkers. Sometimes they would plan attacks against wayward individuals in meticulous detail before confronting them. Lee said he did not like these activities, but he did take part, limiting his activities to yelling political slogans. "They led nowhere. The struggles and the meetings were wasting time that could have been used to build China's economy. The Cultural Revolution was good because we learned a lot about China and its people. But it was bad because it wasted time we could have used to learn more things and do good things for China."

On a cold night in November, 1973, Lee and three close friends swam two miles across Mirs Bay to Hong Kong. Shortly after his arrival in Hong Kong, Lee was taken to a meeting of the International Social Service, one of a handful of organizations catering to refugees from China. The organization helped him contact relatives in Hong Kong and find a job. After one meeting sponsored by that organization, Lee talked with one speaker about the problems of Hong Kong and was urged to go to the United States. He decided then that he would try, and in July of 1975, he was granted an immigration visa and came to the United States. He filed the necessary application forms, including an affidavit from a sponsor (an American-born Chinese from Fresno) whom he had never met.

Life has not been easy for the young men and women who left China and settled in San Francisco. Most of them are working just as hard as they did in China, but for the first time, they say, they are working for themselves. They can spend their money on anything they want. This has given some of them great pleasure. They proudly display some of their recent purchases, including stereo sets, used cars, new dishes, appliances, and televisions.

They are concentrating their energies on self-improvement—learning to speak English, studying at adult schools and trade schools, and working as busboys, waiters, seamstresses, accountants, carpenters, and other jobs, mostly for low pay. Practically all of them are full- or part-time students.

Traditionally, Chinese immigrants in the United States have taken unskilled jobs in the cities and skilled jobs in Chinatowns. These young men and women say they want to leave the Chinatowns where they live as soon as possible in order to make the transition into more "typically" American occupations. They are anxious to take any job as a stepping stone to better employment.

They are zealous about learning English. As high school students in China before the Cultural Revolution, many of them studied foreign languages, but few learned English. Most took courses in Russian. Many of them learned a few English phrases while living in Hong Kong, but few learned to speak the language with any fluency. Within a month or two after they arrived in San Francisco, most of them found their way to schools that offered English as a second language. Some enrolled in courses at adult schools. Others took English classes coupled with job training programs at federally funded schools.

Their teachers say these Chinese immigrants approach their education more aggressively than those from Hong Kong and Taiwan. One English teacher commented that

> the ones from China are more systematic about how they learn. They have a tendency to be more clear about their motivation for learning in the sense that they know they need to learn it, and they put out to do it. They're very thorough about asking questions and they're more analytical about learning grammar. They're also more inquisitive and less accepting of simple answers to their questions. They're always asking 'Why?'"

Their strong analytical powers, their aggressiveness, their argumentative nature, and their strict self-discipline are all traits they learned growing up in China. They have been brought up in a culture where introspection and analysis are part of daily life. Their upbringing in China also taught them a straightforward method to learn new things. The legacy of the Cultural Revolution taught them that they must investigate everything and discover the good and the bad in any given situation.

As a result, there is little doubt that the vast majority of these immigrants from China value education highly and place heavy emphasis on learning English quickly. Many of them encourage their friends from China to spend longer periods of time studying the English language, because, they warn, it is the key to a good future in the United States.

Despite the importance placed on language training, most of them are eager to better their lot quickly, and English lessons are sometimes eclipsed by other activities. One teacher said the students from China were transient— leaving school for a job, enrolling again later, then leaving for another job. These Chinese do not agree. What appears to be capriciousness to her, they said, is merely the most sensible way to secure better jobs and a more secure future. Indeed, for some young Chinese, English language education has taken a back seat to the search for a better job. One young man who came to the United States after spending five years in Hong Kong explained his priorities thus: "Right now I want to do what's most practical. I want to learn English. I have a job as a busboy at Fisherman's Wharf, but I want to find a better job working with leather and making purses like I did in Hong Kong. I know people look down on busboys. But, in the beginning, I have to be practical. I want to start learning English, but I need a job first." His impatience is common to many other young immigrants because all of them are anxious to pursue the host of opportunities they feel are available to them in the United States.

Due to what many say is an abundance of opportunities for work and easy money, some of these former Red Guards opt to take whatever jobs are available so they can begin to earn a steady income. But most of them insist that they should use their first few years in the United States learning new skills and studying the English language. For example, one thirty-year-old man is now taking courses to learn auto mechanics. He attends a local junior college in Alameda. He is an earnest student, and says he goes to class every day with a list of questions about his work—detailed points he insists on understanding thoroughly. Sometimes he bids for his teacher's time to answer his questions. He said he is puzzled by the absence of enthusiasm and the lackadaisical approach of some of his classmates toward their studies. "What I fear most," he said, "is wasting my time—not learning something new each day." This motivation for education is matched by his realization that he needs capital to open his own garage. To raise the money he therefore works four or five nights a week as a busboy at a Chinese restaurant.

Some of these immigrants from China do have difficulty getting jobs that utilize their skills, although they are prepared to work hard and long hours. One social service agency worker who helped many of these young men and women from China settle in San Francisco said that getting decent employment is their first priority. When they arrive, "the most important thing is for them to get a job to start with," he said. "Most of them have a sponsor once they get here who can help them. Then, if they decide to fight on for a better life and more opportunities, they go to the language schools. After that, it takes more than two years for them to get employment."

Teddy Sung is a slight twenty-eight-year-old man from a small village outside of Guangzhou. He leads a rigorous life. At seven o'clock each morning he leaves his room in Chinatown and goes to his English classes. At noon, he goes to work driving a delivery truck that supplies Chinese restaurants throughout the Bay area. He finishes that job at five o'clock and immediately starts his second job, cooking. He works in the kitchen of a Chinese restaurant until about ten o'clock each evening.

Nancy Low worked for almost a year as a maid at the St. Francis Hotel. She managed to hold her job and take English classes at the same time. Recently, she decided she wanted to take accounting courses at the San Francisco Skills Center. She discovered that she had to quit her job and be unemployed for three months to qualify for the federally funded program. She called that requirement "stupid."

Others become depressed at their inability to put skills they learned in China to use in the United States. Frank Chin has lived in San Francisco for almost four years. In his home town of Guangzhou, he was admitted to the prestigious Sun Yat-sen Medical College. He completed his work there, including extensive training in both Western and traditional Chinese medicine. He then finished a year of residency before leaving China. In Hong Kong, he ran his own clinic for more than one year. In San Francisco, he has been taking English courses, then spending hours pouring over medical textbooks to learn English medical terminology. He has held a succession of menial jobs at hospitals and clinics, but he has never been allowed to practice the medicine he learned in China.

He said he was virtually closed off from practicing medicine in the United States due to his language problems and his lack of United States certification, so he has opened an acupuncture clinic of his own. He has built up a small practice, but it is too small to support himself. He is in an uncomfortable limbo, wanting to put his skills to use helping Chinese people and other patients in the medical system here, yet unable to enter that competitive profession.

John Fang, thirty-two, from Shantou (a small town north of Guangzhou) was trained in China as a carpenter. During the Cultural Revolution, Fang did not join the youth who became the Red Guards; he stayed in his city and took a job working in an underground factory. The son of a once-prosperous factory owner who was labelled a capitalist, Fang said he had no future in China. As the son of a former capitalist, he too inherited the capitalist label. It was a harsh stigma that made him vulnerable to criticism and attack during China's political campaigns. "I was raised in the Mao Tse-tung era," he said, "and I ate Mao Tse-tung's food, but still they called me a capitalist because of my father's activities before liberation [in 1949]."

Fang spent five years working in Hong Kong as a carpenter before he came to the United States. He came here unable to speak more than a few phrases of English, an immigrant with a sixth-grade education who had almost ten years of experience as a carpenter. Since arriving in San Francisco, he has taken English classes repeatedly, but has made little progress. He now can speak a few tentative sentences. He has spent the bulk of his time working— ten hours a day, six days a week. "Now I'm a member of the proletariat," he joked. He worked at first as a carpenter for a local Chinese American contractor. Since he finished that job, he has worked steadily as a fry cook in a popular Chinese restaurant.

Despite language and occupation difficulties, Fang has been thrilled by his ability to buy goods with his earnings. For the first time in his life, he said, he can buy whatever he wants. His first major purchase was a large refrigerator that took up a lot of space in his tiny room. Within a year after he arrived in San Francisco, he bought a new car. He spends an hour or two washing his car every Sunday when he is off work.

One man, who left China in 1968 after being sent from his hometown to work in an agricultural commune in another province, explained why many people coming to the United States from China are delighted with their ability to earn money:

> China is lacking in materials. People don't earn much in the cities, much less in the countryside. In a day, people earn about one Chinese dollar. Then they use about $10 a month to eat. Cigarettes are about 20¢ a day. One piece of clothing would cost a few dollars. Here, anyone can easily find a job that pays about $25 a day—even if you're just a janitor or a busboy like me. But that money is enough to eat plenty, buy all you want, and still have some left over for savings. And here it's so much easier to buy things. Nothing is rationed. You just give them your money and you get what you want. I'm convinced that anyone of working age from China would be very content with their earning capability here.

As for American material culture, these Chinese immigrants are extremely satisfied. They also have developed attitudes highly critical of other aspects of American life. While they heatedly disapprove of many of the policies of the Chinese Communist Party, they also find many weaknesses in the institutionalized capitalism of the United States.

Some say the direction of trends in the United States is wrong. One young man, who is studying at a univeristy in Southern California had these thoughts

> In America, people worship movie stars and politicians. This is silly. Nobody here talks about intellectuals—the ones who are really important to any nation and its future. Also, your leaders here don't get much accomplished. I really admire some of the Communists in China because of the way they take command and get things done for the people. I think Chou Enlai was great and so was Mao Zedong.

Another man said he still loved China but hated the Cultural Revolution. He blamed Mao and other Chinese leaders for launching a destructive movement that kept China from transforming itself into a more modern nation. He concluded that

> what they did was ridiculous. Why would anyone want to start a movement like that? It was like playing with the people. They abused the cadres and other leaders. But when they finished, what

did they accomplish? Of course, everyone loves their home, and we love China. So why do people leave? If they weren't forced to do things they didn't like, they wouldn't leave.

He also discerns problems in the United States and feels he should be critical: "Now, I'm here and I think that things are very free. But I still know that everything is not good. Mao said that everything divides into two,[6] and I think that's right. So if I think Carter is bad, I criticize him."

These people brought up in a radically new Chinese society are accustomed to participating in social change. As veterans of the Cultural Revolution, they have come to the United States with a fresh outlook that is different from that of Chinatown's traditional inhabitants. Their thinking is different, but their living and working conditions are the same: high rents for run-down apartments and low wages for long hours of work. One example is Henry Lam. Three or four nights a week he worked for $2.15 an hour as a busboy at a Chinese restaurant. At that time, the minimum wage in California was $2.50 an hour, but the restaurant owners could legally deduct expenses for meals if the workers agreed and signed a statement to that effect. Henry Lam, a straightforward man who likes to argue with his friends, never signed such a statement and never argued with his boss. Lam said he knew he was not being paid enough, but he did not want to risk losing his job. He held that part-time job for more than a year. Then, with the $60 he took home each week he paid his bills, saved a little, and wired the rest to his family in China.

His situation has changed somewhat in the last year. Lam has taken a part-time job as a waiter at an Oakland Chinatown restaurant. He is earning more money for less work, and he is saving as much money as possible.

Home for Lam is an old brick Chinatown rooming house that has been used as a first stop by Chinese immigrants for decades. His small eight-by-ten-foot room is dominated by his single bed. A suitcase, cardboard boxes, a rack of clothes, a few pots and pans, and canned food and tea fill the shelves he built over the door. A new stereo on a metal rack, a few bookshelves and a desk fill the rest of the room. Lam and eight other young immigrants from China live in the same rooming house. They started moving into the building a few years ago, one said, after rumors that the place was occupied by ghosts scared off many of the old tenants. Now these young immigrants, a half-dozen young families, and old men and women live there. The accommodations are ample for their spartan needs. Most of the young Chinese men say they live there to save money. At $35 to $55 a month per room, it's one of the cheapest places in Chinatown. Lam and the others said living in Chinatown cushions their transition into American society, but many of them are anxious to leave Chinatown and get away from the Chinese living there: "They are living according to the old style," said one man from China. "I feel they are backward. I live here, too, but I don't spend much time here."

The residents of Chinatown are largely recent immigrants from Hong Kong and a sizeable number of old men and women who have lived in the United States as laborers for decades but never learned English.[7] Since so many of these elderly workers who have long been totally disenfranchised from American political life have not succeeded in the material sense, these young Chinese immigrants are critical of them. Many of the elderly Chinese virtually never leave Chinatown and the young Chinese believe this makes them even more backward. Some of them say that San Francisco's China-town is the most backward Chinese enclave in the world.

These new Chinese immigrants have no sympathy for the plight of the city's elderly Chinese, the living symbols of a bygone era.[8] They say that they have no connection with them because these old men and women came to the United States several decades ago from a crippled nation. Therefore they are quick to distinguish themselves from the rest of Chinatown's inhabitants. They see themselves as coming from a different generation and a different world. "I think our experience of living in this world is deeper than theirs," said Sally Low, a twenty-six-year-old accountant at the Bank of America who has lived in San Francisco for two years. She lives in a one-bedroom apartment a mile away from Chinatown with her two brothers and a sister, all of whom swam from China. "We've had a big change in our lives. Everything in their lives has been smooth."

Low was referring to their experiences during the Cultural Revolution and their exodus from China. Like her, many of these immigrants believe that they have made harder decisions than their predecessors; they feel that their resolve to leave China and start a new life was stronger than that of the earlier generations.

These young immigrants also believe that the recent immigrants from Hong Kong and the American-born Chinese in San Francisco are fundamentally different from them. Many of the San Francisco Chinese, they say, are backward because they were denied a basic education. They say they were simply never taught Chinese human values, especially how to behave toward their fellows.

Those human values they talk about represent a mix of the moral teachings of Mao Tse-tung Thought and Confucianism, a blend of belief in pragmatic, scientific behavior and a belief in respect and propriety. Sally Low's younger brother, a student at City College, commented that he believed that:

> Some of the ABCs [American-born Chinese] don't have a good
> family education. They grew up alone, with no warmth because they
> can't even talk to their parents. They have no Chinese education.
> Some of them even have problems getting along with whites. Then
> there are two other types of Chinese here. Some of the ABCs do
> have a Chinese education. Even though their parents didn't know
> how to write, they still made their children learn, and that's good.

The ones who want Chinese culture, they're very nice and seldom lie. They're not selfish. They seem like an American countryman—very honest. And many of them were raised like that in Chinatown.

A third group he mentioned were those whose parents were professionals. "They gave their children a good background, and now they're just like Americans. That's good."

The qualities these immigrants prize in others represent aspects of Chinese culture. They admire the American-born Chinese who are adept at dealing with both American and Chinese societies. They pity those who are unable to cope in either society.

Just as these immigrants from the People's Republic of China have distinct impressions about the American-born Chinese, so do other Chinese in San Francisco have opinions about them. For instance, an American-born Chinese who is a social worker who deals with delinquent youths in Chinatown said the immigrants from China are very different from those raised in Hong Kong or San Francisco. "They're not involved in community struggles. They're conservative. They dress conservatively, and they're conservative in that they want to have families and earn enough money to get by on."

Another American-born Chinese said they were easily taken in by the relative freedom in America—so much so that they overlooked social injustices. "Generally, they think that freedom here is really good stuff. Their concept of freedom is based on the seeming availability of education. Many came here because they thought there was no future for them in China, since they weren't able to pursue their interests there." Further, he said that those he has met "tend to shy away from political things. Sometimes we talk about issues like the International Hotel, but they're very cynical. They're leery of the people who claim to do good for the masses. They're skeptical and suspicious that these people are involved more out of self-interest than anything else."[9]

One young immigrant said that he did not understand the issues surrounding the International Hotel, but that he sympathized with the tenants. He also believed that the organizers of the movement to stop eviction of the hotel's tenants did not know how to run a movement: "What they were doing was child's play. We know how to create a movement. We went through the Cultural Revolution. But we're not going to do anything here." The immigrants were exhilarated by their ability to help shape events in China and help benefit selected causes. Many of them learned through the Cultural Revolution that issues were very complex, that factions always emerged, and that solving crises was never easy. However, when it came to launching certain movements, they did so with careful planning. As a result of their experiences, some former Red Guards scoffed at efforts of organizers of the International Hotel movement. Those behind the movement, they said, had failed.

The hotel was coming down. The organizers did not take careful aim and did not devise a workable plan for their cause.

The focus, said one young man, should have been on housing for old and poor people in the neighborhood. With that as an issue, the movement should have been broadened by involving others in the Chinatown neighborhood. Other Red Guards said if the organizers really wanted better housing for old people, they should have welcomed the destruction of the old building, and lobbied for the construction of better housing in its place.

Many of these Chinese immigrants said they have had their fill of political movements in China. Also, their conditional entrance status and their fear that their right to stay in the United States could be jeopardized if they become politically active make them reluctant to participate in local reformist campaigns. They were more concerned with establishing themselves in a new culture. In this respect, a Chinatown social worker said that "they are political refugees, but they don't take part in political activities in the U.S. If they were pro-Communist, then they wouldn't have come here in the first place. They came here to enjoy the freedoms of democracy, so they don't make a lot of demands in the political arena. They're satisfied with just having a decent job."

The sensibilities of these former Red Guards have not been dulled in the United States. They are keenly aware that the American version of democracy, like Chinese-style communism, functions imperfectly. New to the United States, they are fascinated with concepts of civil liberties and individual freedom. Most of all, many said they were impressed by the American legal system.

While the concepts are appealing in themselves, many of these young Chinese have jumped at the chance to see how American legal principles work in practice. For example, Tony Chow, who has lived in San Francisco for almost three years, received several parking tickets in a two-month period. Rather than paying the $10 fines, he went to court. He twice appealed his tickets to a traffic court judge, and twice the tickets were dismissed. He beat his traffic tickets by persuading the judge that he did not understand local traffic regulations. He admitted he was more cunning than the other people in the court, most of whom he said were poor and uneducated. He thought the system was fine for him; the court had listened to him before it made a judgment.

That judicial process was appealing to Chow. It was refreshing compared to his experiences during the Cultural Revolution, when right and wrong were determined on the basis of Mao Thought, which he believes was a capricious system that left important judgments to the whim of the dominant partisans of the moment. Those in power decided the "correct" interpretation of Mao Zedong Thought. There were no fixed standards for judgment then. For this reason, while many of these former Red Guards are themselves the object of discrimination and unfair treatment in the United States, they are willing to rely on a system that contains certain constitutional guarantees.

Henry Lee's case is different. He roamed China during the Cultural Revolution and exposed wrongdoing there. Now he has found himself the victim of certain injustices in the United States. He said that he and others who work as busboys in Chinese restaurants are grossly underpaid and exploited. The busboys should organize to solve the problems, but this would be difficult because "all the busboys are different. Some go to Reno or to Chinatown gambling houses the minute they get paid, others go home to take care of their families, and some of us use our spare time to study."

Lee feels there are two ways to rectify this kind of exploitation: violence or negotiation. "We could blow up one of the restaurants," he joked. More seriously, he said, "it's the simplest thing to do but it wouldn't really solve anything. Or we could use the law and negotiate. The important thing is to educate them [the restaurant owners]. But all the laws here are written in English—that's part of the problem. We're not sure what rights we have yet. I know paying us such low wages is illegal, but we still don't know what to do about it." Still, he would rather rely on the law: "In China there were no standards. There was no law to guide us. But in America, you have laws. There are standards. And that's the difference."

While these young immigrants from China are extremely self-assured and believe that they can use laws to serve their own ends, most of them are in a hurry to advance their own lot and therefore do not want to get mired in confrontations of any sort. What they value highly is economic stability. They want steady incomes and they are willing to work long hours to earn money.

Some of these former Red Guards have a nearly unquenchable wanderlust. During the "link-ups" of the Cultural Revolution they had the rare and exhilarating opportunity to learn about a nation by travelling, so some of them are attempting to learn about American culture by seeing as much of the country as possible. George Wang is a good example. He has been in the United States for almost four years. He wears tight, faded jeans, an open shirt, and his hair is neatly styled. His English is spiced with vulgarisms and curious idioms he has learned during his travels.

Wang worked as a busboy in a Swiss restaurant behind New York's Rockefeller Center for several months. He left the job, he said, because he was slowly starving while he worked there. He hated cheese, and each time he left work he could not wait to eat. As a result, he left New York and held a succession of jobs (usually in restaurants), in Connecticut, New Jersey, Massachusetts, and then Florida. For the last few months he has worked as a bartender at a San Francisco theater.

Wang said that his travels helped him learn about the United States. He liked some aspects of American society and found many people to be very friendly. He also said that his way of thinking was more practical than his American counterparts: "We'll always be different. For one thing, the ways we have fun are different. And we're always thinking of making things better for the future. Young Americans our age don't think of that."

During their first years here, these Chinese immigrants concentrate on learning American values and on making themselves productive citizens. Most of them spend practically all their time working and studying. They cherish the concept of self-reliance they learned growing up in China as children of the "Mao Zedong era." They have discovered that their Chinese education serves them well in American society. Adjustment to American capitalism has proven easy for most of them, although some of them say the only way they can acquire economic power is by cooperating with each other, pooling their resources to start their own businesses.

Four men have made an agreement to go into business together. One is a recent arrival who works as a busboy and still studies English several hours a day; one has completed auto mechanics training and is giving up a job at a garage; one has worked for several years as a busboy and a janitor but cannot speak much English; and one has worked for several years as a waiter at a Persian restaurant. They want to buy a restaurant and sell what they call Cantonese "country-style" food. By cooperating, they say, they have economic power.

The immigrants' personal lives are limited. Some talk of girl friends in Hong Kong they would like to bring to the United States and marry in a few years. Most of them say they want to establish themselves in secure jobs before thinking about marriage. Some of them marry and begin raising families. For the most part they are concentrating on educating themselves and establishing careers before thinking about having families. They lead disciplined lives, but they are full of warmth and humor. They value honesty, daring, and hard work—all attributes that ease their adjustment to American society. But for all of them, the society can never replace their passion for China. The transition into this culture is a new, sometimes trying experience. "Customs here are so different," said Henry Lee. "We hope to learn your customs. We live here, but we're like children—we don't know anything about American society."

Notes

1. The Cultural Revolution was launched in 1966 as a means of keeping the nation's leaders and party authorities from backsliding and forgetting the purpose of the Chinese Revolution. During the heat of the Cultural Revolution, from 1966 to 1969, China was in a period of disorder with rash fits of reform. The Red Guards were the intellectual

youth of the nation, mostly from the cities, who were mobilized by Mao to scour the country, root out those who were abusing their authority, and gain revolutionary experience.

2. None of the refugees fled China without first making elaborate preparations. As one of them said, they knew all the obstacles they might confront by heart long before they undertook the trek. In Guangzhou (Canton) during the early 1970s the atmosphere was such that many young Chinese who had tried to slip out of the country and failed would talk about their experiences openly in tea houses and describe what happened in vivid detail. At that time, these young people who had failed to elude border patrols and had spent a few months in country prisons, were giving advice to their peers who were contemplating escape.

It was impossible to escape without a few bribes and well-chosen friends. To get passes to enter the countryside, most had to pay large sums of money. Some of them tried to pass for peasants returning to their villages as they went through check points beyond the city limits. To do this, some of them spent months sunbathing to get their skin as dark as the peasants. Then they cut their hair short and wore the oldest, most tattered clothing they could obtain. Tossing a small fish net over the shoulder helped build up the image, said one former Red Guard. The idea was to look so much like a peasant that they wouldn't be questioned. If they were forced to speak, their urban accents could have been picked out in an instant.

Once they managed to enter the countryside, they depended on sympathetic peasants to house them and guide them into the hills. One man said he befriended an old peasant who was once a communist guerrilla who fought against the nationalist (Guomindang) troops before China's liberation in 1949. The old peasant had already led several dozen men and women into the hills before. He was known to be dependable, yet extremely circumspect about whom he chose to help.

The young man befriended him over the course of six months, entertaining him each time he came into the city by taking him out for tea and snacks, all the while discussing what would be required to make a safe journey. On such rendezvous the peasant took money from the dissatisfied young Red Guard and used it to buy supplies for the long hike over the mountains.

Such peasant-allies were paid handsomely for the risks they took— sometimes as much as 100 Chinese dollars (about four months' wages).

Once in the countryside, the young Chinese would spot their peasant friend, then follow behind him at a discreet distance as he led them back to his village home. They would stay there for a night before being escorted into the mountains the next evening. Before the peasant left his charges, he would unearth the supplies he had buried for their long journey.

On their own, the young men and women would scamper across the woods and over mountains, travelling only at night, resting in hiding during the day.

Chinese patrol guards and their dogs were the nemesis of the escapees. But once they were eluded, there was more to be afraid of. "First, I feared running into people," said one. "Then I feared stepping onto a trap by accident."

3. All of the former Red Guards interviewed were from Guangdong Province. Many of them claim that young Chinese left their country by fleeing northward to Russia and Korea when they swam to Hong Kong.

4. Many of these former Red Guards were sent to the countryside after they were "demobilized" in the wake of the initial years of the Cultural Revolution. Since they were city youths, they didn't know how to raise crops efficiently. Their inexperience meant that they couldn't produce enough extra vegetables and other foodstuffs to supplement their diets. Most said they depended on their families to send money. They said when they worked on the farms, the worked for long hours and for months on end thought of nothing but sleep and food.

5. For accounts of the experiences of Red Guards in China and descriptions of the climate of the nation at that time, see: William Hinton, "Hundred Day War: The Cultural Revolution at Tsinghua University," *Monthly Review Press* 25 (July-August 1972): 5–278.

6. Most of these young Chinese use the analytical techniques they learned through years of study of Mao Tse-tung Thought and political meetings to examine and criticize their problems in the United States. Many of these concepts, they say, are good tools for examining life in America.

7. For a good anatomy of San Francisco's Chinatown, see Victor Nee and Brett de Bary, *Longtime Californ': A Documentary Study of an American Chinatown* (Boston: Houghton Mifflin Co., 1973).

8. Many of the elderly Chinese who now inhabit San Francisco's Chinatown tenements came to the United States decades ago, some as early as the 1920s. The majority of them speak only a few phrases of English. Many of them are illiterate peasants who came to the United States from small villages in rural China. After working for years at hard jobs in Chinese communities in California, many of them have retired and now live on social security.

9. The International Hotel in San Francisco once house Filipino and Chinese retired workers. But after the property was bought by a foreign developer the hotel was slated for demolition. The residents were sent eviction notices, and the hotel soon became a cause célèbre for some San Franciscans. Those protesting the eviction had several standoffs with the police, but the tenants were finally forced out and the building gradually taken down. Although those supporting the displaced tenants were ostensibly agitating for more housing for the community's elderly residents, they virtually ceased their demonstrations once the International Hotel began to be taken down.

William A. Edwards

Civil Rights, Affirmative Action:
An Incomplete Agenda?

The *New York Times* recently featured a four-part series on Black youth and unemployment.[1] Not surprisingly, *Times* reporters affirmed some of the grim statistics relative to the current economic plight of young Blacks between sixteen and nineteen. As a group, teenage unemployment for Blacks during the first quarter of 1979 was reported at 35.3 percent.[2] This figure compares with a rate of 16.5 percent twenty-five years ago and 24 percent ten years ago. Nationally, the rate of Black youth unemployment for this age category is approximately three times the comparable rate for white teenagers of the same age. The National Urban League suggests that even these figures may understate the actual unemployment picture of Black youth. The League has developed an index which it calls the "Hidden Unemployment Index," indicating that not only is there enormous reported unemployment, but that the figures do not reflect the "discouraged worker" who has given up hope that there are any job possibilities.

The *Times* report informs us that American society pays a high cost for these youth in terms of high crime rates, social services, and most importantly the loss of available talent. This latter point is particularly significant since, contrary to some popular misconceptions, a substantial number of these youths are high school graduates. The National Urban League's study on Black employment reported that in 1946 44 percent of Black youth had either completed high school or had gone on to college (15 percent).[3] Further, the same study indicated that in spite of rising educational attainment for Blacks generally, there still remains a gap between income earning for Blacks and whites. These conclusions were also supported by Dorothy Newman, et al., in their study of Black Americans from 1940-75.[4]

For Black Americans in general, the unemployment figures as an indicator of the health of that segment of the population point out that during the decade of the 1970s unemployment consistently approximated twice the rate for whites.[5] Similarly, Black Americans are significantly affected by changes in the economy. During recent periods of economic upturns (1954-57, 61-69, 75-77), Black employment rises but rarely closes the two-to-one ratio of white unemployment. During economic downturns Blacks are most likely to experience their highest unemployment. In the period 1975 to August 1976, Black unemployment was never lower than 12.2 percent (May 1976) while white unemployment never exceeded 7.8 percent.[6]

Unemployment is not the only area in which Black Americans lag behind their white counterparts. In the area of family income, Blacks still earn less than whites. In 1969, the Black-white income ratio was 61 percent, while in 1976 that ratio had dropped two percent to 59 percent.[7] This decrease occurred in spite of the fact that incomes in dollars rose from a median of $5,999 for Blacks in 1969 to $9,242 in 1976. During the same period, white family median income rose from $9,794 in 1969 to $15,537 in 1976. Even in 1976, Black median family income had not reached the level of white income in 1969. This is all the more important because this time period was one of almost continuous recession. While we are constantly reminded that statistically Black Americans have been entering the middle class ($15,000-25,000) at a faster rate than whites, the Black middle class is not a comparable socioeconomic group.

What these figures suggest is that after more than two decades of sustained civil rights activism, Black Americans, while making progress, are still lagging behind whites. For Black teenagers the picture is even more bleak. As Herbert Hill observed:

> It is evident that a permanent Black underclass has developed, that virtually an entire second generation of ghetto youths will never enter into the labor force. This means that a large part of the young Black urban population will remain in a condition of hopelessness and despair and that the social and psychological costs in wasted lives continues a major tragedy in American life.[8]

That there should be such a degree of hopelessness and despair after a quarter of a century of organized civil rights activity is both unfortunate and quite suggestive. As a major ingredient of the civil rights movement, Black Americans maintained at least an implicit hope that reforms in the society would guarantee them some significant changes in their lives. To a substantial degree this hope was expressed in the belief that through legislative actions, executive leadership, and favorable judicial rulings Black Americans would enjoy the fruits of this society. Many felt that once the legal barriers to racial exclusion were removed, Blacks would become fully integrated. A major thrust of the civil rights movement was therefore directed toward the goals of integration and racial equality.

But what did integration and equality mean during the period of civil rights activism? From a cursory examination of a very rough outline of the economic position of Blacks in contemporary American society, it would seem that both integration and equality are illusory matters. In a time when the cities are experiencing "white flight" and the idea of equality faces stiff challenges, it may be useful to raise some questions concerning the events of the last two decades and their relationship to issues of equality, access, public policy, assumptions, and tactics of the movement. An examination of these issues may provide some clues about the civil rights period as a social movement and the interplay of policy and assumptions. In addition, this examination will attempt to show that there remains an unfinished agenda for Black Americans.

Social Change and Legal Reform

Observers of societies have always been curious about the nature of order and change. One of the age-old questions has been: What are the sources of change within a society? Do all members of a society have equal access to the instruments of change? While the answers to the first question vary significantly, those to the second are more obvious. Within a highly complex, diversified, and technological society such as the United States, all persons or groups do not have equal access to the various sources of change. Neither do all groups in the society perceive change in a similar manner. Change may be seen in relation to such factors as class, race, ethnicity, age, sex, religion, geography, and education.

For Black Americans, social change has historically been complicated by the profound sense in which race has affected the nature of intergroup and intragroup relations. Race has been a major factor in the process of stratification whereby Black Americans have consistently been the victims of structured inequality. It has been from the position of being one of the least privileged groups in American society that Blacks have sought social, economic, and political change. As a historically powerless group, Blacks have lacked the strong social basis for effectively orchestrating those changes which would affect their lives most directly. From the disadvantageous position of a rejected minority, Black Americans have had nominal success in forging changes on the basis of their own agenda. What Black America could do was often a factor of what the larger society would tolerate.

Within this context it has been virtually impossible for Black Americans to set before the country any principles or claims through which they may choose to direct the affairs of their lives. Further, Black America was rarely perceived by the larger society as having any legitimate claim for special consideration in spite of its peculiar history in this country. Black Americans were perceived as having little of significance which should occupy the conscience of America. For the larger society, Black America had no agenda. If there was anything that needed changing, it was that Blacks should devote their energies to self-improvement. This type of thinking has also militated against Black America's push for social change and has been one of the principal reasons why, historically, Black movements have almost always been *protest* movements. As such, the changes which Blacks have effected have come through compromise. Change has been determined more by others than by Blacks themselves.

As a relatively powerless group, Blacks have sought change through their own initiative, through alliances with whites, but most particularly through reforms taken by the branches of the federal government. This strategy has always meant at least two things: first, Black protest has been articulated through group opposition to inequality, and, secondly, it has been presented as a national issue. Whether or not Blacks have accepted Gunnar Myrdal's conclusions that the "Negro problem" is the result of the disparity between America's creed and its deeds, Blacks have recognized that their problems are the problems of America and that they will never be solved until America resolves its own basic democratic contradictions. Out of this position has emerged the argument that social change for Black America represents a challenge to the principle of equality and the social maintenance of racial discrimination.

Underlying these questions of principle and practice is a fundamental question for Black Americans. Once the legal foundation of inequality and discrimination has been undermined, will long-term benefits follow? Recognizing that one of the barriers to social change has been the implementation of Jim Crow laws, Black Americans have sought the federal government's intervention to effect long-term socioeconomic and political benefits. The position taken by Herbert Hill in 1969 reflects this point: "The law is a formidable means for the elimination of group discrimination and for the establishment of conditions that discourage prejudiced attitudes."[9]

It was this belief that prompted many in the civil rights movement to seek the federal government's assistance. Government commitment, it was felt, would legitimize the struggle for civil rights and establish that struggle as a matter of national concern. But government routinely acts politically, and within this context what is demanded is usually not what is granted. Historically, the federal government has responded reluctantly to demands for racial reforms within existing structures.[10]

Two leading figures in the civil rights movement have made some pointed observations about hopes for legal reform. In a thoughtful assessment of the civil rights movement and legal reform, Julian Bond concluded that the first mistake made in the movement "was to assume that racism could be legislated out of existence, that court orders and acts of Congress could change hearts and minds."[11] Martin Luther King, Jr., wrote late in his life that: "The civil rights measures of the 1960s engraved solemn rights in the legal legislation and, proclaiming its historic importance in magnificent prose, the American Government left the Negro to make the unworkable work."[12] Both of these statements implicitly recognize that legal reforms can do no more than deal with matters of principle. As an active participant in what was considered a question of legal rights, the federal government could not have addressed the historic question of structured inequality, nor was this question posed by civil rights leaders as an agenda item. As Bayard Rustin notes, "the Negro's struggle for equality in America is essentially revolutionary."[13]

Revolutionary changes would necessitate changes in the political structure. Reforms, while urgent in the short term, cannot be sustained without eventually addressing the question of the structural nature of racial inequality and its meaning in the history of this country. In its earliest stages (to approximately 1964) the civil rights movement did not perceive itself as a movement attempting a *revolution* in the treatment of Black Americans. Change was envisioned as a removal of the barriers of racial exclusion and the granting of equality. While these objectives can be defended in principle, they do not significantly explain the basis of Black inequality. As an instrument for social change, the national government mitigated the demands of the movement through democratic principles. Vincent Harding summarizes the matter succinctly. "What majority," he asks, "has ever presented a minority with a legislated revolution?"[14]

To suggest that the basic question of structural inequality was not put forth during the early stages of the movement is not to say that the movement was irrelevant. On the contrary, the civil rights movement viewed change as possible. Those in the movement recognized the relatively powerless position of Blacks but nonetheless translated this position into a struggle for racial integration and institutional access. The question of social change was framed as a question of legal reform. Gaining access to the voting booths, public facilities, schools, etc., was assumed to be a necessary step toward racial integration.

The Social Definition of Civil Rights

The United States Supreme Court played a significant role in establishing a national tone for the civil rights movement. In striking down the legal doctrine of "separate but equal," the high court's decision in *Brown* v. *Board of Education* signalled the first round of attacks against institutional racism. Not only did the court overturn the legal basis for racial segregation; it also said that separation inherently assumed a stigma of inferiority. The *Brown* decision suggests that legal segregation manifests an assumption of superiority. The definition of Blacks as a racially inferior group was institutionalized by law in the 1896 *Plessy* v. *Ferguson* decision. This decision became the legal framework of the social practices which followed. More importantly, the *Plessy* decision represents the culmination of a social definition accepted for more than two centuries.

The unanimous decision of the Supreme Court in the *Brown* case put the full force of the Court behind the move toward desegregation.[15] In winning one of its most important cases, the NAACP Legal Defense Fund affirmed its position that racial segregation could be successfully challenged in court. Having established a legal precedent, it faced the major task of implementation. The unanimity of the decision would certainly impel implementation. The reception by the international community would also accelerate the pace of change. C. Vann Woodward has written that: "Within a few hours after the Supreme Court's decision was read in 1954, the Voice of America had broadcast the news to foreign countries in thirty-five separate languages."[16] The *Brown* decision was proclaimed one of America's proudest moments in the defense of the democratic principle of equality.

Equality was a key word in the liberal response to the *Brown* decision. Striking down legal restrictions was interpreted in many quarters as opening wide the door of equal opportunity: "Access to equal education, it was thought, would ensure equal access to the starting line in life."[17] Education was perceived as one of the major avenues to upward mobility. Having been denied equal access to this avenue, Black Americans lagged behind the country as a whole. Civil rights advocates argued that through the educational system, Blacks would enter the American "mainstream." Stated as an "if-then" proposition, the *Brown* decision would vindicate America's faith in education.

Shortly after the second *Brown* decision in 1955, America was confronted with the first episode of direct collective action since the 1940s. Following the arrest of Mrs. Rosa Parks in Montgomery, Alabama, for failing to give her seat to a white rider on a public bus, the Montgomery Improvement Association staged a successful one-year boycott of the local transit system. Again the United States Supreme Court was asked to intervene and again the Court ruled, in sustaining the lower court, that state and local laws requiring racial segregation on public busses were unconstitutional. Another national legal assault had been launched against institutional racism. The decision seemed to reinforce the idea that the national government was responsive to Black Americans' demands for redress of historical injustices. One should not, however, overlook the targets of civil rights protest. As Bayard Rustin observes, "in desegregating public accommodations, we affected institutions which are relatively peripheral both to the American socioeconomic order and to the fundamental conditions of life of the Negro people."[18]

The Montgomery boycott had a major impact on the future of the civil rights movement. First, it affirmed the viability of organized protest. Second, it sustained the international interest in civil rights and democracy in America. Third, it established nonviolence as the major tactic for social change. Fourth, it launched the civil rights career of Martin Luther King, Jr.

Fifth, it affirmed the idea that Black Americans were only seeking those rights guaranteed by the Constitution. Finally, along with the systematic resistance of the Southern states to school desegregation, the Montgomery boycott focused attention on the South as the country's center of overt racial prejudice. This last point was amplified in the Emmett Till murder case.

The *Brown* decision, the Montgomery boycott, and the Till murder case stimulated public support of civil rights, but they also drew attention to what the larger society would perceive as the major issue confronting Blacks in America: discrimination, Southern style. The full thrust of liberal support converged on Southerners as the "ugly Americans." America did not ask, nor did the civil rights movement demand, that this assumption be scrutinized from an historical perspective. Discrimination was viewed as the Southern attempt to deny by law the rights which Black Americans were presumed to have by virtue of their citizenship. If civil rights were guaranteed by constitutional authority, how could Black Americans be further denied their rights? Southern opposition to attempts at desegregation was crucial in determining how Black Americans were to be treated as a matter of national policy.

After months of sporadic confrontations and violence directed toward Blacks, the two national political parties gave tacit support to civil rights. In the 1956 presidential campaign the Democratic party recognized school desegregation as mandated by the Supreme Court while simultaneously rejecting the use of force to implement the Court's decisions. Among their pledges, the party promised "continued efforts" to eliminate *illegal* [emphasis mine] discrimination in the areas of employment, voting, and education. The party rejected, however, a plank that called for strong government action to implement the Court's decision and federal civil rights legislation.[19]

The Republican party platform likewise affirmed the Court's decisions. It also supported the enactment of the 1956 civil rights measure proposed under President Eisenhower. Eisenhower's program called for the formation of a bipartisan Commission on Civil Rights. This Commission was to investigate charges of the denial of the right to vote and possible illegal economic pressures exerted against Black Americans. The program also asked for legal statutes to protect voting rights.[20]

Several interesting issues emerge from an examination of the platforms of the two national parties. One such issue involves the Democratic party platform statement regarding continuing efforts to eliminate illegal discrimination in the areas cited. Aside from executive actions taken by Presidents Roosevelt and Truman, Congress had not passed a civil rights bill since 1875. This inaction hardly bespeaks "continuing" efforts. Both parties explicitly supported efforts to eliminate laws sustaining discrimination but left implementation of those efforts to state and local governments. This is a peculiar stand in view of the Compromise of 1877, which left the Southern states in a position to act according to their own discriminatory wishes. On the other hand, this position seems politically wise in an election year. In spite of national and international sentiments, both parties were seeking victory at the polls. Therefore, they were not in a mood to allow issues of civil rights to interfere with reelection. If, on the other hand, political advantage could be gained from civil rights issues, both parties were ready to seize the opportunity.

Civil rights were being transformed by both political parties into what was essentially an expedient. Black America played a minor role in establishing the party agenda of both Republicans and Democrats. The irony of this situation was that Blacks were being excluded from participation in forming the national agenda, while they were seeking legislative reform as a major source for social change. What Black America did demonstrate was the extent to which their fundamental needs could be subverted by political expediency. Hence, the emphasis of both parties on the issue of voting. In a political climate tempered by the demands for racial change, both parties looked toward Black Americans as party supporters, but this support could not be solicited at the expense of alienating white voters. An interesting national forum on civil rights was emerging.

It should be remembered that only two years had passed since the *Brown* decision. The civil rights movement was in its infancy, without any unified ideological stand other than a commitment to nonviolent protest and a desire for racial integration. Within that context the structural basis of inequality was rarely addressed. Black Americans, desirous of change, were in no position to challenge politically the manner in which civil rights were being changed.

Coalition Politics

The successful challenge to institutional racism by the Montgomery boycott opened a new chapter in Black protest. It presented the South with an organized protest unparalleled in history. Boycotts and organized protests were not new, but during the 1950s the mobilization of middle-class, professional Blacks for direct action gave the movement a character that proved to have some interesting results. The middle-class nature of the leadership emerging in the South during the post-Montgomery confrontation[21] presented a moral tone which quickly gained the support of many whites.

That support was not lost in 1960 when Black students throughout the South staged repeated sit-in demonstrations. The sit-in tactic mobilized several civil rights organizations and their sympathizers, most notably the Southern Christian Leadership Conference (SCLC), under the leadership of Martin Luther King, Jr., and the Congress of Racial Equality (CORE). Northern white students also joined the protest and staged their own demonstrations.[22] They were joined by religious leaders, union leaders, and others in carrying out their demonstrations against racial exclusion.

During the same year, the country experienced the Freedom Rides. Mobilized to attack the issue of segregated seating in interstate travel, Freedom Riders were converging on the South in massive numbers. The Freedom Riders came from all age groups and included family members of noted politicians. For many this was their first taste of Southern discrimination. More importantly, these coalitions demonstrated their desire to end segregation in transportation and lunch counters. Again, in terms of the fundamental problems of inequality, these protest efforts could easily be absorbed within the context of a moral crusade. Being able to sit where one pleases is important in principle but does not change the nature of more pressing matters. As many people in the civil rights movement came to agree, acquiring the means to eat where one pleases was a more fundamental issue.

Because 1960 was also an election year, the major parties were preparing to address the matter of civil rights. Unlike the 1956 campaign, there was a growing constituency dedicated to pushing forward with sociopolitical change. Civil rights activism intensified, and the issues it raised were expected to occupy front stage in the national agenda.

Prior to the 1960 presidential campaign, Congress did pass a civil rights act. This act was essentially an extension of the 1957 act and reflected the intention of Southern legislators to minimize, if not defeat, any civil rights proposals. Although the act provided penalties for bomb threats and crossing state lines to transport bombs, the major civil rights clause authorized judges to appoint referees to aid Blacks in registering to vote.[23] In view of the national climate surrounding civil rights protest, the provision of this act appears quite modest. Congress again demonstrated its reluctance to act forcefully on civil rights.

The reluctance of the Congress to act on civil rights, as well as the kinds of actions it did take, further raises the question of the movement's reliance on legal reform. By 1960 it was clear that any reforms instituted by the Congress would be the result of considerable compromise. Southern legislators were acting out of their commitment to maintain the status quo. Northern politicians had not felt the political pressures to act because the focus on civil rights had been considered a Southern issue. The liberal coalitions being formed aimed their exclusive attention at breaking the patterns of the most blatant expression of racial discrimination. What these coalitions were not prepared to attack was the national dimension of racial practices as they affected Black Americans as a group. To do this, the civil rights movement would have had to alter its character as a protest movement and put forth political issues that touched the foundation of structured inequality. This would have meant, in part, a confrontation of union leaders and others who comprised the civil rights coalition. Such a confrontation was viewed as inappropriate because the movement felt that it was important to maintain its allies in order to gain momentum.

When the two major political parties addressed the issue of civil rights there was a decidedly stronger tone to their platforms. Both parties made platform pledges to support voting rights, school desegregation, equal opportunity in housing, and fair employment. After the Republican convention, President Eisenhower made a final gesture to civil rights by proposing a President's Commission on Equal Job Opportunity and federal financial assistance to schools undergoing desegregation. A Senate bill designed to legislate these proposals was defeated. Responding to the defeat of the Senate bill, the Democrat's nominee for President, John F. Kennedy, joined twenty-three other Democrats in drafting a statement on civil rights. In part, the statement read: "We pledge action to obtain consideration of a civil rights bill by the Senate early next session (1961) that will implement the pledges of the Democratic platform."[24]

Kennedy's senatorial actions were symbolically important, but he shifted his attention to the question of moral principles. He intervened in the arrest and mistreatment of Dr. King in Atlanta during the fiercely contested demonstration that greatly enhanced his image and had a tremendous impact on the movement. Black voters took advantage of their newly acquired voting rights to swing the election for Kennedy and the Democratic Party. For the first time since the Truman administration Black Americans felt that they had a friend in the White House who would actively push for civil rights.

During 1960 there surfaced several factors which would complicate the process of change. One of these factors was the growing militancy of student demonstrators. Their impatience with the legal approach of the NAACP and the moral, Gandhian approach of SCLC, was creating internal tension within the movement. Although their goals were not revolutionary, their militancy was disturbing to some who felt that these students might accelerate the movement too fast and alienate liberal support. While their actions did not pose a radical civil rights agenda, they were nonetheless determined to reject the idea that change inevitably meant "go slowly." Students were likewise determined to expose Southern racism at its worst, and, like the Freedom Riders, they were successful. They also were exposing a national embarrassment which Kennedy was determined to eliminate.

While internal issues continued to boil within the movement, John Kennedy was attempting to focus primary attention on voting rights. Robert Brisbane concludes that in order to subvert the student militancy and to redirect the movement, Kennedy felt what was needed was "an alteration in the political balance of the deep south, and this could be brought about only by a significant increase in the black vote."[25] When the emphasis in the movement focused on voter education, some of the students felt that this action was a retreat from direct action confrontation.[26] The emerging factionalism was only the beginning of a much broader confrontation.

Facing a reluctant Congress and conservatives in control of key committees, Kennedy resorted to executive actions to carry through his commitment to civil rights. In the field of employment, he established the Equal Employment Opportunity Commission to combat racial discrimination in the government and also in agencies holding federal contracts. But it was in the area of voting rights that the president was most active.

It is important to examine the process of civil rights actions, definitions, and policy in the context of a movement for change. The coalitions that were being formed from the 1950s to the early 1960s were clearly defining civil rights as an issue of democratic principle. Their focus on the South suggested that there was little attention being paid to the issue of racism as a national phenomenon and all of its manifestations. Equality of opportunity was either an implicit or explicit expression of the movement. An assumption underlying this expression was that Blacks would become equal with the elimination of racist laws. One major issue not addressed was whether Blacks would become equal by merely eating at a lunch counter, riding in the front of a bus, or having an opportunity to vote for presidential candidates. Black inequality was not a matter that could be rectifed by removing legal restraints. The great attention to voting rights as a civil rights issue certainly had its benefits for Blacks, but the most immediate payoff was to those elected.

From the Montgomery boycott to the events surrounding the election of John Kennedy as president, the civil rights movement did not confront America with a national challenge. The liberal perception of civil rights was being shaped by the essentially regional nature of the movement. If there was a national agenda emerging from the movement, it suggested that this country's most pressing problem was defeating Southern racism. Without the necessary political leverage, Black protest could not have been converted into a political movement. Without the vote, Blacks posed little or no political threat. During the latter days of the Kennedy administration there were a number of skeptics who felt that the civil rights movement was being orchestrated from Washington and that the leadership of King, Roy Wilkins, and Whitney Young impeded radical challenges to American society. This feeling was gradually articulated by young civil rights activists who felt that gaining the vote and protesting was not enough. They felt that as long as Washington called the shots, Blacks would remain victims of political expediency.

Civil Rights in Transformation

Throughout the early stages of the movement there remained an abiding faith in nonviolent, direct action. Even in the face of reactionary violence, Blacks were asked to remain nonviolent. As the intensity of the movement heightened and the racist forces became more entrenched, it was inevitable that the nonviolent strategy would be tested. If there were Blacks who were less than enthusiastic about this approach, it would raise important questions about the viability of the civil rights coalitions and how the national response would alter the perception of the issues.

Civil rights, nonviolence, and the future of the movement converged in Birmingham, Alabama, in 1963. After a Supreme Court decision declaring state laws requiring segregation unconstitutional, white reaction included the bombing of the home of Martin Luther King's brother. Shortly afterward, enraged Blacks took to the streets breaking windows, setting fires, and attacking local police. One result of these actions and the behavior of local police during the several days of protest was a national announcement from the president. In strong language the president proclaimed that the recent events in Birmingham had forced the country into a moral crisis. Neither violent actions, tokenism, or mass demonstrations would address the problem. In his attempt to take the leadership in the civil rights movement, the president submitted a bill to Congress guaranteeing access to public accommodations, allowing for the discontinuation of federal programs in areas where discrimination was practiced, committing the government to filing suit to desegregate schools, establishing a Community Relations Service, and strengthening efforts to prevent discrimination by government contractors. In presenting his bill to Congress, the president asserted that: "We are confronted primarily with a moral issue. . . . The fires of frustration and discord are burning in every city, North and South, where *legal remedies* [emphasis mine] are not at hand."[27]

The recognition of the national scope of the crisis facing America was occasioned by the outbreak of violence following the ambush slaying of Medgar Evers, state executive secretary of the Mississippi NAACP. Black Americans were expressing an anger and frustration that transcended the issue of equality and access. Their anger was directed towards the pervasiveness of racism in America. The violent outbreaks also revealed that not all of Black America shared the premise that integration was the primary goal. They also revealed a class dimension to their protest, which had major implications for national organizations such as the NAACP, SCLC, and the Urban League. Important also was the fact that the violence of northern and western Blacks questioned the direction of leadership and the politics of coalition. In a *Newsweek* poll taken in 1963, 42 percent of rank and file Blacks responding felt that most whites wanted to keep Negroes down, while only 9 percent of those identified as leaders felt the same.[28] When whites were asked what Negroes wanted, 41 percent nationwide answered "equal treatment."[29] In the same poll, 62 percent of whites nationwide supported a federal law enforcing an end to job discrimination but overwhelmingly rejected (31-1) a suggestion of preferential treatment.[30]

When *Newsweek* published a comparative poll in 1979, it showed that in 1966, 66 percent of whites agreed that Blacks tend to have less ambition than whites.[31] Forty-one percent of those sampled felt that Blacks want to live off of handouts. As racial conflict accelerated in 1963 several different perceptions of race relations emerged. Black civil rights leaders were optimistic about change and thought that whites were primarily interested in giving Blacks a better break. Rank and file Blacks were far less optimistic about this possibility and felt that racism was the main issue. White America in general agreed at least on the principle of equality but strongly opposed any suggestions that Blacks experienced any unique problem which would require special treatment. If there were any reservations about Blacks, they were expressed in terms of personal failures. White America was not willing, in the main, to submit to the proposition that the problems of Blacks were rooted in the nature of the social structure. Equality was perceived as a right due to the individual as a matter of principle; for Blacks to demand an alteration in their group position was considered unacceptable.

By the close of 1963, an interesting amalgam was surfacing. Demonstrations had taken place in approximately 800 cities, north, south, and west. The culminating event, however, was the March on Washington for Jobs and Freedom on August 28. At that time 200,000 persons gathered in the nation's capital to petition the country in general and the government in particular to act immediately and comprehensively on civil rights. A formidable coalition of Blacks and whites created an international climate in which major reforms were demanded. The demonstration also was a strong show of support for the civil rights intentions of the president.

The assassination of President Kennedy in November was an unexpected blow to the civil rights movement and its belief in the moral leadership which Kennedy had established. Legislatively, the president's record left much to be desired, but for many Blacks he was a significant symbolic figure. Blacks were far less sure of the vice-president, Lyndon Johnson—a Southerner. There were fears of a possible retrenchment of civil rights, but these fears were allayed for many when President Johnson gave his first address to Congress. "No memorial oration or eulogy," said the president, "could more eloquently honor President Kennedy's memory than the earliest possible passage of the civil rights bill for which he fought so long."[32]

On July 2, 1964, the president signed into law the Civil Rights Act of 1964. Celebrated by many civil rights activists as the most comprehensive step to assure equal opportunity for Blacks, the Civil Rights Act of 1964 was considered the highwater mark in the civil rights movement. For some, the struggle was now over. Black Americans had finally gained their freedom. Equality of opportunity had been indelibly impressed upon the nation's conscience. Alexander Bickel summarized the law by saying that it established national goals "that reach beyond minimal constitutional requirements."[33]

In spite of the enthusiastic support for the 1964 act, it still appeared that the bill had a regional intent. "Its address," notes Bickel, "is largely to the South."[34] Although this was not its overall intent, the regional perception of the law raised questions concerning its national implications. Blacks were particularly concerned about the implementation of Title VI, which prohibited discrimination in any program or activity receiving federal assistance. Title VII of the act also broadly prohibited discriminatory employment practices. How would these provisions apply outside of the South? Increasing Black unrest outside of the South established the basis for much uncertainty.

Some liberal civil rights coalitions perceived the 1964 act primarily as a blow against entrenched Southern racial prejudices. When the matter turned to areas outside the South, these factions were far less enthusiastic about implementation. Stokley Carmichael and Charles Hamilton addressed this issue in their critique of civil rights coalitions.

> They [some northern liberals] could be morally self-righteous about
> passing a law to desegregate Southern lunch counters or even a law
> guaranteeing Southern black people the right to vote. But laws
> against employment and housing discrimination—which would affect
> the North as much as the South—are something else again.[35]

Several factors related to the 1964 act should be pointed out. First, there was a discrepancy between what Blacks expected as a group and what the act provided for in terms of the individual. Implicit for many interpreters was the idea that equality of opportunity restored the principle of meritocracy, which assumes that merit should be the only legitimate basis for treatment.[36] Many Blacks, particularly those of the lower class, believed that merit was a false premise and that race was a more important factor in terms of who received the spoils of society. Second, there was a growing discontent among disaffected Blacks, because changes for a few Blacks did not mean racial progress for the group. Their problems ran much deeper than the larger society would admit. But the question was: How does one legitimize special need for a group when the larger society perceives the problem as an individual matter? Therefore, many supporters felt that with the passage of the 1964 act, civil rights had been accomplished. If Blacks suffered a disadvantage because of the law, removing the legal barriers would result in equality. Third, there were some voices claiming that passing a law did not make unequal persons equal.

President Johnson expressed some of the national ambivalence about civil rights actions that has persisted to the present. In a commencement address at Howard University on June 4, 1965, the president noted that one cannot take an individual who has been hobbled by chains for years and place him at the starting line of a race and declare him equal. It was not enough, he said, simply to provide openings for opportunity. One must also be provided the ability to take advantage of those opportunities. The president felt that legal equality had to be coupled with human ability. Therefore, equality must be a fact and not a theory. In closing his speech, the president said that the task now was to give Blacks "the same chance as every other American to learn and grow . . . share in society, to develop their abilities . . . and to pursue their individual happiness."[37]

Although President Johnson correctly identified the problem that history had left Blacks unequal, he concluded with an appeal to equal opportunity. Some social scientists, such as Daniel Moynihan and Edward Banfield, hastened to point out that equality of opportunity must not be confused with equality of result. As a matter of principle, these observers agreed that preferential actions could not be justified constitutionally. Therefore, special treatment would give Blacks an unearned advantage over others. Out of this argument came the popular labels "reverse discrimination" and "preferential treatment."

Affirmative Action

Unlike previous legislation, the 1964 Civil Rights Act was a legal landmark. In order to demonstrate the president's intention to give its provisions some "teeth," Johnson issued Executive Order 11246 in September of 1965. This action subsequently became known as the affirmative action order. It was the president's intent, through the encouragement of Vice-president Hubert Humphrey, to offer leadership, guidance, and support in the coordination of compliance with the terms of the act. The president consequently established the Council on Equal Opportunity. Relative to Title VI of the 1964 act, affirmative action embodied the idea of voluntary compliance. If agencies failed to act, the Council could recommend steps to cut off federal support. This represented some of the strongest actions yet taken by the government in the field of civil rights.

The president's actions were not totally altruistic. Just one month prior to the issuance of his executive order, he had signed into law the Voting Rights Act of 1965. Much of the agitation for stronger voting rights protection derived from the violence attending the Selma March led by Martin Luther King, Jr., during the same year. Less than a week after the Voting Rights Act was enacted, the first of continuous outbreaks of urban violence erupted in the Watts section of Los Angeles. Most Americans were stunned by the violence and attempted to discredit these outbreaks as the work of "riffraff" committed to lawlessness, not justice.

As white America watched the cities burn through the long, hot summer, the contradictions that plagued America were becoming a living reality. In spite of the celebration of the 1964 act and the president's gesture for affirmative action, it was becoming increasingly clear that the passage of laws would not reach the depth of Black discontent. What many Blacks were trying to tell the country was eventually echoed by the Kerner Commission: "Our nation is moving toward two societies, one black, one white—separate and unequal."[38] The commission concluded that the single most important reason for the violence in the cities was white racism.[39]

The climate surrounding affirmative action was volatile at worst and anxious at best. White America had yielded to what it felt was the solution to the "Negro question." What was left was implementation, and that would challenge the national commitment beyond the elimination of legal restraints. In addition, the country was being asked to provide both "guns" for the Vietnam conflict and "butter" for the dispossessed. President Johnson's promises of both could not be fulfilled, and many Black Americans felt their cause was being pushed aside in the interest of the war priorities. The national war program relegated any proposal for a Black agenda to the back burner. It was considered "treasonous" in some quarters for Black militancy to challenge the national agenda.

Largely as a result of these confrontations, affirmative action was more of a promise than a reality for many Blacks, especially those of the lower class. For these persons it was not enough to hear the recitation that Blacks are "making it," that there is an increasing Black middle class. They were not convinced of the "learn and earn" equation because too many of them had learned but were not earning. As victims of racial discrimination they were often the very last hired and the first fired. After gaining access to the starting line of life, they were not equipped with the necessary skills to run the race. Facing an ominous future, many of these persons felt that the only way for America to hear them was to make a loud noise in the street. As for the national war agenda, many felt no compulsion to fight a war abroad when they perceived their greatest fight in this country.

What did affirmative action mean? For those with the skills it meant opportunity. For those without them it mattered not whether one argued for quotas or goals. They were summarily excluded. But even for many who "made it" the price they paid caused them to question the results. King, in his final days, reflected on this situation and concluded: "Some of the most tragic figures in our society now are the Negro company vice presidents who sit with no authority or influence because they were merely employed for window dressing in an effort to win the Negro market or to comply with federal regulations in Title VII of the 1964 Civil Rights Act."[40] Unfortunately, this situation was not new to the Black experience. William Kornhouser pointed out the predicament of the Black union official who is powerless to act[41] and Ralph Bunche bemoaned the Black politician who is not his own person.[42]

Contrary to the claims of Diane Ravitch,[43] the issues of the 1970s are not more complex than those of the 1950s and 1960s. They are regrettably the result of the historical failure to deal effectively with structured inequality. The Supreme Court's rulings in the *Bakke* and *Weber* cases give affirmative action an uncertain future. Already there are retrenchments in some of the efforts to aid minorities in higher education. Tight fiscal policies in an age of "Proposition 13 fever" are depleting special education programs at the grade school levels. These are the places where individuals do gain those skills which make them productive citizens. As long as Black Americans and other minorities continue to swell the ranks of the lower class, there will always be an unfinished agenda.

Notes

1. *New York Times*, 11–14 March 1979.
2. Ibid., 11 March 1979, p. 1.
3. Robert Hill, *The Illusion of Black Progress* (Washington, D.C.: National Urban League Research Department, n.d.), p. 7.
4. Dorothy Newman, et al., *Protest, Politics, and Prosperity* (New York: Pantheon, 1978), pp. 71–98.
5. Ibid., p. 64.
6. Ibid.
7. Hill, *The Illusion of Black Progress*, p. 40.
8. Quoted in John Herbers, "Changes in Society Holding Black Youth in Jobless Web," *New York Times*, 11 March 1979.
9. Herbert Hill, "State Laws and the Negro: Social Change and the Impact of Law," *African Forum* 1 (Fall 1965): 92.
10. Mary Berry, *Black Resistance/White Law* (New York: Appleton-Century-Crofts, 1971).
11. Julian Bond, "Martin Luther King: Again a Victim—This Time of History Revised," *Los Angeles Times*, 14 January 1979.
12. Martin Luther King, Jr., *Where Do We Go From Here?* (New York: Harper & Row, 1967), p. 81.
13. Bayard Rustin, "From Protest to Politics: The Future of the Civil Rights Movement," *Commentary* 39 (February 1965): 28.
14. Vincent Harding, "Black Radicalism: The Road from Montgomery," in *Dissent: Explorations in the History of American Radicalism*, ed. Alfred Young (Dekalb, Ill.: Northeastern Illinois University Press, 1968), p. 334.

15. Richard Kluger, *Simple Justice* (New York: Alfred A. Knopf, 1976).
16. C. Vann Woodward, *The Strange Career of Jim Crow*, 3rd ed., rev. (New York: Oxford University Press, 1974), p. 132.
17. Bond, p. 1.
18. Rustin, p. 25.
19. *Revolution in Civil Rights* (Washington, D.C.: Congressional Quarterly Review Service, 1965), p. 26.
20. Ibid., pp. 26–27.
21. Martin Luther King, Jr., *Stride Toward Freedom: The Montgomery Story* (New York: Harper & Row, 1968); Preston Valien, "The Montgomery Bus Protest as a Social Movement," in *Race Relations: Problems and Theory*, ed. Jitsuichi Masuoka and Preston Valien (Chapel Hill, N.C.: University of North Carolina Press, 1961), pp. 112–127; Ralph Hines and James Pierce, "Negro Leadership After the Social Crisis: An Analysis of Leadership Changes in Montgomery, Alabama," *Phylon* 26 (Summer 1965): 162–172.
22. Robert Brisbane, *Black Activism* (Valley Forge, 1974), p. 49.
23. For a discussion of the provisions of the 1960 Civil Rights Act, see *Revolution in Civil Rights*, pp. 31–35.
24. Arthur Schlesinger, Jr., *A Thousand Days* (Boston, Mass.: Houghton Mifflin, 1965), p. 929.
25. Brisbane, pp. 57–58.
26. Ibid., p. 58.
27. *Revolution in Civil Rights*, p. 39.
28. William Brink and Louis Harris, *The Negro Revolution in America* (New York: Simon & Schuster, 1963), p. 126.
29. Ibid., p. 146.
30. Ibid., p. 149.
31. Dennis Williams, Jerry Buckley, and Mary Lord, "A New Radical Poll," *Newsweek*, 26 February 1979.
32. *Revolution in Civil Rights*, p. 41.
33. Alexander Bickel, "The Civil Rights Act of 1964," *Commentary* 38 (August 1964): 38.
34. Ibid.
35. Stokely Carmichael and Charles Hamilton, *Black Power* (New York: Vintage Books, 1967), p. 76.
36. Daniel Bell, "On meritocracy and equality," *The Public Interest* 29 (Fall 1972): 29–68.
37. Quoted from Richard Bardolph, *The Civil Rights Record* (New York: Thomas Crowell, 1970), p. 355.
38. *Report of the National Advisory Commission on Civil Disorders* (Washington, D.C., 1968), p. 1.
39. Ibid., p. 91.
40. King, *Where Do We Go From Here?*, p. 119.

41. William Kornhauser, "The Negro Official: A Study of Sponsorship and Control," *American Journal of Sociology* 57 (March 1952): 443–452.
42. Ralph Bunche, "The Negro in the Political Life of the United States," *Journal of Negro Education* 10 (July 1941): 567–584.
43. Diane Ravitch, "Color Blind or Color Conscious?," *The New Republic*, 5 May 1979, pp. 15–18, 20.

David Chanaiwa and Jack Bermingham

Education for Alienation: The African Versus the American Worlds of the Educated Elite

This essay is an analysis of the goals, implementation, and effects of Western education in colonial mission schools and in American universities upon the African educated elite. It emphasizes the experience of African professionals and intellectuals who have immigrated to the United States since World War II. We shall explore the attitudes, ideologies, and life-styles of African professionals in relation to the traditional world of the African masses among whom they lived and worked and to the Western world of white missionaries, settlers, and administrators who educated them, formally or informally.[1] We shall then examine the motivations, expectations, and experiences of the educated elite that managed to come to the United States for overseas study and then remained.

A further concern of this study is the Africans' search for both personal and collective identities in an alien, colonial situation.[2] Whether traditional or Christian, rural or urban, the Africans were placed in a culturally and psychologically oppressive system. They were told that they had no civilization or history, that their future depended on their readiness and ability to acquire Western customs and values. It was in response to such condescension and to the problems of African dignity, unity, and freedom that the educated elite developed new attitudes, ideologies and strategies.

Colonial Education in Africa

Education was probably the most pervasive instrument of colonial control in Africa.[3] We are referring here to the different forms of education: academic and experiential, secular and religious. Education was the means by which the Europeans transmitted their technology, religion, customs, and values, as well as their colonial culture of domination, racism, and capitalism. Thus, education is an appropriate barometer of the effects of European colonialism upon African life, even in the new socioeconomic formations of postindependence Africa.

The education we are discussing was born of the exigencies of colonial domination and exploitation.[4] Socioeconomic realities demanded that some Africans be educated to occupy secondary positions in government, missions, and industries. Africans were indispensible auxiliaries in the administration and exploitation of the colonies. To be effective, however, the education had to produce Africans who were both efficient and obedient, who would submit to subordinate positions in a social system based on white supremacy. Thus a major component of colonial education was its deliberate attempt to alienate the student from the African masses and their heritage. The educated African was supposed to be a self-deprecating, black-skinned European whose highest ambition was to emulate the colonizers in whose image he had been molded. Whether it was at a missionary, government, or private school, colonial education tended to be an indoctrination process leading to alienation and dependency.

The most typical educational institution was the mission boarding school.[5] African education was generally perceived as an essential part of the Christian missionary's responsibilities. At mission schools, impressionable African youths were indoctrinated with specifically Western values that were presented as being universal. They were given religious, academic, business, and civic education, all of which provided them with their guiding principles and values. They were also indoctrinated with colonialist notions of elitism, class distinctions, and "proper manners." In short, colonial education was not just a process of acquiring knowledge; it was also a way of living and feeling. It was essentially a capitalist, middle-class, Christian ideology and life-style.

Consequently, the mission-educated African elite adopted the religious values of the missionaries, the secular values of white liberals, and the ideology of capitalism. More importantly, its education subsequently determined its perception of both the African and Western worlds. Like its missionary and white liberal mentors, the elite despised the traditional African world which it considered heathen and backward. Having categorized the African masses as primitive, the elite assumed the responsibility of overhauling traditional Africa to reflect Christian and capitalist values. Before the end of World War II, the elite feared racial, political, and cultural consciousness among the African masses.

In relation to the African masses, the educated elite appears to be alienated from its African heritage and inured to Christianity and Western culture.[6] In reality, however, its character is very complex. The principles of brotherhood, of individualism, of free enterprise, and of cultural assimilation inherent in both Christianity and colonial education conflicted with the practical realities of colonialism. The flagrant contradiction between the myths and realities of the so-called White Man's Burden were thus exposed. The denial of economic opportunity and racial equality represented an inescapable embarrassment for the missionaries and white liberals and a source of frustration for the Africans.

Having been denied acceptance and equality, the educated elite also turned against the colonial world. Thus, it was not merely seeking acceptance in the white man's world or aping his values. Its commitment to individual dignity, racial equality, free enterprise, and parliamentary democracy was both a philosophy of life and a moral crusade against evil, ignorance, and racism. Its ideology actually transcended both the African and colonial worlds. Even its notion of education was much broader than the mere production of bureaucrats and other professionals. Education had to include programs for elevating the material, political, and moral well-being of the whole community. Above all, it had to aim at providing the community with well-trained, conscientious leadership capable of improving the quality of life:

> When I completed my mission school years, I genuinely believed I
> would help lead the masses to freedom. My education showed me
> concepts free of racism and exploitation. In fact, I thought African
> countries would quickly surpass Europe because we would end
> oppression. . . . I thought we were already better human beings than
> the missionaries. . . . They didn't practice most of what they
> preached.[7]

Thus, the main failing of the educated elite was not that it rejected fellow Africans in favor of the white man's world, but that its humanistic outlook overlooked the cruel realities of settler colonialism. It created a utopian vision of its own, which embraced both the African and European worlds. Throughout the colonial period, the elite formed national, nonethnic political movements, such as the African National Congress of South Africa (1912) and the National Democratic Party of Nigeria (1920), which were based on the Christian ideals of racial equality, nonviolence, and equal opportunity.

But its cultural and psychological alienation from the African masses and the rejection of the settler society caused the elite to lose its power base and legitimacy. Consequently its ideology became mere self-expression, a negligible force in colonial Africa. However, this elite made the first attempt to undermine ethnicity and sectional collaboration among African chiefs, groups, and individuals.

Ultimately, the bitter experiences and prolonged frustrations of the educated elite, as well as the liberating influence of World War II, led to African nationalism and to the militant denunciation of colonialism, racism, and Western values. Those of the elite who did not make the ideological shift became conservative and even counterrevolutionary. The post-World War II leaders such as Kwame Nkrumah and Julius Nyerere, as well as the political movements, have been committed to mass support, total independence, racial equality and Pan Africanism.[8] For those who did not fit in after independence, there was the option of emigrating. Their motivation was often political or economic. But many Africans who remain outside their homeland now believe that their education alienated them from their society. As an African intellectual from Nigeria succinctly put it, "I no longer felt comfortable at home. For me there was no going back after I got my education."[9]

However, this African environment did provide an important cultural and educational background for African students who came to the United States to study and live:

> My mission school training helped me fit into America because the values with which I was imbued were compatible with American society. I gained the necessary foundation to compete educationally and economically. . . . My class status was equivalent to middle- or upper-middle-class Americans.[10]

The Educated Elite as Foreign Students in the United States

An understanding of the cultural background of the foreign student from colonial Africa is essential for an understanding and appreciation of African students, intellectuals, and professionals in the United States. Most of the African students who were products of missionary schools regarded themselves as Christian ladies and gentlemen. At the boarding schools they had adopted the Western middle-class value system characterized by the capitalist-Protestant ethic of piety, thrift, industriousness, sobriety, independence, and social mobility. Their middle-class values were largely theoretical and not necessarily related to their family background. Their middle-class values were predicated upon idealism and high expectations. In fact, the generational and cultural gap between them and their parents was often very wide. Like most true believers, some of them acquired an almost fanatical view of Western education and technology as the solution to all social problems and to self-fulfillment.

> I remember thinking that America really was a place to accomplish success easily. There was so much wealth, and when I finished school, I quickly got a good paying position. It seemed that all I needed was the education. . . .[11]

On the whole the African foreign students were self-made, self-confident, and elitist individuals. Their educational careers were success stories in their communities, in their boarding schools, and even in ther countries: they were accustomed to being put on a pedestal. They perceived themselves as select individuals who were being groomed for future leadership roles, for success and fame. Like many affluent immigrants, the African foreign students had much in common with middle-class America. They were programmed for integration and assimilation, and they had no ideological commitment to ethnicity, bilingualism, or biculturalism.[12] The most enthusiastic among them even shared the Puritan, middle-class biases against big government, the welfare system, and communism. Because of their value system, African students, like the bourgeois American Black, Chicano, or Asian, were also likely to have difficulty relating to lower-class Americans.

> It is difficult for me to understand the problems of lower-class
> Blacks. My background gave me little in common with them besides
> my color.[13]

African foreign students, especially those from English-speaking British colonies, were well prepared to undertake university education in the United States. Even if they were from French- or Portuguese-speaking colonies, they were already fluent in an African and a European language and easily acquired some level of competency in English. Furthermore, their colonial education mainly consisted of the study of European and American history, science, and culture. In some subjects their preparation was better than that of the American students:

> For me specifically, coming from South Africa, I had an advantage
> of living in a mixed society. Since I left before many of the laws
> changed, I went through an education that was the same for whites
> and Africans. I had both educational and social advantages, given
> my knowledge and experience in a racialist environment.[14]

The actual educational and cultural experiences of individual African students varied considerably, according to the institutions they attended and their individual ability, diligence, and temperament. But whether they were sponsored by their missionary mentors, their colonial governments, humanitarian organizations, or relatives, the students considered their overseas educational studies rare opportunities. For the vast majority of African foreign students, coming to the United States depended upon competition for a sponsor. Even the universities and degree programs to be attended were often determined by the sponsors. Thus, depending on the sponsor, a student could be sent to Britain, France, or any other European country, as well as to Canada, Russia, Australia, or India.[15] Our particular concern, however, is with the student who came to the United States.

The prospect of overseas study in the United States was exciting for most of the selected candidates and their families. Through their colonial education, through movies, and through the United States Information Service, the students had learned to perceive the United States as "the promised land of milk and honey." To most of the mission-educated elite, the United

States was the antithesis of both the traditional and colonialist worlds in Africa. It represented wealth, democracy, racial equality, equal opportunity, and self-determination, all of which were lacking in their homelands. The African foreign student may have experienced less cultural shock because of his Western orientation. His rude awakening was to the practical and sometimes harsh realities of capitalist and racist America. "Discrimination was shocking to me. It was the most shocking thing. I don't think the whole experience of slavery could have been put in a starker perspective."[16] Negative experiences, such as being forced to ride at the back of the bus,[17] bred disillusionment and frustration that served as an impetus to return to Africa. For others these problems were assessed as less significant, because discrimination was rampant in their homeland.[18] Economic opportunity also motivated many to stay.

> The state of development was astonishing. From afar it was like a
> fantasy; but to see that it was real, so much wealth, affluence,
> was shocking. . . . It provided genuine economic prospects for people
> with my background.[19]

These economic opportunities, coupled with the legal victories achieved by the civil rights movement in the 1950s and 1960s, reinforced the idealism and westernization acquired in colonial mission schools. They provided convincing reasons to like American society and to consider establishing an American residence.

On the positive side, most African students found better educational opportunities, curricula, counseling, and sponsorship than they had back home. Even the few like Kwame Nkrumah[20] who were self-supporting still appreciated the opportunity to be able to work and go to school. The middle-class values that the African students had acquired in colonial schools were instrumental in enabling them to weather the trials and tribulations of learning in a new environment. Their education and life-styles at mission boarding schools had taught them to evaluate new situations, take initiatives, and apply self-discipline. In short, they had been programmed for success in capitalist America.

> My engineering degree quickly gave me a chance to make money
> which I could invest and make more money. . . . I think my up-
> bringing at mission school let me understand the system and moti-
> vated me to want to make money. . . . For a while I may have been
> a better capitalist in America than most Americans. The colonial
> experience and my education showed me the way.[21]

Invariably, the African foreign students, like all other immigrants to the United States, were deeply impressed by American science, technology, and efficiency.[22] Most of them were amazed by the technological accomplishments such as elevators, automatic doors, fast-food restaurants like Jack in the Box and McDonald's, amusement parks like Disneyland, and the day-to-day contact with a multitude of "modern" conveniences. Like most other immigrants in the United States, many of the students were soon accustomed, if not addicted, to the hamburger, french fries, coca cola, cars, and television. In time, the students were able to establish some lasting friendships with Americans and other foreign students, and many of them ended up marrying Americans. The high level of technology and material comfort in America reinforced the students' previous realization that European colonialism was retarding African advancement. Thus both the academic and experiential aspects of the students' education in America provided some liberating influences.

On the other hand, nearly all of the students were surprised at the negative image that Americans had of all Africans, which contradicted the students' middle-class orientation and elitism.[23] There was the image of Africa as the "Dark Continent" and of Africans as Stone Age cavemen. Several of the Africans took offense at such ignorant questions as "When did you first put on clothes?" and "Are you a cannibal?" Furthermore, many of the students experienced racial discrimination both on campus and in the community at large, which shook their idealized perception of the United States.[24] The students' experiences and responses were further complicated by the fact that while they suffered racial discrimination with Black Americans, most Black Americans held the same negative stereotypes of Africa and the Africans as the whites.

> I was astonished how little Black Americans knew about Africa.
> Most Blacks that I met weren't even sure that there were different
> countries in Africa. All they could talk about was natives and
> tribes.[25]

Given their ideological commitment to racial equality the African students readily empathized with Black Americans and liberal whites in the civil rights struggle. However, they were always singled out and treated as "Africans," which created some degree of identity conflict among the students. Instead of encouraging assimilation, pluralist America emphasized their uniqueness and, therefore, stimulated their cultural, historical, and ethnic consciousness, generally referred to as Negritude. Their apparent exile and alienation in America caused a few of the foreign students to turn to their African traditions, especially of diet and dress. Considering the breakdown of African traditions that was taking place back home due to industrialization and urbanization, these students became superficially more traditionalist than many Africans living in Africa.

The African students observed various aspects of American society, especially of the capitalist system, that left permanent impressions. They came face to face with the abject poverty of the urban ghettos and skid rows of big cities such as New York, Chicago, and Detroit. They also noted the surprisingly high level of rural poverty and underdevelopment, especially in the South. Their individual reactions to these unpleasant realities of life in America varied considerably. Some individuals like Kwame Nkruma perceived the poverty and apparent government neglect of the poor as a failure of the capitalist system and a vindication of socialism.[26] They empathized with the poor and with the militant Black leaders such as Marcus Aurelius Garvey. Some maintained their middle-class orientation and empathized with the civil rights movements seeking gradual and constitutional reforms of the capitalist system.[27] A few adopted the Puritan ethic of conservative America and blamed the poor for their supposed ignorance and lack of motivation and self-discipline. These varied reactions to lower class poverty can be found within the Black American, Chicano, and Asian middle classes. To a considerable degree the Africans transferred their elitism and paternalism towards the African masses to the lower class of America.

> It's hard for me to understand why there are poor people in America. There are so many jobs. All one has to do is work hard. . . . Some Africans at home have the same problem. They are not willing to take a job I did to help me to get an education. . . . Many just want a handout.[28]

The Educated Elite: Effects of the American Experience

The vast majority of African students who came to the United States before the 1960s returned to their countries of origin upon graduation, partly because of the conditions of their sponsorships and partly because of attractive employment opportunities back home. However, in the postindependence period, there has been a steady increase in the number of graduates who have taken up permanent employment and residence in the United States, especially among those who originally came from nations such as Nigeria and Zaire, which have experienced civil wars, or from the settler colonies of Rhodesia and South Africa.

Clearly, American education has had a major impact on Africa. American universities have produced some of Africa's most outstanding leaders, such as Kwame Nkrumah of Ghana, Dr. Namdi Azikiwe of Nigeria, John Dube and Pixely Seme of South Africa,[29] and Ndabaningi Sithole[30] and Bishop Abel Muzorewa of Zimbabwe.[31] Together with their counterparts educated in African, European, and Asian universities, the American-educated elite has dominated modern African leadership. In postindependence Africa it has displaced both the Euorpean colonizers and the traditional African chiefs.

Therefore, the destiny of Africa and, to an extent, of the world, will be affected by its leadership, ideologies, and development programs.

Modern African leadership and nationalism stemmed from an ideological and cultural environment created by Western religion, education, and capitalism. But the educated elite has always had the political and moral support of the African masses, especially the partially transformed urban proletariats. Both formal and informal education managed to establish Western cultural values among Africans. Consequently, the capitalist self-determination and individualism exemplified by the elite found support among the masses, who saw in its self-confidence and material success the embodiment of their own dreams and desires. Until both had learned from bitter experiences and frustrations, the elite and the masses generally agreed that the ideals of racial equality and nonviolence represented a viable alternative to the racist world of European colonialism. The failure of these ideals partially accounts for the militant demands and armed struggle against colonialism by all segments of the African population that began in earnest after World War II and led to political independence.

With independence came a political struggle within African countries for government positions. Many Africans who were students in the United States at that time missed their opportunity to gain positions proportionate to their qualifications.

> I saw people get important political appointments because they were friends or relatives of the president or an important minister. Even uneducated people who were active in the independence movement got better positions than I would have gotten—even though I had a Ph.D.[32]

Some of the African students in America had come after failures in politics at home. They became refugees, but with a class base that suggested they would not starve.

> I lost in the political infighting at home . . . but I already had a B.A. degree. The United States is a place where I can use my education to make money. First, I'm going to get the M.A.[33]

Recently, several Africans who had taken up permanent residence or citizenship in the United States have begun to return home, at least for lengthy visits. As the political and economic situation in Africa changes, it becomes more attractive to those African immigrants who felt exiled. It will be interesting to see how many return to Africa permanently. In my interviews with Africans who have stayed in America, many contend that they will go back to their homeland someday.

I never lose sight that I will go home to Nigeria. Now I'm making enough money here to help my family out at home and still live comfortably. I think my family would be disappointed if I left this opportunity to go home. There's just too much money here; besides my kids are getting a good education. . . . But someday I'll go back to stay.[34]

Nonetheless, several African university graduates have established permanent residence in the United States and are making their living here as professionals. They have either married Americans or brought their spouses from Africa. As parents they are now concerned with even the elementary and secondary school levels of American education and with bilingual/bicultural programs. As professionals and taxpayers they are directly affected by affirmative action policies and programs. Culturally and psychologically they have to confront the problems of their dual lives as Africans in America and the gap between them and their children, as well as between them and their African relatives and friends.

Apparently, many of them have in turn sponsored their relatives for educational study and personal visits to the United States. The result has been a relative increase of African foreign students and residents in the United States. Both the objectives of African immigrants and the process of selecting them are more diversified in the postindependence period than in the colonial period. During the colonial period, few Africans came to the United States to visit or to take up permanent residence. Now many choose to remain in America. The impact of this trend on the brain drain on African countries deserves study. Surely, America has benefitted and has become a richer plural society thanks to the contributions of these recent Black immigrants.

Notes

1. The African educated elite has been discussed before, primarily in the context of African nationalism and leadership. See for example J. F. A. Ajayi, *Christian Missions in Nigeria, 1841-1891* (London: Longmans, 1965); Robert W. July, *The Origins of Modern African Thought* (New York: Praeger, 1967); Peter Walshe, *The Rise of African Nationalism in South Africa: The African National Congress, 1912-1952* (Los Angeles, Ca: University of California Press, 1971); Helen Kitchen, ed., *The Educated African: A Country-by-Country Survey of Educational Development in Africa* (New York: Praeger, 1962); Agrippah T. Mugomba and Mougu Nyaggah, eds., *Independence Without Freedom: The Political Economy of Colonial Education in Southern Africa* (Santa Barbara, Ca.: Clio Press, 1980); and David Chanaiwa, ed., *Profiles of Self-Deter-*

mination: African Responses to European Colonialism in Southern Africa, 1652-Present (Northridge, Ca.: California State University Foundation, 1976).

2. For a discussion of this concept of the search for identity consult Raymond Betts, ed., *The Ideology of Blackness* (Lexington, Mass.: Heath and Company, 1971); July, *Origins of Modern African Thought*; and David Chanaiwa, "African Humanism in South Africa: The Utopian, African, and Colonialist Worlds of the Mission-educated Elites," in *Independence Without Freedom*, ed. Mugomba and Nyaggah.

3. Chanaiwa, "The Political Economy of Colonial Education," in Mugomba and Nyaggah.

4. Martin Carnoy, *Education as Cultural Imperialism* (New York: David McKay Company, 1974).

5. See for example Ajayi, *Christian Missions in Nigeria*; E. A. Ayandele, *The Missionary Impact on Modern Nigeria 1842-1914* (London: Longmans, 1966); and Chanaiwa, "African Humanism in South Africa."

6. For more details consult, July, Mugomba and Nyaggah, Chanaiwa, and Leo Kuper, *An African Bourgeoisie* (New Haven, Conn.: Yale University Press, 1957).

7. Interview 33, p. 7. All interviews referred to in these notes were confidential and were conducted by Jack Bermingham in California in 1978-79. The page numbers refer to the transcript.

8. For detailed analysis of African nationalism consult, Thomas Hodgkin, *Nationalism in Colonial Africa* (New York: New York University Press, 1971); Ndabaningi Sithole, *African Nationalism* (London: Oxford University Press, 1969); Walshe, *The Rise of African Nationalism in South Africa*; Immanuel Wallerstein, *Africa: The Politics of Independence* (New York: Vintage, 1961); George Padmore, *Pan Africanism or Communism* (London: Dobson, 1956); C. Legum, *Pan-Africanism* (New York: Praeger, 1965).

9. Interview 29, p. 11.

10. Interview 30, p. 10.

11. Interview 32, p. 7.

12. Interview 32, p. 8; interview 27, p. 4.

13. Interview 41, p. 14.

14. Interview 28, p. 12.

15. Interview 27, p. 6.

16. Interview 29, p. 7.

17. Ibid.

18. Interview 28, pp. 13-14.

19. Interview 29, p. 7.

20. See Kwame Nkrumah, *Ghana: The Autobiography of Kwame Nkrumah* (New York: International Publishers, 1971).

21. Interview 40, p. 7.

22. For autobiographical notes on experiences and impressions of individual African students in the United States see for example, Nkrumah, *Ghana*; Nnamdi Azikiwe, *My Odyssey: An Autobiography* (New York: Praeger, 1970); and Muzorewa, *Rise Up and Walk: The Autobiography of Bishop Abel Tendekey Muzorewa*, ed. Norman E. Thomas (Nashville, Tenn.: Abingdon, 1978).

23. Interview 28, p. 5; interview 31, p. 3.

24. See for example Nkrumah, *Ghana*.

25. Interview 24, p. 14.

26. See for example Kwame Nkrumah, *Neo-Colonialism: The Last State of Imperialism* (London: Heinemann, 1968).

27. See for example Azikiwe, *My Odyssey*.

28. Interview 37, p. 13.

29. See Walshe, *The Rise of African Nationalism in South Africa*.

30. Sithole, *African Nationalism*.

31. Muzorewa, *Rise Up and Walk*.

32. Interview 19, p. 15.

33. Interview 41, p. 9.

34. Interview 40, p. 5.

Part II

Programs for Pluralism:
Towards an End to Racism

Introduction

Efforts to alleviate tension between ethnic groups in the United States have focused largely on educational reform that would allow minorities equal access to the education system as a whole. However, the ethnic minorities themselves have fought for broader changes in an attempt to make cultural pluralism a reality. In doing so they have expended much energy attempting to broaden educational reform in such fashion as to bring appreciation of the cultural diversity of American society. The shortcomings of this strategy once again demonstrate the importance of socioeconomic background. Class relationships are crucial in determining the power to implement and enforce reforms. Consequently, minorities do not have significant discretionary powers to define and execute reforms.

This section examines recent educational reforms which reflect the evolution of laws resulting from court decisions in support of minority rights and cultural pluralism. Implicit in the essays is the recognition that public policy has not altered basic socioeconomic disparities; therefore cultural pluralism is still not a reality.

Laura Miller examines pupil placement in public schools, tracing the use of race and ethnicity to deny access to education. She explains how placement standards such as language, ability, achievement, and handicaps, which may be theoretically defensible, are potential and real causes of ethnic segregation. In Professor Miller's view, the courts and legislatures are centralizing power, enabling them to determine placement and procedures for outlining parental involvement in specific placement decisions.

Using his experience as an administrator in the Bilingual Education Department of the San Francisco Unified School District, Douglas Lee discusses the reality of cultural pluralism and its implications for education. Although his essay comments on East Asian immigrants in general, it focuses on the Chinese immigrant student. He describes the routine of an administrator and comments on the position's limitations, suggesting changes needed to make programs more effective.

George Roberts offers an analysis of textbooks in public education and their impact in promoting pluralism. As former chairperson of California's

State Committee on Textbooks and a member of the California State Board of Education Task Force, Roberts draws on the commission's research findings to discuss this crucial aspect of schooling. Within this context the essay examines what needs to be done to achieve cultural pluralism in California.

Laura Means Pope Miller

Race or Ethnicity as Determinants of Pupil Placement in Public Schools*

Introduction

Public school administrators routinely assign students to various programs, groups, or schools. Federal and state laws, amplified by local school district policies, govern most aspects of these judgments. This "sorting" process serves many purposes, including convenience, efficiency, child benefit, the economic system, or majority prejudice. Though a law may be neutral on its face and a particular placement considered "best" for the child, the long-run effects often belie the beneficial intent. The child may be stigmatized and lose opportunities; the society may waste human potential and reap civil strife (Washington Research Project, 1974). This paradox is part of an enduring dilemma for any society, but it is particularly poignant in the United States.

When our forefathers declared that "all men are created equal, that they are endowed by their creator with certain unalienable Rights, that among these are Life, Liberty and the Pursuit of Happiness,"[1] their basic premise was more self-serving than "self-evident," as proclaimed. Over 200 years later, Justice William J. Brennan, Jr., in his dissent to the *Bakke* decision, argued: "Yet candor requires acknowledgement that the Framers of our Constitution, to forge the Thirteen Colonies into one Nation, openly compromised this principle of equality with its antithesis: slavery. The consequences of this compromise are well known and have aptly been called our 'American Dilemma'".[2]

Government classification of people on the basis of race, sex, language, ethnicity, wealth, mental ability, or physical disability inevitably risks conflict with the American ideal of equal treatment under the law. People are not created equal in terms of wealth, health, or capacity, nor is all ascribed

*This chapter is largely excerpted, with permission, from "State Statutory and Administrative Regulation of Pupil Placement in Public Schools," *Advances in Law and Child Development*, vol. 1 (Greenwich, Conn.: JAI Press [Forthcoming]).

status equally valued. Unfortunately, equal treatment of unequals may be outrageously inequitable. The United States Constitution prohibits Congress and the states from denying any person's right to life, liberty, or property without due process of law.[3] It also promises equal protection under the law,[4] but not equal distribution of status, which is generally based on wealth, power, or prestige. Presumably, the right to pursue happiness, touted as "unalienable" in the Declaration of Independence, includes the right to join the competition for status. Those participants impeded by acts of government increasingly invoke the equal protection and due process clauses of the federal and state constitutions to attain equal opportunity, especially for education. Sociologists consider education an important determinant in the status stratification process, a view shared by litigants and courts alike. The oft-quoted *Brown* decision observes: "In these days, it is doubtful that any child may reasonably be expected to succeed in life if he is denied the opportunity of an education. Such an opportunity, where the state has undertaken to provide it, is a right which must be available to all on equal terms."[5]

The United States is committed to a competitive race for rewards tied to finite, physical resources, despite any inequities in the natural endowments of the competitors. The outcome could be no less brutal than the law of the jungle, but for mutually accepted restraints on the exercise of power. Since the powerful have long legitimized and amplified their power through governments, we have amended our federal constitution over the years to limit governmental powers and set standards of behavior for the exercise of power by both the public and private sectors.

"Fairness" is the *sine qua non* of acceptance of the competition and the consequent stratification. Throughout our history, people have organized to use the judiciary to force changes in behavior. Today the courts are increasingly using the constitutional doctrines of due process and equal protection of the law as amplified by civil rights legislation to force governmental agencies to neutralize or overcome handicaps caused by cultural and lingual diversity, poverty, racial prejudice, and physical or mental disability.[6]

This essay will review first the struggle to eliminate the use of race or ethnicity as a primary determinant of pupil placement in public elementary and secondary schools. It will then examine some of the other criteria for placement which are plagued with implications of racial or ethnic discrimination. As used here, "placement" means classification of persons for the purpose of determining access to or exclusion from free public education in whole or part. Legislators and administrators at federal, state, and local levels adopt statutes and regulations which determine the standards used to sort children into schools and programs. The interplay of the decisions at various levels and among the branches of government often determines who wins what and who is stratified where.

Using Race or Ethnicity for Pupil Placement

PRE-CIVIL WAR PRACTICES

Classifying people according to race or ethnicity to determine eligibility for a public education or assignment to a school, program, or class is totally arbitrary, yet it has been done for centuries in our land. The struggle by Black men and women to change such injustice is magnificently chronicled by Richard Kluger.[7] His book begins with a quote from a petition from parents to the legislature of the Commonwealth of Massachusetts Bay in 1787. They decried the fact that their children did not benefit from the free schools in Boston and concluded: "we, therefore, must fear for our rising offspring to see them in ignorance in a land of gospel light when there is provision made for them as well as others and yet can't enjoy them, and no other reason can be given than they are black. . . ."[8]

The legislature apparently was unmoved, but Boston established a separate school for Negroes in 1820. Five-year-old Sarah Roberts had to walk past five elementary schools for white children to reach the Negro school. The school committee ignored her father's pleas for reassignment, so he took the matter to court. Despite the eloquent arguments of his abolitionist attorney, Charles Sumner, the 1849 decision upheld the Boston School Committee's power of assignment.[9] It was another six years before the Massachusetts legislature outlawed segregation in the commonwealth schools.

Support for segregated schools in the North had deep roots in slavery. For example, "African schools" were long sustained on the Quinnipiak plantations. The New Haven Board of Education eventually assumed responsibility for the African School with the assertion that "the children of this class should have privileges equal in all respects to those of other schools."[10] Segregated schooling, however, persisted in Connecticut until after the Civil War.

Segregated schooling, however, was not always attributable to slavery. A continent away from the fires of Atlanta, the political rhetoric on abolition scorched political candidates in California. Under a pre-Civil War statute, state funds for education were apportioned on the basis of white enrollment, so local districts shouldered all cost of any schooling accorded nonwhites. While blacks pressed successfully in many communities for their own schools and Mexican-Americans were counted as white in those days, the Orientals and Indians were rarely admitted to schools. Despite scathing proslavery opposition, the California voters elected a moderate Republican State Superintendent of Instruction in 1862, who argued that nonwhites—Chinese, Negroes, and Indians—should be educated in their own schools. Although the education laws were amended in this direction, Blacks continued to press not only for their own schools, but for admission to schools for whites.

While Northerners and Westerners debated about whether and how non-whites should be educated, the Southern elite scorned the very idea of public education for anyone before the Civil War and were too poor to support it after the war. Northern philanthropies financed the postwar schools for Blacks as two separate systems of education developed in the South: one Black, one white.

POST-CIVIL WAR SEGREGATION

Among other things, the Fourteenth Amendment provides for equal protection under the law.[11] Just what that meant when applied to segregated education or exclusion from education was unclear. When the amendment was ratified in 1868, the laws in thirteen states were either silent about segregated education or prohibited it. Eight states provided separate schools or local option, and five Yankee states excluded Black children either directly or implicitly by law.[12] Concerned about the meaning of the Equal Protection Clause, legislators in Connecticut, Florida, Louisiana, Michigan, and South Carolina prohibited segregated schools soon after ratification of the Fourteenth Amendment. Three of those states eventually reinstated the practice.

Frustrated by the slow pace of legislative reform of the school laws in California and encouraged by the possibilities under the new amendment to the federal constitution, California Blacks turned to the courts in 1872. Their attorney chose the experience of Mary Ward, who was denied entrance to the San Francisco school nearest her home, as the vehicle to charge that segregated education violated the Equal Protection Clause. Relying on *Roberts,*[13] the California Supreme Court anticipated *Plessy*[14] when it decided in 1874 that the board of education violated no constitutional rights by providing racially segregated schools. The Court ruled, however, that ". . . each [race], though separated from the other, is to be educated upon equal terms with that other, and both at the common public expense."[15] Because the sparse population of Blacks was scattered, this ruling meant an integrated education for many of them even before the legislature acted in 1880 to open all public schools, unless otherwise provided by special statute, to "all children between five and twenty-one years of age, residing in the district."[16]

School administrators in this period needed no law to exclude the Chinese. The superintendent in San Francisco simply closed the Chinese school in 1870. Hendrick observes: "So thoroughly were Chinese residents socially excluded from American institutions that it is likely some members of the legislature failed to notice that Chinese had neither been excluded nor segregated in the school laws of 1872, 1874, or 1880. They were simply ignored."[17] A native citizen of Chinese descent finally challenged such exclusion. The San Franciso school administrators denied school admission to Mamie Tape, one of over 1000 Chinese children totally barred from public education. The lower court ordered her admission pursuant to the 1880 state law. Because the legislature had not excluded any race, "the question whether it might have done so does not arise in this case."[18] During the two-month period of appeal, Superintendent Moulder turned to the legislature. The California Supreme Court upheld the decision[19] on March 3, 1886, and within days the legislature classified the Chinese as a group which could be segregated.

THE PLESSY DOCTRINE AND BROWN

The "separate but equal" doctrine enunciated in the *Plessy* v. *Ferguson*[20] transportation case in 1896 by the United States Supreme Court lent the imprimatur of constitutionality to a plethora of governmental decisions classifying people according to race. No constitutional brakes impeded expression of arbitrary racial prejudice in public decisions until the mid-1900s. Hendrick's study of public policy toward the education of nonwhites in California found that racial prejudice increased with the concentration of each minority. Economics took precedence over prejudice in most school board decisions, but whenever minority concentrations made separate schools economically feasible, prejudice often triumphed. The advent of discriminatory covenants in deeds of private property restricted land purchases by minorities. The resulting residential concentration of minorities, especially Blacks and Mexican-Americans, made boards of education vulnerable to public pressure for segregated schooling. As Hendrick observed about the trend in the 1920s:

> The Los Angeles school board and administration reluctantly cooperated with white neighborhood groups in creating segregated schools during this time. Because state law clearly did not sanction a dual school system (for Negroes), and because it was difficult to maintain that Negroes required separate facilities on educational grounds, all deliberate segregation was accomplished through the manipulation of school boundaries, the location of new schools, and a selective transfer policy.[21]

Under the *Plessy* doctrine, states freely classified people by race. California law permitted local districts to provide separate schools for Chinese, Indian, and "Mongolian" children. With a rise in Japanese immigration, the legislature added the Japanese to the list in 1921. Mexican-Americans had long been considered "white," but when the California Attorney General offered the opinion in 1927 that they were Indians, local districts were free to isolate them. The United States Office of Indian Affairs in the meantime was pressing hard for integration of Indians. Concurrently, a wave of Mexican immigration generated pressure to segregate Mexicans. The legislative response was a twisted statute which desegregated American Indians without mentioning Mexicans, which left school districts free to segregate the latter: "The governing board of the school districts shall have power to establish separate schools for Indian children, excepting children of Indians who are wards of the United States government and children of all other Indians who are descendants of the original American Indians of the United States, and for children of Chinese, Japanese or Mongolian parentage."[22]

The battle to attain equal facilities, let alone equal education, was a losing one for minorities. In a democracy in which a Caucasian majority believed race and ethnicity determined intelligence, increasing poverty among minorities further isolated them. Only the constitution could protect minorities from acts of the majority, so members of the National Association for the Advancement of Colored People (NAACP) used their "lesser" intelligence to mount the long campaign to reverse the *Plessy* doctrine. Attacking through those bastions of rationality, the state law schools, they chipped away at the premise that separate educational facilities could be equal. First, the United States Supreme Court agreed that paying the tuition of Black students to attend out-of-state law schools did not justify a denial of entrance to a public law school within the state.[23] Another suit filed in Texas sent legislators scurrying to set up a separate law school for Blacks, who were not allowed to attend school with whites, but the United States Supreme Court ruled that separate law schools could provide neither equal library facilities nor an equal education.[24] Part of becoming a lawyer is matching wits with peers, and Black lawyers would need to know how to work with white lawyers, witnesses, jurors, judges, and other officials.

The NAACP strategy included simultaneous assault on an Oklahoma statute which permitted Negroes to attend white colleges but required that instruction be segregated. McLaurin, a Black Oklahoman enrolled in a course leading to a doctorate of education, was assigned to classroom seats "reserved for colored students" and a special table in the cafeteria. The Supreme Court ruled that "state-imposed restrictions which produce such inequalities cannot be sustained."[25]

The final assault on *Plessy* involved four cases from Kansas, South Carolina, Virginia, and Delaware which were considered together by the United States Supreme Court as *Brown* v. *Board of Education*.[26] In three cases, the lower courts upheld constitutional or statutory segregation. In Kansas, relief was denied because facilities were found to be equal; in South Carolina, the federal district court ordered equalization of facilities but denied interim admission to white schools; and the federal district court in Virginia ordered both equalization and interim admission to white schools. The Delaware lower court found segregation resulted in unequal education and ordered admission of Blacks to white schools, but the Delaware Supreme Court, in affirming the decision, hinted that modification of the order might be possible if equalization were accomplished. The United States Supreme Court abandoned the *Plessy* doctrine and ruled that separate schools do not provide equal protection under the law.

Brown v. *Board of Education* changed the standard. All constitutional, statutory, or administrative provisions for racially segregated education became vulnerable to legal attack. The NAACP strategy succeeded in turning the tide and marked the beginning of the third major stage in black/white relations in the United States. The first sanctioned slavery or the servant role for free Blacks; the second accorded freedom and equality in theory but gross inequality in practice; the third provided the legal leverage needed to achieve real civil equality.[27]

POST-BROWN CASELAW

The battle for equality has been doggedly fought in the board rooms, legislative halls, and courtrooms since 1954. Courts have no command of physical means by which to enforce their decrees. They depend on the legislative and administrative branches of government to aid them. The response of political leaders to judicial decisions makes all the difference.[28] President Eisenhower often opined after *Brown*, "It is difficult through law and through force to change a man's heart."[29] Stanford psychologist D. J. Bem disagrees, arguing that legislation and court decisions *can* change attitudes by forcing changed behavior and that when behavior is changed, attitudes tend to follow.[30] Time and the Gallup Poll substantiate Bem's view. The opposition of white parents to school integration has dropped dramatically since the parents' march on Washington on August 28, 1963. When asked whether "you, yourself, have any objection to sending your children to a school where a few of the children are black? Where half are black? Where more than half are black?," the percentage of Southern parents objecting in 1963 was 61 percent, 78 percent, and 86 percent respectively. Today the percentages are 7 percent, 28 percent, and 49 percent. Northern parents showed the same decline in objections: 10 percent, 33 percent, and 53 percent in 1963 versus 5 percent, 23 percent, and 38 percent, respectively, today.[31]

The Supreme Court's decisions, without physical force, change the behavior not only of the socially dominant, but of the subordinate. Voluntary desegregation in 750 school districts occurred within four years of *Brown*,[32] and by 1976 more than 50 percent of the schools in the South were "relatively free of segregation."[33] In the decades following *Brown*, minorities used physical, economic, legal, and ballot box resistance to all forms of segregation. Even Eisenhower backed the judiciary with federal paratroopers when Governor Faubus defied a 1956 desegregation order to admit Blacks to Little Rock's Central High School.

In its implementation decision regarding *Brown*, the Supreme Court remanded the cases to lower courts for orders "to admit to public schools on a racially nondiscriminatory basis with *all deliberate speed* the parties to these cases."[34] In one such case,[35] Judge Parker intoned that neither the Constitution nor the *Brown* decision took away from the people the *freedom to choose* the schools they attend. Relying on these two phrases, administrators dawdled over desegregation for a decade. In the 1964 *Griffin* decision,[36] the Supreme Court declared there was no more time for "deliberate speed." In the 1968 *Green* ruling,[37] the high Court found *ineffective* freedom-of-choice plans to be unconstitutional. Even President Nixon's chosen Chief Justice, Warren Burger, joined by a unanimous Court, wrote bluntly in the 1969 *Alexander* opinion: "Under explicit holdings of this Court, the obligation of every school district is to terminate dual school systems at once and to operate now and hereafter only unitary schools."[38]

The Burger Court ruled, again unanimously, in 1971 that a "racially neutral" assignment plan based on existing neighborhood schools was inadequate to remedy segregation in the nation's largest school district, Charlotte-Mecklenberg, North Carolina. Declaring that the use of quotas to achieve racial balance in every school is not constitutionally required, the Court nevertheless ruled that "the very limited use made of mathematical ratios" as a starting point was within the equitable remedial discretion of the court.[39] Gerrymandering of districts to desegregate schools was also approved as a remedy for the past history of segregation. The lower court had ordered a transportation plan which provided for average distances of seven miles with the longest route taking thirty-five minutes. The Supreme Court approved the busing and commented that it compared favorably with the former plan involving an average of fifteen miles one way for an average trip of over an hour.

The tactic of forming a new school district was declared unconstitutional in *Wright*,[40] and in *Keyes*[41] the Court ruled that the finding of intentional segregation of a portion of the district raises a presumption of segregation in the whole. For the first time, the Court also expressly recognized Mexican American students as a minority to be protected from segregation. From Boston[42] to Denver[43] and Los Angeles,[44] the judiciary gaveled the point home.

Members of the U. S. Supreme Court divided sharply in 1974 when they ruled that the lower federal district court could not order interdistrict assignment of pupils to desegregate the heavily black school population in Detroit because there was no finding of state or local action concerning school districting based on a segregative intent, i.e., de jure segregation. *Milliken* v.

Bradley[45] thus limited the power of the federal judiciary to remedy segregation caused by the administrative acts of a school district in which the "minority" has become a majority. State supreme courts generally echo the U. S. Supreme Court when interpreting equal protection clauses in state constitutions; but the California Supreme Court appears to deviate from the *Milliken* rule requiring a finding of de jure segregation. In an ambiguous decision which acknowledged the lower court finding of de jure segregation in Los Angeles, the state supreme court argued that regardless of the cause, the board of education must do whatever is "reasonably feasible" to remedy racial segregation.[46] Subsequently, the First District Court of Appeals interpreted this language as empowering it to order an interdistrict remedy in a case involving nine San Francisco Bay area school districts.[47]

LEGISLATIVE AND ADMINISTRATIVE RESPONSE

The federal legislative response began with establishment of the Civil Rights Commission in 1957 and a Civil Rights Division in the Justice Department with the power to bring suit on behalf of Negroes denied the right to vote.[48] Under Presidents Kennedy and Johnson, the administrative leadership for civil rights crescendoed to a climax with adoption of the 1964 Civil Rights Act,[49] which permits the Department of Justice to require school desegregation under Title IV. Title VI prohibits discrimination in the distribution of benefits from any program or activity receiving federal financial assistance. Pursuant to authority granted under the act, the United States Office of Education eventually issued a Statement of Policies for School Desegregation, known as "guidelines."[50] When Congress adopted the Elementary and Secondary Education Act (ESEA) of 1965,[51] it provided the Department of Health, Education, and Welfare a carrot/club with which to encourage nondiscrimination. (For a detailed discussion of the Title IV experience, see United States Commission on Civil Rights, 1973; for judicial discussion of Title IV, see *United States* v. *Jefferson County Board of Education*, 372 F. 2d 836 (5th Cir., 1966.) The Nixon and Ford administrations were much less enthusiastic about desegregation. The number of HEW investigations of communities to determine whether school desegregation guidelines were being met dropped steadily from twenty-eight in 1968 to none in 1974.[52]

Congress, fired by growing public opposition to busing and by the Nixon leadership, quickly adopted the *Milliken* approach in the 1974 Equal Educational Opportunities Act.[53] The act simultaneously forbids discrimination based on race, color, sex, or national origin; forbids use of ESEA funds for busing to overcome racial imbalance in the schools; and prohibits remedies which ignore school district lines unless the discriminatory effect was caused by intentionally discriminatory state action.

State legislative response to the *Brown* decision varied widely. One of the *Brown* cases involved Black high school students in Prince Edward County. Both the Virginia constitution and statutes required segregation of Negroes and whites.[54] The Virginia legislature tried "massive resistance" by banning mixed schools and providing tuition grants for private nonsectarian schools. The state supreme court invalidated the legislation as unconstitutional, so the legislature repealed the compulsory attendance law and enacted a new tuition grant law. From 1959-63 Black children in Prince Edward County were totally without schools. The United States Supreme Court reviewed the events and supported the injunction of the payment of the tuition grants and tax credits while public schools were closed and suggested that an order to lay taxes and open schools might be needed.[55]

In contrast, the California State Board of Education approved a succession of policy statements encouraging desegregation. The state board escalated its actions, with minimal effect, during the 1960s, beginning with adoption of an administrative regulation in 1962 admonishing decision makers to consider seriously the "policy of elimination of existing segregation and curbing any tendency toward its growth."[56] In 1963 another section added the requirement that school districts consider ethnic factors.[57] Two months later the Board added a section requiring county committee consideration of the effect of proposed boundaries of new school districts on achieving racial integration.[58] In 1963 the board established a Commission on Equal Opportunities in Education, opposed the fair housing law in 1964, and instituted a statewide racial and ethnic census, beginning in 1966.[59]

Despite the election of Governor Reagan in 1966, the board continued to press desegregation. As the racial census program documented the increasing racial and ethnic isolation in California, the board escalated pressure by ordering school districts with racial imbalances to "prepare plans to eliminate such imbalance."[60]

None of the Board's actions aroused public opposition until February 1969, when the board adopted a new policy defining a school as "racially imbalanced" when its minority student enrollment differed by more than 15 percent from the percentage of minority children in that school district.[61] The public saw busing as the correction required by such a definition. The resulting backlash brought enactment of a statute in September 1970, which provided: "No governing board of a school district shall require any student or pupil to be transported for any purpose or for any reason without the written permission of the parent or guardian."[62] The California Supreme Court construed the statute to require parental consent for a child to use school transportation, but not to limit the school district power of assignment.[63] The legislature then deleted it from the Education Code.

In Massachusetts the legislature enacted a racial imbalance law after a federal district court ordered the Springfield School Committee to take into consideration the fact that racial imbalance impared the educational opportunities of Negro students suffering under de facto segregation.[64] The act required school committees to provide the Commissioner of Education with statistics on racial imbalance and to prepare plans for elimination of racial imbalance, which was "deemed to exist when the percent of nonwhite students in any public school is in excess of fifty percent of the total number of students in such school."[65] To encourage compliance, the act provided additional aid for necessary construction and a potential cutoff for non-compliance.[66] The Massachusetts Supreme Court upheld the constitutionality of the act,[67] but the legislature repealed the reporting provisions and added incentives for voluntary transfer among districts to decrease imbalance in 1974.

The Connecticut General Assembly enacted a racial imbalance statute requiring a periodic racial census in the schools and defining racial imbalance as: "a condition wherein the proportion of pupils of racial minorities in all of the grades of a public school of the secondary level or below taken together substantially exceeds or falls short of the proportion of such public school pupils in all of the same grades of the school district."[68] The remedy includes state board notice of racial imbalance to the local district, local preparation of a plan subject to state board approval, assistance, and monitoring. The state board has regulatory power.[69]

RESULTS

Notable success in desegregation of the public schools has occurred since *Brown*. In California, voluntary compliance, locally inspired, successfully desegregated schools in Berkeley, Riverside, and a number of smaller California school districts, while others such as San Francisco, Pasadena, San Diego, and Los Angeles responded to court decisions. Only Oakland was helpless to correct de facto segregation because of the steady influx of Blacks. The 120-year history of California evidences considerable improvement in the legal and social rights of nonwhite students, but the ultimate irony is that the net disadvantage created by segregation and poverty has never been so severe.[70] The latest statewide survey of racial and ethnic isolation of students in public schools reveals that the number of minority students attending predominantly minority schools has increased 27 percent in the last four years and now totals nearly one million students. The State Department of Education study documents a steady rise of segregation of minority students since the first survey was made in 1967.[71]

Similar problems exist throughout the nation. Twenty years after *Brown*, more than half of the minority children in New York attended schools with more than 90 percent nonwhite enrollment. In Chicago nearly half the schools enrolled more than 90 percent nonwhite, and in Washington, D.C. 96 percent of the children in public schools were Black. The four school districts which spawned the *Brown* decision were little changed. The public schools in Prince Edward County, which were closed from 1959 to 1964, subsequently enrolled nearly all Blacks, although by 1974 about one-third of the whites left their private schools to return. In Topeka more than half the Black students were concentrated in one-sixth of the elementary schools. In Delaware white flight from Wilmington, combined with other factors, converted the population to nearly half Blacks, and the schools were 90 percent Black. In Clarendon, North Carolina, the focus of the *Briggs* case, the public schools enrolled 3,000 Blacks and one white child.[72]

A Southerner, acknowledging growing problems such as diminishing numbers of whites in city schools, socioeconomic segregation, exclusion of children from school, increasing violence in schools, and increasing resistance to desegregation, nevertheless found that:

> The public schools of Hemingway and Williamsburg (for example) offer dramatic proof that equal educational opportunity, quality education and desegregation can be achieved, even under the most difficult conditions.[73]

The U. S. Commission on Civil Rights flatly announced after a national study that "desegregation works." The commission credits local leadership:

> These communities have learned that through positive, forceful leadership and careful planning by a broad cross-section of the community, school desegregation can be implemented smoothly. School districts which have experienced desegregation for several years generally report that minority student achievement rises and that these students often exhibit greater motivation that ultimately leads to pursuit of higher education. Majority group students hold their own academically and they commonly report that experiences with minority students have dispelled long-held stereotypes.[74]

Racial and Ethnic Implications
of Other Placement Criteria

The use of race or ethnicity as an open criterion for student assignments is unconstitutional and outlawed by federal and state statutes. A so-called second generation of racial and ethnic discrimination problems, however, infects decisions based on other criteria such as language, ability, achievement, and handicap.

—→ LANGUAGE

English has long been the language of instruction in most schools in the United States, and the public schools have been the medium for Anglicizing our population. State laws frequently require instruction in English,[75] although the United States Supreme Court ruled in 1923 that the State could not coerce the use of the English language by prohibiting the use of another in teaching.[76] The Nebraska statute in question prohibited teaching any subject in any private or public school in a language other than English until the student had graduated from the eighth grade.

Unfortunately, the problem of teaching chilren who speak little or no English has been used elsewhere to isolate students along ethnic lines. Until 1947, California law permitted separate schools for Chinese, certain Indians (interpreted to mean Mexican American), Japanese, and Mongolians.[77] As the concentration of Mexican Americans in California cities increased, the white population pressed for separate schools, especially at the elementary level. Typically, the espoused justification for separation of the Mexican Americans was the need for special instruction in English and a concern for the progress of other children, but the result was generally segregated and inferior education for the non-English-speaking child.

The 1964 Civil Rights Act, Title VI, and the regulations thereunder, sowed the seeds of change. Section 601 provides: "No person in the United States shall, on the ground of race, color, or national origin, be excluded from participation in, be denied the benefits of, or be subjected to discrimination under any program or activity receiving Federal financial assistance."[78] Although the initial HEW regulations accepted a court desegregaton order or an HEW-approved voluntary desegregation plan as evidence of compliance, in 1968 the department broke new ground with a comprehensive regulation asserting that: "School systems are responsible for assuring that students of a particular race, color, or national origin are not denied the opportunity to obtain the education generally obtained by other students in the system."[79] In 1970, the HEW Office of Civil Rights sent a memorandum[80] to selected school districts "to clarify" the regulation to the effect that, among other things, the school district has an affirmative duty to rectify any language deficiency in order to open its instructional program to non-English-speaking students.

Congress responded to pressure for financial aid with the "Bilingual Education Act of 1968," which became Title VII of ESEA.[81] The philosophy underlying Congressional action was modified in 1974 to recognize multicultural backgrounds and "that a primary means by which a child learns is through the use of such child's language and cultural heritage."[82] Such a philosophy is in strong contrast with the "melting pot" or assimilationist view long dominating public policy in the United States and represents the spreading success of the Black revolt which championed cultural pluralism.[83] The turnabout in policy should eventually reverse the prevalent practices of discouraging the speaking of Spanish in the classroom and, in many schools, punishing its use.[84] Despite the fact that almost 50 percent of the Mexican American first-graders do not speak English as well as white students, they are forced to learn simultaneously English and all the other subjects which are taught only in English.[85] The frustration and discouragement experienced by such children can be turned into success in the classroom with the bilingual-bicultural approach.[86]

The United States Supreme Court upheld the HEW regulation and memorandum in 1974, when it ruled in *Lau* v. *Nichols*[87] that the Chinese Americans had suffered discrimination in educational opportunity. Regardless of intent, the San Francisco school *in effect* excluded them from the benefits of academic programs because they did not understand English, the medium of instruction. This landmark case prompted further Congressional action to extend the ruling to all school districts, including those which spurn federal funding, through the Equal Educational Opportunity Act of 1974.[88]

Following the federal lead in this area, Massachusetts was the first state to adopt a statute mandating bilingual education in 1970. By 1976, nine more states legislated such a mandate and sixteen states adopted statutes expressly permitting it. Fourteen states tacitly permitted it, and only ten prohibited bilingual education.[89] The growth of the programs is reflected in state appropriations totalling over $68 million and federal funding of nearly $148 million for the 1975–76 school year.[90] The magnitude of implementing appropriate bilingual-multicultural programs in many school districts was dramatically illustrated by the president of the Los Angeles Board of Education when he startled an audience at RAND Corporation with the remark that there are at least eighty-six languages spoken in the homes of Los Angeles school children and possibly as many as ninety-six.[91]

Language as a criterion for placement is becoming much more prominent under the pressure of civil rights legislation and judicial enforcement of a right to an equal opportunity for education. No longer can it be used to place groups of children in isolated, inferior classes or schools. The challenges to educators and the community will be difficult, as the decision makers attempt to implement multiple values which increase the variables considered in placement. The stakes are high in terms of a potentially enriched cultural pluralism and expanded individual achievement, but removing the language barrier to a meaningful education is only one step in the quest for equal opportunity. Unfortunately, nearly every criterion used for pupil placement, though to some extent defensible on educational grounds, can be shown to reflect or entrench social or ethnic separation. The next subsection examines the effects of using ability as a sorting criterion.

ABILITY

Schools for over a century have used ability to group children for educational purposes. It is closely related to, but distinct from, achievement, although in school administration and state law they may be intertwined. State laws have not used ability to classify children except those at either end of the ability curve. Both the retarded and the gifted are by definition such a minority that local school boards have tended to ignore their needs in favor of programs appropriate for most students. Parents of the neglected minorities therefore turned to the state legislatures, Congress, and the courts for redress.

Ability grouping takes many forms. The grouping and regrouping for instructional purposes within a classroom is commended as a teaching practice and is generally accepted according to Findley and Bryan,[92] but they note that other common varieties are more controversial. Practiced in about 77 percent of the public schools by 1970, ability grouping was lauded as a means to provide for individual difference, to simplify teaching, and to facilitate curriculum planning.[93] It is as popular today among public school teachers as it was in the 1920s, despite inconclusive empirical evidence as to its efficacy.[94]

Critics of the use of "ability" to sort students into homogeneous classes or programs attack the effects, the inferred ulterior motives, and the premises of the concept. From a social perspective, the harshest criticism of ability grouping, especially in the form of tracking students into different educational programs, centers on the demonstrated effects of racial, ethnic, and socioeconomic segregation.[95] In the most famous judicial scrutiny of tracking, Judge Wright described the four-track curricula in Washington, D.C., during the 1960s, as consisting of "separation of students into rigid curricula, which entails both physical segregation and a disparity of educational opportunity; and for those consigned to the lower tracks, opportunities decidedly inferior to those available in higher tracks." He continued: "A precipitating cause of the constitutional inquiry in this case is the fact that those who are being consigned to the lower tracks are the poor and the Negroes, whereas the upper tracks are the provinces of the more affluent and white."[96] The U. S. Commission on Civil Rights found a similar pattern of placement in the Southwest: "An analysis of schools which practice some form of ability grouping shows that Chicano students are grossly overrepresented in low ability group classes and correspondingly underrepresented in high ability groups."[97]

Regardless of the motivation for tracking, it appears to be constitutional to discriminate among students if *in fact* they are classified according to ability.[98] The Washington, D.C., school authorities failed to prove that their system rested on distinctions in ability, because the federal district court was persuaded that the standardized aptitude tests used to sort students were "completely inappropriate for use with a large segment of the student body."[99] The court agreed with the plaintiffs:

> Because these tests are standardized primarily on and are relevant to a white middle class group of students, they produce inaccurate and misleading test scores when given to lower class and Negro students. As a result, rather than being classified according to their socioeconomic or racial status, or—more precisely—according to environmental and psychological factors which have nothing to do with innate ability.[100]

The court found the track system in operation violated its own premise that placements were made according to ability and ruled that it unconstitutionally discriminated against the poor and the Black. The circuit court of appeals refused to overrule the lower court's order to abolish the track system, but viewed the order as narrowly related to the specific program in effect at the time and refused to speculate about the proper balance of educational goals or permissible methods of testing.[101] The decision is binding only in Washington, D.C., but raises doubts about the constitutionality of any tracking plan which has the same effects.

That people differ in mental ability is obvious to just about everyone, but no one has satisfactorily defined the essence of intelligence, nor is there agreement about its components or how to measure it. The concept of an intelligence quotient or IQ score developed by Binet and Simon has facilitated a ranking of chronological age peers according to their "mental age." It is computed by dividing mental age by chronological age and multiplying by 100. An IQ of 100 means one's performance on the test is average for one's age. This basic model was used for many years and numerous competing tests and special purpose tests have been developed.

Ingalls notes that no commonly accepted theory of intelligence supports these tests. The earlier versions assumed that intelligence was a unitary concept and that performance of quite varied tasks reflected the same innate ability. More modern tests use subsets of items to measure multiple abilities and provide scores for these subsets as well as an overall IQ score. Ingalls asserts that since the word "intelligence" does not describe a psychological entity or operation, it cannot be used to explain behavior. The tests are useful evidence of what people can do, but are not conclusive evidence of what they cannot do.[102]

Research shows that intelligence tests predict reasonably well the future academic performance of both black and white children in schools geared to white middle-class values.[103] Yet, other research suggests that no more than 50 percent of academic performance is associated with intelligence test scores.[104] At a technical level, the tests are useful for identifying unrecognized ability in children who are not performing as well as they could in school or predicting for the short term a child's success in a traditional school. They can alert administrators to discrepancies in teachers' judgments and are helpful in identifying exceptionally endowed or seriously retarded children. Danger in their use, at an operational level, may arise from improper administration, blind trust in the scores, stereotyping of children, and lowered expectations. Not only may the latter affect a child's performance in fulfillment of the prophecy, but educators can shift blame for poor achievement from their own teaching to the presumed defects in the child's ability. Whether intelligence testing is dangerous to the future of individual children appears closely linked in practice to the goal of testing, i.e., diagnosis of weaknesses and strengths, as opposed to stratification of students along a superior—inferior continuum of ascribed status. Unfortunately, placement on the continuum is often confused with human value.

From an egalitarian perspective, the most egregious abuse of test scores stems from the assumption that the tests indicate innate, inherited mental ability. Many studies confirm, for example, that Blacks as a group score about one standard deviation lower than whites as a group.[105] Adherents of the eugenics movement in the early 1900s used such data to buttress arguments for segregation of Blacks and Mexican Americans,[106] sterilization of "mental defectives,"[107] tightening of immigration laws, and anti-miscegenation laws. Social Darwinism, a belief in the inheritance of acquired characteristics and the survival of the fittest, gained popularity as Goddard used intelligence tests to "prove," after World War I, the mental inferiority of Blacks and the superior intelligence of Western versus Eastern Europeans. Anglo-Saxon Americans accepted his studies as confirmation of their superiority and passed laws to protect their racial purity.[108]

Whether one believes intelligence is genetically fixed, environmentally determined, or a bit of both has important implications for social policy. Ingalls reports that although there has been more educational research on the issue of the relationship between social conditions, race, and school failure than on any other issue in the 1960s and 1970s, no solution has been found for the problem of school failure, and the rate of failure among Blacks, Hispano-Americans, and the poor has not declined.[109] His analysis of the three dominant theories which have been advanced to explain the discrepancies in test scores correlated with race and socioeconomic status illustrate the impact on policy.[110]

The most generally accepted theory hypothesizes that child-rearing practices and the economic environment foster success in middle/upper-class children and failure for the poor, a large proportion of whom are racial minorities. The concept of cultural deficit sparked massive spending on compensatory education programs in the 1960s.

The genetic theory holds that heredity is the greatest determinant of intellectual potential, that weaker intellects tend to be found among the poor, and their condition is inherited. According to this view, compensatory education programs are useless. Ingalls asserts that this theory is not widely supported, partly because it is politically untenable and partly because of accumulating evidence that child-rearing practices have considerable impact on the mental ability of the child.

The newest and increasingly popular theory argues that there is no intellectual deficiency among children of low-income and minority families. They only appear less intellectually competent when measured by white middle-class persons and institutions with tests reflecting the skills, values, and behavior of the white middle-class population used to standardize the tests. Adherents of the cultural difference hypothesis oppose all compensatory education as superfluous, because there is no deficit, and unacceptable, because it proceeds on the assumption that the white middle-class culture is superior. The alternative approach urges acceptance of cultural differences, organization of multicultural schools, and placement practices which assume that an equal proportion of gifted and retarded children will be found in all cultural groups.

Though brief and oversimplified, this treatment of the problems associated with intelligence testing at least alerts the reader to the subtle dangers and reasons for debate about statutes and regulations which rely on intelligence tests to classify students. Hobbs cautions that intelligence tests are actually achievement tests in the sense that they measure what a person has learned.[111] Presumably, everyone has had an equal opportunity to learn the answers to the questions asked and the more "correct" answers given, the more intelligent the person. Such assumptions do not hold crossculturally. The circumstances surrounding the testing experience can also profoundly influence an individual score.[112]

This subsection has discussed grouping by ability for different programs, the problem of a concomitant racial segregation and unconstitutional discrimination, the difficulties in measuring intellectual ability, and conflicting concepts of intelligence. The next subsection considers briefly the implications of the national trend toward conditioning grade placement on demonstrated achievement.

ACHIEVEMENT

An analysis of education statutes in effect in the mid-1970s revealed that local school districts enjoyed greater autonomy in the area of grade promotion policies than in any other of the thirty-six areas reviewed.[113] Thirty-five states had no laws concerning promotion requirements. Spearheaded in

California, Florida, and Oregon, the accountability movement suddenly shifted focus from the system to the student. By early 1978, thirty-three states had enacted laws or regulations to mandate specific standards for grade promotion or graduation from the public schools. While issues of discrimination are political problems amenable to redress through the judicial or legislative process, the problem of low academic achievement is more technical than political. Wise argues that intervention by higher levels of government is unlikely to work.[114]

In the traditional annual spring placement rites, school administrators and teachers determine who will teach whom during the following year. Inevitably, regardless of the process used, there is a problem of what to do with those children whose achievement lags, most often cumulatively, year by year. Grade repetition, and the concomitant problem of "overageness" for the class assignment, is a hotly debated solution.[115] Most often, teachers recommend retention because a child's mastery of the subject matter is insufficient to enable the student to handle the materials in the next grade, but sometimes a child is judged too emotionally immature, or prolonged illness has interfered with school attendance. Retention, particularly if repeated, separates the students from peers of the same age, subjects them to humiliation, and worse still, to more of the same subject matter and teaching which failed to help them achieve at an acceptable rate in the first place.

The United States Commission on Civil Rights found that in Texas more than 22 percent of the Mexican Americans and nearly 21 percent of the Blacks repeated the first grade, compared to less than 6 percent of the whites, and that there was a strong relationship between grade repetition and low student achievement.[116] The commission report underscored the fact that the number of Mexican American eighth grade students reading below grade level was much higher in Texas, which had a high retention rate in grades one and four, than in California, where fewer Mexican Americans repeated a grade. The report also cites the high correlation of grade retention to school dropout rates, as discovered by the United States Department of Labor study of seven communities. It revealed that 53 percent of the dropouts were two or more years older than their classmates and 84 percent were at least one year older.[117] The local school response to such criticism has been social promotion of underachieving students.

Unfortunately, social promotion is no more a complete solution to the problem of low achievement than is grade repetition. One socially promoted graduate recently sued the San Francisco public schools because he was functionally illiterate, but the court refused to award money damages.[118] Peter W.'s malpractice suit nevertheless focused attention on expectations of the public schools, and future litigants may succeed in obtaining redress in other forms.

The California law differs[119] from the Florida act[120] by delegating to local school districts the task of setting standards and devising assessment procedures with the guidance of an "assessment framework" developed by the state department of education.[121] Nevertheless, the same penalty is levied for failure to demonstrate proficiency in reading, writing, and mathematics on graduation: no diploma. Ultimately, only the student is penalized. Critics of the minimum competency legislation, intended to solve the problem of functional illiteracy, warn that fear of the penalty will cause many students who would have remained in school against formidable odds to give up their quest for the high school diploma as a passport to employment.[122]

The advent of the minimum competency testing laws raises the specter of compounding all the "sorting" problems of student placement; e.g., racial, ethnic, or socioeconomic separation. Yet, to the extent that the success of schools and professionals is tied to the success of these minorities, the laws will have the effect of allocating more resources to the task of helping them achieve. Reportedly, the state of Washington expects to spend $43 to $47 million in 1978–79 on remedial programs in reading and math; Michigan is spending $28 million, and Florida initially allocated $10 million.[123] Nevertheless, students on the lower end of the scale may find that no matter how much they improve, "it's never good enough," as school districts or states raise the standards. One official in the Gary, Indiana, minimum competency program reports that they expect to raise the cutoff scores as students improve so that students leaving Gary schools will be able to perform at an increasingly higher level.[124] He sees the program as providing "high school diplomas with meaning." That meaning may be the labelling of a fixed proportion of the student body as incompetent, regardless of how its performance improves. Inevitably, the cutoff score is arbitrary, and the impact on individuals in the system is serious.

A minimum competency testing program that denies standard high school diplomas to persons who have persisted in school attendance and may have learned other useful skills not measured by the test may operate as the economic gatekeeper for controlling competition for jobs. This may be the widespread effect despite judicial decisions requiring employers to show the relevance of their standards, such as a high school diploma, to the job to be performed.[125] Viewed from another perspective, if the high school diploma purports to signify competency in certain skills but is not valid for use by employers to screen applicants, why allocate large amounts of time and public funds to sort so-called functional literates from illiterates? Life will do it freely and more accurately.

Testing procedures need to be balanced carefully against their social implications. Glass charges that the minimum competency testing movement feeds racial prejudice (see note 3), and he is not alone in his criticisms of both the technical and social implications of the trend.[126] Rejection of social promotion in favor of performance progression stigmatizes laggards through labelling, grade retention, and tracking, but enthusiastic advocates cite the potential for systematic attention to the problem of achievement, funding of remediation, motivating students, and upgrading education.[127] The cost of devising, validating, and administering the tests will mount at the same time the cost of remediation escalates, and, predictably, pressure on Congress to adopt nationwide standards and provide funds has begun. The choice is political and may hinge on beliefs about human behavior, the purpose of public education, and the causes of low achievement, or possibly the economics of the business of testing and education.

Minimum competency testing chiefly affects placement decisions about marginal students who nevertheless are able to function in a regular classroom. When children suffer mental, physical, or emotional handicaps to the degree that they need help or services which cannot be provided by the regular classroom teacher, placement decisions based on their handicap must be made. The use of this criterion to place or exclude children has been revolutionized in the last decade.

HANDICAP

Statutory exemptions from compulsory education laws have been, in practice, tantamount to exclusion. By 1974, such laws in forty-seven states exempted children with mental, emotional, or physical disabilities,[128] so it is not surprising that Congressman Brademas asserted in 1975: "Fully 1 million of the 6 million school aged handicapped children are denied entrance to any publicly supported education, and only 40 percent of these children are receiving special educational services appropriate to their needs."[129] Classification of children on the basis of their handicaps is inevitably a two-edged sword. Theoretically, it can be used with the care, ethics, and professionalism necessary to provide a precise educational diagnosis followed by prescriptive teaching or for social control to "cut out" deviates from the norm for isolation or change. The cultural values of the majority are institutionalized in the mechanics of the classification system.[130] Increasingly aware of these potentials, legislators, adminstrators, and judges are consciously trying to balance societal and individual goals.

The problems encountered by handicapped children in need of education include denial of access to public education, inadequate programs of instruction, misclassification, segregation, stigmatization, and meager funding. Some of the answers advanced by courts and legislatures are explored in this subsection. Advocates for the education of the handicapped have been remarkably successful. Testifying before a congressional committee, the Executive Director of the Council for Exceptional Children, Frederick J. Weintraub, commented in 1975: "It is worth noting that the first comprehensive [state] legislation on behalf of the education of handicapped children was enacted in 1967; it would be a fitting capstone to a decade of effort and concern on the part of Congress to enforce [the] right to an education before 1978."[131]

The Council's records showed that within three years following the Connecticut action in 1967, Georgia, Indiana, Kentucky, Texas, Utah, and Wyoming adopted a full program of special education.[132] Three states, Hawaii, New Jersey, and Pennsylvania, had mandated such programs in 1949, 1954, and 1956, respectively. Another four states acted in 1971, the year the *PARC* (Pennsylvania Association of Retarded Children) decision enjoined Pennsylvania school districts to provide appropriate educational programs for all handicapped children.[133] During 1972, the year that the *Mills* decision[134] ordered the Washington, D.C., schools to open the doors to handicapped children, another ten states legislated programs. By August, 1974, eighteen more state legislatures responded to the political and judicial pressures. According to Barbacovi and Clelland, the Council for Exceptional Children reported that all but two states had mandated special education by 1975.[135]

The proponents of massive federal aid for special education argued that despite the surge of state laws mandating special education, data collected from the state departments of education showed that many children were still excluded from school and, in most states, less than 50 percent of the handicapped children were receiving an appropriate education.[136] The recession and lack of sufficient state and local funds were blamed for the plight of the handicapped children. The crescendo of concern for the handicapped grew to forte levels when Congress passed sixty-one bills for the handicapped between January 1970 and November 1975.[137] The Education for All Handicapped Children Act,[138] climaxed the legislative response with massive federal aid and regulations which will encourage an almost instant uniformity in the legal framework for special education across the nation.

The early 1970 cases, *PARC* and *Mills*, set the tone and standards for subsequent cases and legislation.[139] The "silent minority," so called by the President's Committee on Mental Retardation (1973), has successfully waged "the quiet revolution" (Dimond, 1973) to confirm a constitutional right to equal opportunity for public education and to pass legislation governing its provision.[140]

There seems to be little disagreement that special education labelling stigmatizes the child despite the fact that identification is prerequisite to special help. The risk of stigma may be acceptable, however, if in fact, accurate diagnosis and appropriate teaching are the rewards, but the Children's Defense Fund charges that racial and language minority children apparently suffer arbitrary and discriminatory treatment in special education placement, especially those labelled educable mentally retarded (EMR).[141] Mercer's research reveals that the key factor in disproportionate minority enrollment in EMR classes was a clinical diagnosis relying almost exclusively on an IQ test.[142] She reported in 1971 that in Riverside, California, Mexican Americans were overrepresented in special education classes by four to five times times and Blacks by two to three times their proportion in the school population. She explained:

> We found that Anglos with IQs of below 69, in general, were also
> failing in adaptive behavior in their social roles. But this was not true
> of persons from Mexican American or Negro background. . . . we
> could predict 25 percent of the variance in IQ simply by knowing
> the cultural setting from which the person came—a very large
> percent of the variance, enough to account for all the differences
> which have systematically been found between different cultural
> groups.[143]

The 1970 United States Commission on Civil Rights investigation of San Diego schools disclosed the same pattern of disproportionate placement.[144]

The California legislative response, in 1971, to these discoveries swiftly reaffirmed the principle of equal opportunity for students of all ethnic, socioeconomic, and cultural groups and a preference for regular class assignment.[145] The change in California law requiring annual reevaluation and use of a variety of placement criteria dramatically reduced EMR enrollment from over 57,000 in 1968-69 to under 30,000 by 1973-74, but the disproportionate representation of minorities only slightly improved.[146] Spanish-surnamed students still comprised 23 percent of the EMR enrollment, but only 17.2 percent of the total number of students, and Blacks represented 25 percent of the EMR enrollment, but only 9.8 percent of all students.[147] Transition programs returned some pupils to regular classrooms or other special education programs.[148] The California Advisory Committee to the United States Commission on Civil Rights nevertheless expressed alarm about a simultaneous increase in enrollments in classes for the educationally handicapped which was proportionate to the decrease in EMR enrollments and urged more effective monitoring by the State Department of Education.[149]

The California problem is not unique. In a 1974 report on the Southwest, the United States Commission on Civil Rights attributed the disproportionate representation of Mexican Americans in EMR classes to the use of inaccurate, unfair criteria such as IQ tests. The commission deplored the resulting misclassification, infrequent reevaluation, and lost opportunity.[150] It also charged that such placement practices, common in the Southwest, violate federal regulation.[151] Of the southwestern states, California has experienced the most legal challenges concerning tracking and placement practices for Chicanos and Blacks.[152]

Minority advocates successfully challenged placement in EMR classes in San Diego[153] and San Francisco. In *Larry P.* v. *Riles,*[154] Black San Franciscan students claimed that placement in EMR classes on the basis of IQ scores denied them equal protection of the law under the Fourteenth Amendment. The court granted a preliminary injunction in 1972 which restrained school officials "from placing black students in classes for the educable mentally retarded on the basis of criteria which place primary reliance on the results of IQ tests as they are currently administered, if the consequence is racial imbalance in the composition of classes."[155] The court found that Blacks constituted 28.5 percent of all students in school, but 66 percent of the enrollees in EMR classes. Evidence of such disproportionate representation shifted to the defendants the burden of proving that the tests were rationally related to classification of students according to ability. The court ruled that they failed to sustain the burden.[156] Kirp interprets the decision as appropriately placing on the school the burden of showing that its classifications serve a "substantial educational purpose," meaning they benefit the affected students.[157]

Influenced by the progress of judicial intervention, California administrative regulations subsequently provided for different interpretations of test scores for students whose primary language was not English and continued to require other comprehensive assessments.[158] By February, 1975, however, the Department of Education further modified its instructions to local school districts in response to developments in the *Larry P.* case. The department "disapproved," until further notice, of the use of intelligence tests as a criterion for placement in EMR classes or reevaluation of EMR students, but permitted their use for evaluation, placement, and reevaluation of exceptional pupils in other classes.[159] Comprehensive evaluation components other than intelligence testing are approved.

From an educational perspective, professionally handled intelligence testing is too useful diagnostically to ban but so vulnerable to misuse that alternative diagnostic and decision-making procedures should be required despite the increased administrative cost. This value judgment is not universally shared. In an analysis of the California Master Plan for Special Education, the State Department of Finance found that during the pilot program, the new procedures increased per pupil administrative costs by over 77 percent. Although acknowledging that "adequate pupil assessments, written, individualized instructional plans, annual reassessments, parental involvement, and parent and child rights are all important," the analysts were still "not convinced that the benefits that reputedly stem from the proposed set of admission procedures justify such an increase in expense."[160] No doubt the federal regulations under the Education for All Handicapped Children Act will set the pace for procedural safeguards.[161]

Intervention to solve the problem of identification and placement of mentally retarded children is a matter of perspective. The intra-school battles of the Larry P.'s in this world are but a microcosm of the social stratification struggle in our society from a social system perspective. Mercer's perceptive academic comparison of the social system versus clinical perspectives on mental retardation[162] pale before the blistering analyses of the Braginskys.[163] Based on their studies of institutionalized adults labelled mentally ill and children labelled mentally retarded, they charge that such classifications ostensibly rest on a clinical concept of defectiveness, but are in reality a sociopolitical phenomenon. They assert that just as the "helping" professionals unwittingly transform surplus adults into emotional defectives, they assist in the metamorphosis of discarded children into intellectual defectives warehoused in segregated classrooms and state institutions. Their research demonstrated the ability of institutionalized "retardates" to manipulate IQ scores to appear "bright" or "dumb" at will and to control significant aspects of their environment against formidable odds. They contend that any child of the surplus poor is a potential retardate who will be recognized as such when it is necessary to justify placement in a training school. The urge focusing resources on understanding the politics of deviancy.

The President's Committee on Mental Retardation echos this assessment less pejoratively. Noting that mild retardation without detectable organic pathology is concentrated in the most marginal socioeconomic groups, it calls for culture-sensitive tests and warns that "genuine mental retardation, usually mild, often appears in conjunction with poverty, cultural deprivation, and familial deterioration."[164] Whether mental retardation is inherited is no longer the main issue. Current issues of research and practice center on the learning-developmental process, the environment in which it occurs, and the techniques and timing of intervention to achieve the best outcome. According to the committee, definition, identification, and treatment of mild, sociocultural retardation, which accounts for 90 percent of the retarded, are the surface issues. The basic issues in effective intervention relate to ethnic discrimination and the environment of poverty; i.e., the "socioeconomic-political-educational waterfront."[165]

Drucker and others report that while minorities are overrepresented in EMR and slow learner tracks, whites are overrepresented in classes for the learning disabled. They attribute the problem to the statutory language which defines learning disabilities by excluding problems "due primarily to ... mental retardation, emotional disturbance or to environmental disadvantage."[166] The exclusionary clause eliminates classification of many minority children as learning disabled. The use of IQ tests for screening for mental retardation operates to compound the disadvantage of racial and linguistic minorities because of the cultural and language biases of the tests.

Despite advances in objective testing and the level of professional judgment suggested by Keogh and Tchir,[167] Kirp argues that regardless of who undertakes the study, they find substantial overrepresentation of minorities in programs for children classified as educable mentally retarded, slow learners, or non-academic. He concludes that the phenomenon relegates lower socioeconomic and racial or ethnic minorities to a basically inferior education.[168]

Conclusions

The common administrative act of classifying students for purposes of educational placement is a governmental act fraught with legal and social ramifications. School officials are agents of the state bound by the federal constitutional injunction not to deny any person equal protection of the law, but the meaning of the phrase is still evolving. It is a "prophecy" unfulfilled, but powerfully pervades the social conscience and exerts a magnetic, if erratic, pull on the direction of statutes, regulations, and judicial decisions. A dynamic interplay among citizens, legislatures, administrative agencies and courts continually reshapes the means and the meaning of the ends sought.

Individuals, often in concert, have turned to courts to force change in legislative and administrative rules which placed students in racially segregated schools and classes, or which have a racially segregative impact but are not rationally related to legitimate educational goals. The judicial arena is particularly appropriate for forging a right of access, but is not as well suited to negotiating the reallocation of resources. Judicial affirmation of a basic right to equal educational opportunity nevertheless provides impetus for political solutions to equity-based claims.[169]

Since the *Brown* v. *Board of Education* decision in 1954, this dynamic process has produced statutes, regulations, and court decisions concerning desegregation, bilingual education, and education for all handicapped children. State legislatures or departments of education are usually first to respond with laws and regulations pressed by constituents, and ultimately Congress and HEW are involved to provide resources and a national uniformity of response. The courts in turn interpret the new statutes and regulations in light of the constitution, if necessary, but prefer to examine administrative action in terms of the legislation.

Because placement decisions have enormous impact on social stratification processes in the United States, they can no longer be left to the subjective judgment of local school officials. As competing interests seek to structure the "rules of the game" at the state level, new legislation and regulations are rapidly imitated by other states. The competition quickly moves to the national arena as the participants seek funds and uniformity of decision. Legal precepts about fairness are permeating judicial and statutory law as judges and legislators rely on "due process" concepts to mediate the clashes between entitlements and scarce resources. The essentially adversarial legalistic processes developd by courts and legislatures to bring equity to placement decisions may bring order, provide the potential for influence on resource allocation, and engender greater acceptance of the decisions. Reliance on form alone, however, will fail unless the participants understand the real issues, are open to influence, and are mutually committed to the ideal of equality of opportunity.

The rapid trend toward centralization of power over decisions about pupil placement in state or federal legislatures and courts has been consciously balanced by requiring involvement of the parent and child in decisions about particular placements. The trend carries the seeds of real individual influence on traditionally autocratic school decisions, but only if the parents have private resources, the help of an association, or governmentally provided advocates. Entitlement is but one facet of power. Parents also need knowledge, time, and persistence. Without help, many of the poor or racial and ethnic minorities will miss their "equal" opportunity "to place" in the social stratification race.

Notes

1. U. S., *Declaration of Independence*, July 4, 1776.
2. *Regents of the University of California* v. *Bakke*, 98 S.Ct. 2773, *2767* (1978).
3. U. S., *Constitution*, Amends. 5, 14, § 1.
4. Ibid., 14, § 1.
5. *Brown* v. *Board of Education of Topeka I*, 347 U. S. 483, *493* (1954).
6. For cultural and lingual diversity, see *Lau* v. *Nichols*, 414 U. S. 563 (1974); *Serna* v. *Portales Municipal Schools*, 499 F.2d 1147 (10th Cir. 1974); *United States* v. *Texas*, 342 Supp. 24 (E. D. Tex. 1971), *aff'd.*, 466 F.2d 518 (5th Cir. 1972); *Aspira* v. *Board of Education of the City of New York*, 58 F.R.D. 62 (S. D. N. Y. 1973). For poverty see *Serrano* v. *Priest*, 5 Cal. 3d 584, 487 P.2d 1241, 96 Cal. Rptr. 601 (1971), *decision on remand aff'd*, 18 Cal. 3d 728, 557 P.2d 929, 135 Cal. Rptr. 345 (176); *Robinson* v. *Cahill*, 62 N. J. 473, 303 A.2d 273, *cert denied*, 414 U. S. 976 (1973); *Horton* v. *Meskill*, 31 Conn. Supp. 377, 332 A.2d 113 (Super. Ct. 1973), *aff'd.*, 376 A.2d 359 (Conn. 1977). (School financing system violates state constitution.) But see *San Antonio Independent School District* v. *Rodriguez*, 409 U. S. 822 (1973), *rehearing denied*, 411 U. S. 959 (1973). (Texas school finance law does not violate the U. S. Constitution.) See also Lehne, 1978. For racial prejudice, see *Brown* v. *Board of Education*, note 5. See also notes 10–30; for the role of the courts in combatting racial prejudice nationally, see note 7; for the role of racial prejudice in educating racial minorities in California, see note 16; for physical and mental disability, see *Pennsylvania Assoc. for Retarded Children* v. *Pennsylvania*, 343 F. Supp. 279 (E. D. Pa. 1972) modifying 334 F.

Supp. 1257 (E. D. Pa. 1972); *Mills* v. *D. C. Board of Education*, 348 F.
Supp. 866 (D.D.C. 1972).

7. Richard Kluger, *Simple Justice: The History of Brown v. Board of Education and Black America's Struggle for Equality* (New York: Alfred A. Knopf, 1976).

8. Ibid., p. 1.

9. *Roberts* v. *City of Boston*, 5 Cushing Reports 198 (1849).

10. O. J. Sweeting, "Roots of Education in Connecticut" (Paper before the annual meeting of the Connecticut Association of Boards of Education, Hartford, 1969).

11. U. S., *Constitution*, Amend. 14, § 1.

12. Kluger, *Simple Justice*, pp. 633, 634.

13. See note 9.

14. *Plessy* v. *Ferguson*, 163 U. S. 537 (1896).

15. *Ward* v. *Flood*, 48 Cal. 36, *52* (1874).

16. N. E. Hendrick, *Public Policy Toward the Education of Non-White Children in California, 1849–1970* (National Institute of Education, Project No. NE-G-00-3-0082, Riverside, Ca., 1975), pp. 53, 72.

17. Ibid., p. 70.

18. Ibid., p. 72.

19. *Yick Wo* v. *Hopkins*, 118 U. S. 356 (1886).

20. See note 14.

21. Hendrick, *Public Policy*, p. 190.

22. California Statutes, 1935, C. 488, sec. 33, as quoted in Hendrick, p. 179.

23. Missouri *ex rel Gaines* v. *Canada*, 305 U. S. 337 (1938).

24. *Sweatt* v. *Painter*, 339 U. S. 629 (1950).

25. *McLaurin* v. *Oklahoma State Regents*, 339 U. S. 637 (1950).

26. See note 5.

27. Kluger, *Simple Justice*, p. 748.

28. U. S., Commission on Civil Rights, *Fulfilling the Letter and Spirit of the Law: Desegregation of the Nation's Public Schools* (Washington, D. C.: U. S. Commission on Civil Rights, 1976).

29. Quoted in Kluger, *Simple Justice*, p. 753.

30. D. J. Bem, *Beliefs, Attitudes, and Human Affairs* (Belmont, Ca.: Brooks/Cole, 1970), p. 69.

31. *Los Angeles Times*, 28 August 1978.

32. Kluger, *Simple Justice*, p. 754.

33. M. Weinburg, et al., *Three Myths: An Exposure of Popular Misconceptions About School Desegregation* (Atlanta, Ga.: Southern Regional Council, 1976), p. 1.

34. *Brown* v. *Board of Education II*, 349 U. S. 294, *301* (1955).

35. *Briggs* v. *Elliott*, 132 F. Supp. 776 (1955).

36. *Griffin* v. *County School Board of Prince Edward County*, 377 U. S. 218 (1964).

37. *Green* v. *County School Board of New Kent County, Virginia*, 391 U. S. 430 (1968).

38. *Alexander* v. *Holmes County, Mississippi, Board of Education*, 396 U. S. 19, *20* (1969).
39. *Swann* v. *Charlotte-Mecklenburg Board of Education*, 402 U. S. 1, *25* (1971).
40. *Wright* v. *Council of the City of Emporia*, 407 U. S. 451 (1972).
41. *Keyes* v. *School District No. 1, Denver, Colorado*, 413 U. S. 189 (1973).
42. *Morgan* v. *Hennigan*, 379 F. Supp. 410 (D. Mass. 1974), *aff'd*, 409 F.2d 580 (1st Cir. 1974), *cert denied, sub nom Kerrigan* v. *Morgan, White* v. *Morgan*, 421 U. S. 963 (1975).
43. See note 41.
44. *Crawford* v. *Board of Education of City of Los Angeles*, 551 P.2d 28, 130 Cal. Rptr. 724 (1976).
45. 418 U. S. 717 (1974).
46. See note 44.
47. *Los Angeles Times* (April, 1979).
48. Public Law 85-315; Kluger, *Simple Justice*, p. 754.
49. P.L. 88-352; 42 U.S.C. & 2000c (1970).
50. K. Alexander, R. Corns, and W. McCann, *Public School Law* (St. Paul, Minn.: West, 1969), p. 682.
51. 20 U.S.C. §§ 236-244, 311-332b, 821-827, 841-848, 861-870, 881-885 (1976).
52. Kluger, *Simple Justice*, p. 764.
53. Elementary and Secondary Education Amendments of 1974, P.L. 93-380; 20 U.S.C. §§ 1701 et seq., 1741 et seq. (1976).
54. See note 5 at *483*.
55. See note 21.
56. California Admin. Code, Title 5, § 2010; Hendrick, *Public Policy*, p. 227.
57. California Admin. Code, Title 5, § 2011.
58. Ibid., § 135-3 (3).
59. Hendrick, *Public Policy*, p. 228.
60. Ibid., p. 229.
61. Ibid., p. 230.
62. Cal. Educ. Code § 1009.5 (West 1970).
63. *San Francisco Unified School District* v. *Johnson*, 3 Cal.3d 937, 479 p.2d 669, 92 Cal. Rptr. 309 (1971).
64. *Barksdale* v. *Springfield School Committee*, 237 F. Supp. 543 (1965), *vacated*, 348 F.2d 261 (1965).
65. Mass. Stat. 1965 ch. 641. See, Ann. L. Mass. ch. 71 37D (1978).
66. Alexander, et al., *Public School Law*, pp. 710-711.
67. *School Committee of Boston* v. *Board of Education*, 352 Mass. 693, 227 N.E.2d 729 (1967), *appeal dismissed*, 389 U.S. 572 (1967).
68. Conn. Gen. Stat. § 10-226b (1977).
69. Ibid., §§ 10-226a through 20-226e (1977).
70. Hendrick, *Public Policy*, pp. 121-244.
71. *Los Angeles Times* 19 October 1978.

72. Kluger, *Simple Justice*, pp. 777, 778.
73. J. Egerton, *School Desegregation: A Report Card From the South* (Atlanta, Ga.: Southern Regional Council, 1976), p. 47.
74. U. S., Commission on Civil Rights, *Fulfilling the Letter*, pp. 293, 294.
75. E.g., Conn. Gen. Stat. § 10-17 (1977), amended only in 1971 to permit bilingual instruction, Conn. Pub. Act No. 432 Cal. Reorg. Educ. Code § 30 (West 1977).
76. *Meyer v. Nebraska*, 262 U. S. 390 (1923).
77. Cal. Ed. §§ 8003 and 8004 (repealed 1947).
78. U.S.C. § 2000d (1970). For the HEW regulations, see, 45 C.F.R. § 80.1 et seq. (1977).
79. 33 Fed. Reg. 4955, *4956* (1968).
80. 35 Red. Reg. 11595 (1970).
81. 20 U. S. C. § 880b et seq. (1976).
82. 20 U. S. C. § 880b (a) (3) (1976).
83. J. A. Banks, *Multiethnic Education: Practices and Promises* (Blooming-ton, Ind.: Phi Delta Kappa Educational Foundation, 1977), pp. 12, 13.
84. U. S., Civil Rights Commission, *The Excluded Student: Educational Practices Affecting Mexican Students in the Southwest* (Washington, D.C.: U. S. Government Printing Office, 1972), pp. 13-20.
85. Ibid., p. 48.
86. F. Sotomayor, *Para Los Ninos—For the Children: Improving Education for Mexican Americans* (Washington, D.C.: U. S. Government Printing Office, 1974), pp. 18-23.
87. 414 U. S. 563 (1974).
88. 20 U. S. C. § 1701 et seq. (1976).
89. Development Associates, Inc., *A Study of State Programs in Bilingual Education* (Washington, D.C.: Development Associates, 1977), Table 4.
90. Ibid., Table 16.
91. H. Miller, "Presentation at RAND Corporation Seminar" (Santa Monica, June 1978).
92. G. W. Findley and M. M. Bryan, *Ability Grouping: 1970 —Status, Impact, and Alternatives* (Athens, Ga.: University of Georgia Center for Educational Improvement, 1971), p. 2.
93. Ibid., p. 18.
94. B. J. Wilson and D. W. Schmits, "What's New in Ability Grouping?," *Phi Delta Kappan* 59 (April 1978): 535-36.
95. Findley and Bryan, *Ability Grouping*, pp. 45-54; Alexander, *et al.*, *Public School Law*; and U. S., Commission on Civil Rights, *Toward Quality Education for Mexican Americans* (Washington, D.C.: U. S. Government Printing Office, 1974), pp. 24-28.
96. *Hobson v. Hansen*, 269 F. Supp. 401, *513* (1967), *aff'd sub nom Smuck v. Hobson*, 408 F.2d 175 (1969).
97. U. S., Commission on Civil Rights, *Toward Quality Education*, pp. 21, 22.
98. Ibid.,
99. Ibid., at 514.

100. Ibid.
101. *Smuck* v. *Hobson*, 408 F.2d 175, *188* (1969).
102. R. P. Ingalls, *Total Retardation: The Changing Outlook* (New York: John Wiley & Sons, 1978), pp. 17–51.
103. Ingalls, *Total Retardation*.
104. N. Hobbs, *The Faces of Children: Categories, Labels, and Their Consequence* (San Franciso, Cal.: Jossey-Bass, 1974), p. 46.
105. Ingalls, *Total Retardation*, pp. 48, 163; R. C. Nichols, "Implications of Racial Differences in Intelligence for Educational Research and Practice" (Paper at a symposium at the American Educational Research Association, Los Angeles, 1969).
106. Hendrick, *Public Policy*, pp. 183, 184.
107. President's Committee on Mental Retardation, *Mental Retardation: Trends in State Services* (Washington, D.C.: U. S. Government Printing Office, 1976), p. 33.
108. A. Joseph, *Intelligence, IQ and Race—When, How, and Why They Become Associated* (San Francisco, Cal.: R&E Research Associates, 1977), p. 41.
109. Ingalls, *Total Retardation*, p. 169.
110. Ibid., pp. 162–187.
111. Hobbs, *The Faces of Children*, p. 47.
112. T. J. Cottle, *Barred From School: 2 Million Children* (Washington, D.C.: New Republic Book Co., 1976).
113. F. M. Wirt, "What State Laws Say About Local Control," *Phi Delta Kappan* 59 (April 1978): 520.
114. C. Pipho, *Education Commission of the States Update VI: Minimal Competency Testing*, ERIC Document Reproduction Service, No. ED 144 961 (Denver, Col.: 1977), p. 598.
115. U. S., Commission on Civil Rights, *Ethnic Isolation of Mexican Americans*, pp. 35–38, 70–93.
116. Ibid., p. 35.
117. Ibid., p. 38.
118. *Peter W.* v. *San Francisco Unified School District*, 60 Cal. App. 3d 814, 131 Ca. Reptr. 854 (1976). See, Comment: Educational Malpractice, 124 U. Pa. L. Rev. 755 (1976).
119. Cal. Reorg. Educ. Code §§ 51215–51217, 51225 (West 1978).
120. Fla. Laws 1976, ch. 76–223, as amended by Fla. Laws 1977, ch. 77–174; Fla. Stat. Ann. §§ 229.555 to 229.58, 232.245 (West 1977, Supp. 1978).
121. G. K. Hart, "The California Pupil Proficiency Law as Viewed by its Author, *Phi Delta Kappan* 59 (May 1978), p. 593.
122. G. V. Glass, "Minimum Competence and Incompetence in Florida," *Phi Delta Kappan* 59 (May 1978): 605, and W. Van Til, "One Way of Looking at It: What to Expect if your Legislature Orders Literacy Testing," *Phi Delta Kappan* 59 (April 1978): 556.
123. B. D. Anderson and P. Lesser, "The Costs of Legislated Minimum Competency Requirements," *Phi Delta Kappan* 59 (May 1978): 607.

124. D. J. Henderson, "Gary, Indiana: High School Diploma with Meaning," *Phi Delta Kappan* 59 (May 1958): 614.
125. *Griggs* v. *Duke Power Company,* 401 U. S. 424 (1971) (requiring high school diploma and general intelligence test violated Title VII of 1964 Civil Rights Act, because the disproportionate impact on blacks was caused by use of criteria unrelated to job performance). But see, *Washington* v. *Davis,* 426 U. S. 229 (1976); *Albemarle Paper Company* v. *Moody,* 422 U. S. 405 (1975).
126. G. V. Glass and M. McClung, "Presentation" (Seminar on Competency, Proficiency Testing, University of California, Los Angeles, 1978).
127. S. H. Stapleton, "Where School Promotions Have to be Earned," *Reader's Digest* (September 1978).
128. Washington Research Project, *Children Out of School* (Washington, D.C.: U. S. Government Printing Office, 1974), pp. 224–225.
129. U. S., Congress, House, Subcommittee on Select Education, *Extension of Education of the Handicapped Act* 94th Cong., 1st Sess., 1974, p. 1.
130. Hobbs, *The Faces of Children*, p. 41.
131. U. S., Congress, House, Subcommittee on Select Education, *Extension of Education*, p. 30.
132. Ibid., pp. 177–190.
133. See note 6.
134. See note 6.
135. D. R. Barbacovi and R. W. Clelland, *Public Law 94-142: Special Education in Transition* (Arlington, Va.: American Association of School Administrators, n.d.).
136. U. S., Congress, House, Subcommittee on Select Education, *Extension of Education*, pp. 177–188.
137. Barbacovi and Clelland, *Public Law*, p. 3.
138. Education of the Handicapped Act. P. L. 91–230, as amended by the Education for All Handicapped Children Act of 1975, P. L. 94–142, 20 U. S. C. § 1401 et seq. (1976). For regulations, see 45 C.F.R. 121a (1977).
139. For a briefing on such cases, see U. S., Congress, House, Subcommittee on Select Education, *Extension of Education*, pp. 193-239.
140. P. R. Diamond, "The Constitutional Right to Education: The Quiet Revolution," *The Hastings Law Journal* 24 (1973): 1087-1127.
141. Washington Research Project, *Children Out of School*, p. 93.
142. J. R. Mercer, *Labelling the Mentally Retarded: Clinical and Social Perspectives on Mental Retardation* (Berkeley, Cal.: University of California Press, 1973), p. 120.
143. President's Committee on Mental Retardation, *A Very Special Child* (Washington, D.C.: U. S. Government Printing Office, 1971), p. 8.
144. J. Booker-Jones, *Evaluation of Educable Mentally Retarded Programs in California* (Washington, D.C.: Department of Health, Education, and Welfare, 1977), p. 2.
145. Cal. Reorg. Educ. Code § 78804 (West 1978).
146. J. Booker-Jones, *Evaluation of Educable Mentally Retarded*, p. 3.

147. Ibid., Chart 1.
148. Ibid.
149. Ibid.
150. U. S., Commission on Civil Rights, *Toward Quality Education for Mexican Americans* (Washington, D.C.: U. S. Government Printing Office, 1974), p. 31.
151. Ibid., p. 29, citing HEW Memorandum of 25 May 1970; 35 Fed. Reg. 11595 (1970).
152. V. Sierra, *Recent Litigation in the Placement of Minority Group Children in the Southwest* (ERIC, Document Reproduction Service No. ED 122 559).
153. *Covarrubias v. San Diego Unified School District*, Civ. No. 70-3945 (S. D. Cal. 21 August 1972).
154. 343 F. Supp. 1306 (1972), *aff'd* 502 F.2d 963 (1974).
155. Ibid., at 1315.
156. Ibid., at 1314.
157. D. L. Kirp, "Law, Politics, and Equal Education Opportunity: The Limits of Judicial Involvement," *Harvard Educational Review* 47 (1977), p. 770.
158. Los Angeles Unified School District, *Educational Support Services Bulletin*, 45 (1 July 1974).
159. Ibid., Addendum No. 1, 45 (1 April 1975).
160. California Department of Finance, *The California Master Plan for Special Education* (Sacramento, Cal.: California Department of Finance, 1977), pp. xvii–xviii.
161. 45 CFR § 100b et seq. (1977).
162. Mercer, *Labelling the Mentally Retarded*, pp. 1–37.
163. B. M. and D. P. Braginsky, "The Mentally Retarded: Society's Hansel's and Gretels," *Psychology Today* 7 (March 1974).
164. President's Committee on Mental Retardation, *Mental Retardation: Trends in State Services* (Washington, D.C.: U. S. Government Printing Office, 1976), p. 11.
165. Ibid., p. 12.
166. H. Driecker, L. Parker, E. Thompson, and A. Burns, "Learning Disability and Ethnic Discrimination" (paper presented at the annual international convention, The Council for Exceptional Children, Chicago, 1976), p. 3.
167. B. K. Keogh and C. A. Tchir, *Teacher's Perceptions of Educationally High Risk Children* (technical report prepared under contract from California State Department of Education at UCLA, September 1972), pp. 53, 57.
168. D. I. Kirp, "Schools as Sorters: The Constitutional and Policy Implications of Student Classification," *University of Pennsylvania Law Review* 121 (1973): 760–761.
169. Kirp, "Law, Politics, and Equal Educational Opportunity," p. 121.

Douglas W. Lee

Pluralism and Public Policy in Public Education: The Case of San Francisco Unified School District and East Asian Immigrant Students

The case for pluralism in education is nowhere more evident and valuable than in the area of public education at the primary and secondary levels. The concept of pluralism is a useful multidimensional approach to the basic task of problem solving. It has a great deal to offer by way of broadening our perceptions and possibilities in the critical area of servicing the many special needs and interests of an immigrant student population.

Pluralism has been an essential part of public policy strategy addressing the complex problems of a pluralistic society. In public education, it has served as both a philosophical and a methodological approach to the difficult task of resolving controversial and delicate issues. It provides a positive, flexible approach to such situations and their changing conditions. These factors have made the concept especially attractive and useful for educators who have had to formulate public policy in such sensitive areas as integration plans, bilingual education, and ethnolinguistic minority rights.

The notion of pluralism is of value only if we apply it to concrete problems and situations, rather than explore its theoretical probabilities and possibilities. There is the real possibility that through widespread and indiscriminate use, the term will become all things to all people and will lose its value as an approach to problem solving. Indeed, it could itself become a "problem." Such terms as "assimilation," "identity," and "integration" already suffer from overuse and thus appear to many as vague or rhetorical. Instead of precision and clarity, we obtain nothing more than a cliché that explains nothing. I fear that the notion of pluralism may end up this way. Our efforts to understand the concept and its meaning for public policy should be applied to a given problem or issue. This paper consequently focuses on the case of the San Francisco Unified School District (SFUSD) and the concept of "pluralism" as it applies to the public policy issues involved in that case.

San Francisco, the site of an unusually large and diversified student population has long been at the forefront of the struggle for education that is responsive to ethnolinguistic minority student needs. The Supreme Court decision in the *Lau* v. *Nichols* case made San Francisco a cause célèbre in the early 1970s. San Francisco was thus the setting for a landmark case in legal history, but it was also to become a leader in the area of American public education's pioneering work with ethnolinguistic minorities.

There are many parts of the country that also have large ethnolinguistic minorities. San Francisco, however, is unique in that it has the largest and fastest growing East Asian immigrant student population in the United States, with the possible exception of New York. SFUSD public policy is significant because it goes beyond the immediate problem of the language that separates this student group from the majority of students in the American public education system.

San Francisco has a reputation as a "cosmopolitan" city, but the term means more than the popular fantasies conjured up by the tourist industry. It has meant conflict and confrontation in community politics and division within the professional community of educators, to say nothing of the schisms among politicians and local governmental bureaucrats. At the heart of the matter has been the steady increase in the number and diversity of East Asian immigrant students.

SFUSD has not met this challenge with unqualified success, yet it has moved in the right direction with vision and effectiveness. It has become an example of a local institution formulating and implementing public policy that focuses on variables intimately associated with the notion of racism in its many forms and degrees, not the least of which is the concept of "reverse discrimination." Through its application of the idea of pluralism, it has achieved a leadership position in American public education.

My comments will focus specifically on the events and developments of the 1977–78 school year. It was during this period that I served in an administrative capacity in the Bilingual Education Department of SFUSD and thus had the opportunity to observe and in many instances participate in the execution of public policy that underscored pluralism and confronted racism. More importantly, the 1977–78 school year was significant because it was the last school year in which SFUSD operated its many programs under "normal" fiscal and political criteria. The situation in the SFUSD has changed dramatically with the passage of Proposition Thirteen, the statewide tax initiative. The observations advanced in this study reflect prevailing conditions and problems in the pre-Proposition Thirteen era. My comments on the nature and role of pluralism in the area of public policy will focus on: (1) pluralism and public policy with regard to the East Asian immigrant student; (2) public policy and management in the SFUSD Office of Bilingual Education (OBED); and (3) public policy and the educational process.

In June of 1977 I joined the staff of the OBED as the Coordinator of the Comprehensive Employment Training Act (CETA) Bilingual aides. It was also my responsibility to supervise the screening, testing, and initial assignment of all new foreign students entering the SFUSD. In addition, I was a staff aide of the director of OBED, Mr. Ray Del Portillo. As a staff aide I was assigned various tasks by the director. The staff of the OBED was a highly professional and dedicated group that extended to me every encouragement and support.

I remained at this position for just over a year, from June 1977 to September 1978. In this single brief year I learned about the complexities of public education. I was able not only to observe the intricacies of public school administration but also to become involved in this exciting and controversial realm of local community politics. I am neither an educator nor an administrator by training. I entered into my position with an open mind, somewhat idealistic and naive as far as organization policies and politics were concerned. In this light, my comments represent an "outsider's" view from the inside. They are the reflections of a concerned individual who had the fortunate opportunity to be associated with SFUSD as it confronted the issues discussed in this paper.

Pluralism, Public Policy, and the East Asian Immigrant Student

In the early 1970s SFUSD was propelled into conflict and controversy as a result of the United States Supreme Court decision in the *Lau* v. *Nichols* case. The school district, like nearly every element of American society, has been caught up in the revolution of America's ethnic and racial minorities. In part this was a result of the civil rights movement of the 1960s. More specifically, however, radical changes in American immigration laws in 1965 created a new educational environment in San Francisco. The city was experiencing difficulties in meeting the demands of Black and Hispanic minority students, but it was not at all prepared to cope with the rising tide of East Asian immigrant students, especially those from China.

The massive influx of East Asian students into the school system generated new problems and challenges to the school district's understanding—or its lack of understanding—of ethnolinguistic minority student needs. The *Lau* v. *Nichols* case demonstrated above all the new assertiveness and influence of the heretofore "docile" and "compliant" Chinese community in San Francisco. The result of this new spirit of concern and combative politics was the generation of new public policy based on pluralistic criteria.

In the decade of the 1970s the SFUSD hardly had any time to reflect upon the dramatic change of events which so revolutionized the nature of public education in San Francisco. The decade started with the landmark *Lau* v. *Nichols* decision, and ended with the equally significant passage of the California statewide tax initiative, Proposition Thirteen. Both events resulted in conflict and controversy.

The initial result of the Supreme Court decisions in the cases that involved ethnolinguistic student minority rights was a flurry of activity by SFUSD, as it tried to comply with mandates of the federal courts which rendered infinitely more complex and controversial the already hot issue of desegregation. Yet the problem posed by ethnolinguistic minority rights could not be resolved by simplistic mechanical or logistical maneuverings, such as school busing.

It was clear from the start that a whole new orientation and policy was needed to meet the challenges involved in servicing an ethnolinguistically plural student population. The crisis created by the court decisions of the early 1970s affected all ethnolinguistic minorities in the city, the largest of which are Hispanic and Asian. The Asian students posed additional special problems, not the least of which was the fact that they constituted not one but several groups, each with a politically articulate community and its own language.

When confronted by the Chinese in Chinatown, SFUSD was caught in a dilemma. In attempting to meet the needs of this one group on the basis of court mandates, the school district opened a "Pandora's Box." The Chinese community had undergone a revolutionary change as a result of the liberalization of immigration laws in 1965. The massive influx of Chinese immigrants from Hong Kong, Taiwan, and portions of Southeast Asia upset the well-established ratio between foreign-born and American-born Chinese Americans. After the 1930s, American-born Chinese had consistently outnumbered foreign-born Chinese. Thus, the problems of immigrants who spoke little or no English placed new demands on the school system.

In this period after 1965, the Philippine, Korean, and Japanese communities also grew significantly. The emergency immigration and settlement of Vietnamese and other Indochinese after 1975 further added to the complexity of the situation. In the years 1977–78 it was also apparent that there were increases in the number of immigrant students from the Arab world, especially from Lebanon and Palestine, and Jews from Russia.

All of these groups clamored for full and fair treatment by the school district. Out of this situation the SFUSD formulated and adopted a public policy in which the notion of pluralism became a guiding force.

Public policy in the SFUSD came from the Board of Education. This governing board was traditionally white and conservative. In the 1970s, the board went through a series of changes in both its composition and the policies that it developed. Its efforts at desegregation reflected dynamic new policies in regards to racial minorities. In particular, various developments after 1974 manifested an intensification of pluralism in public policy by the Board of Education for the SFUSD. The board meetings may have degenerated into confusion and feuds, but new positive and pluralistic policies emerged. Mr. Ben Tom, current board president, has pointed to such new policies in the areas of affirmative action, bilingual education, desegregation-integration, and multicultural education.[1]

The changes in public policy reflected changes in the composition of the board itself. In the 1970s there was a continued effort to infuse new blood into the board. Community politics were persistently controversial, and designations of "conservative" and "radical" were blurred. Ben Tom chronicles this "board revolution" from the time of his candidacy in 1972 to his final victory in 1976, when three liberal members were elected in place of three conservative incumbents.[2] These changes brought individuals who were willing and able to formulate public policy that responded to the growing force of pluralism.

The result has been the development of policies that support minority students in general and ethnolinguistic immigrant minority students in particular. These policies involve curriculum, staffing, funding, programming, school sites, paraprofessionals, and administration. Ethnolinguistic minority rights have become central issues in the system, and pluralism is the basis of new policies.

Public Policy and Management in the SFUSD Office of Bilingual Education (OBED)

The board of education and the office of the superintendent worked together to draft new policies that brought increased attention to the many new problems associated with the rapidly increasing East Asian immigrant student population in San Francisco. These policies specifically recognized the special needs and problems of this group. It must be admitted that it took the prodding of the Supreme Court, the pressure cooker politics of the ethnic community, and large state and federal grants to bring about such changes in policy. But once the writing was on the wall, the board (after a change in its membership) and the administration of SFUSD (after a new superintendent took office in 1975–76) began to establish new pluralistic policies. By 1976, the district had adopted a Bilingual Education Master Plan in response to the consent decree mandated by the *Lau* v. *Nichols* decision. Thus, it remained for the bureaucratic apparatus of mid-level management to implement the new far-reaching policies.

A special office had been set up earlier to tackle the controversial problem of desegregation, but ethnolinguistic minority student demands were handled by a regular sector of the SFUSD bureaucratic apparatus, the Office of Bilingual Education (OBED).

The OBED had its origins in the late 1960s, largely as an ad hoc organization. In that period there were teachers and some administrators that felt the need to respond to ethnolinguistic minority needs, at least in the area of curriculum. The temporary, somewhat shabby quarters of the OBED reflected the low priority and perhaps even lower status of such activities in SFUSD policies at that time.

OBED was quite different in 1977–78. In place of an ad hoc organization, there had emerged a genuine bureaucracy with all the attendant strengths and weaknesses. The director of OBED, Mr. Ray Del Portillo, was persistent in his efforts to keep OBED tightly centralized. The many program managers and specialists serving under him all sought a measure of autonomy, thus straining the centralization. As an administrative agency of SFUSD, OBED was mandated to implement and monitor the new pluralistic policies of SFUSD. It did this at the central headquarters and in the field. At the headquarters, OBED had its staff and offices divided between two floors in a wing of the central office complex. The director's office and those of a few key staff members were in the basement. The windows of their offices were at ground level, and the fumes of car exhausts blended with cigar and cigarette smoke in the conference room where departmental politics centered on the immediate difficulties of trying to implement policies of the board and administration. (Table 1 highlights the organization of the OBED. Note that the department was divided between CENTRAL OFFICE STAFF at the central office, and CENTRAL OFFICE STAFF, located in the field.)

The staff at both the central office and in the field was divided into three categories. The lifeblood of the organization was those technical specialists who monopolized the system's bewildering jargon and statistics. Resource teachers, program managers, program assistants, evaluators, proposal specialists, legal experts, bilingual-multicultural specialists, and mid-level management experts were all involved in the complex and endless task of translating policy into programs servicing the immigrant students. In addition to the professionals or specialists, there was a full complement of classified personnel: secretaries, clerks, clerk-typists, receptionists, and various assistants. Finally, there was a legion of paraprofessionals scurrying about. In the year I was at OBED, I observed that the paraprofessionals were often the indispensible labor force upon which the successful completion of innumerable projects and programs depended. While specialists dashed off memos and proposals, the classified staff and paraprofessionals made the translation of policy into program a day-to-day reality.

I observed that activity took place in a three-phase process. First, there was the setting of agenda and tasks by the director with his "cabinet." His cabinet met once a week, in the aforementioned gas- and smoke-filled room. Here the director outlined courses of action, deadlines, projects on the front burners, and those on the back burners. From my own perspective, the meetings were elaborate strategies in which staff and director alternated between giving each other support and ulcers. On the surface, the director projected an image of the well-informed administrator, on top of everything. The staff

Table 1.   **ORGANIZATION OF THE OFFICE OF BILINGUAL EDUCATION OF SFUSD 1977-78**

Board of Education SFUSD
Superintendent of Instruction SFUSD
Assistant Superintendent of Instruction for Curriculum

OFFICE OF BILINGUAL EDUCATION (OBED)
Director, Mr. Ray Del Portillo

Second Floor Room 22 component	Director's Office (basement)	Central Office OBED staff in the field
Compliance Officer	Director's secretary/office manager	*Title VII Bilingual Education* Program Managers
Technical Advisor	Loreto	*Title VII Chinese Bilingual*
Trouble Shooter	*Federal & State Grants Coordinator*	Ms. Anna Wong at
1977-78 Language Census	Ms. Cathy Marconi	Commodore Stockton
Survey Coordinator	*ESAA (Emergency School Assistance Act)*	Elementary School
OBED Resource Teachers	Program Manager	*Title VII Spanish Bilingual*
ESL Resource Teacher	Ms. Kathy Reyes	Mr. Ed Garvin
Ms. Jean Ramirez	(1977-78 head of Bilingual	Horace Mann Junior
Spanish Bilingual Resource Teacher	teacher competency certification)	High School
Ms. Margaret Wells	*Hispanic Community Liaison Person*	*Title VII Philippino Bilingual*
Chinese Bilingual Resource Teacher	J. Gonzales (until Spring '78)	Dr. Eli Robles
Ms. Doris Wong until Spring '78	J. Jacamo (after Spring '78)	John Swett
Mr. Jones Wong after Spring '78		Elementary School
Filipino Bilingual Resource Teacher		*Title VII Japanese Bilingual*
Ms. Cora Ponce		Mr. Tetsu Hojo
STAFF Inservice training		Columbus/Sunshine
Ms. Lydia Stack		Elementary Schools
IRAP (Indochinese Refugee Assistance		*Title VII Korean Bilingual*
Program		Dr. Harry Bang
Coordinator—Mr. Cal Haena		Sunset Staging
(Moved to the field fall of 1977)		Elementary school area
Title VII evaluators		*IRAP* ...Fall 1977 moved to
Mr. Luis Herendez		Golden Gate
Ms. Paula Martin		Elementary school
CETA Bilingual Aides Program		
New Foreign Students Testing and		
Screening		
Mr. Douglas Lee		
(also staff aide to the director)		

Dr. John Lum

INDEPENDENT, CITY WIDE EDUCATION CENTERS

Principals or representatives attend weekly OBED staff meetings at OBED central office.

Chinese Education Center
Dr. Mike Kittridge (until Fall '77)
Ms. Claudia Jeung (after Fall '77)
Spanish Education Center
Mr. Rosendo Marin
Philippino Education Center
Mr. Ross Quema

presented a similar image of specialists, all in secure control of their area of responsibility and properly respectful and supportive of the director.

In reality, there was an elaborate and persistent charade being performed by the director and the staff. The director sought to avoid any possible discrepancy between the appearance and the reality of his control over the OBED. To this end he rattled on about policy, programs, and projects. As is the case for many administrators, it was impossible for him to be fully informed, much less in full control, of the many activities of OBED. The director appeared to be the mastermind, and the staff of specialists discussed and debated for appearances' sake.

The second phase of departmental activity centered on the relations and activities among the administrative personnel. Real know-how, the "brains" of the outfit, was distributed among the cadre of specialists, each of whom held complete control over his/her area of specialization. They had their own level and medium of communications, independent but related to that of OBED's director. I observed many a program manager or specialist who came to the weekly meetings to make a perfunctory report, did a bit of socializing, and played out the ritual of being a staff member of OBED. Each such individual arrived like a feudal lord, at Camelot, secure with his own staff and program.

On the second floor there were the four resource teachers, each charged with the monitoring of a major component of the OBED. These resource teachers oversaw the areas of English as a second language (ESL) and Chinese, Spanish, and Filipino bilingual programs at SFUSD. There was clamoring for bilingual programs in other language areas, some of which had "soft money" but not the "hard money" of officially established programs.

The third phase of activity occurred in the field, where OBED personnel interacted with personnel of SFUSD in other departments and agencies of the school system. In this area, OBED personnel represented the policies and programs of OBED. They interpreted policy, explained technical aspects of programs and their financing, resolved conflicts between OBED field staff and non-OBED staff, and established and monitored OBED soft money programs in all of the schools of the system.

The staff at central office represented in large measure the "regular" component of OBED, financed largely by hard money. The specialists were paid from hard money, but many of the classified staff and paraprofessionals were on soft money that came from a number of federal and state sources.

At the top of the pile was the director's chief advisor and troubleshooter, Dr. John Lum. Dr. Lum served as the director's "national security advisor." He was specifically charged with monitoring SFUSD's compliance with various federal court decisions and acted as a liaison between SFUSD's ethnolinguistic activities and various state and federal regulatory agencies, such as the United States Office of Education in Washington, D.C., and the Office of the Superintendent of Instruction in Sacramento, California. Dr. Lum also served as the director's chief advisor for matters of policy, in especially difficult and sensitive areas where the department and the administration (school district superintendent's office) conflicted.

In 1977-78 Dr. Lum was in charge of SFUSD's administration of a state mandated language census. The California legislature had passed a new law which required all school districts to make an annual language census of the students in their district. This would ideally result in more accurate and reliable statistics on which to base fiscal and educational decisions with regards to servicing immigrant ethnolinguistic student minorities. SFUSD adopted a testing procedure commonly known as the San Diego Instrument (SDI), a testing procedure first developed by the San Diego school district. This testing procedure was a one-to-one affair, with one tester per student. It had to be administered in both English and some twenty-odd languages and dialects. The district had some 64,000 students and a staff of a few hundred to do the testing.

Training for the testers began in the fall, and the last examinations were given in March. The test results yielded data about non-English-speaking students (NES) and limited English-speaking students (LES) and indicated which students were bilingual and/or biliterate. The testing procedure was far from perfect; indeed, many found that it often acted as a "catch 22," imposing a classification that was not entirely accurate or appropriate. An example would be a student that was perhaps shy or inarticulate. His/her inability to converse at length often resulted in being classified as a LES-NES student. Often students could speak English but lacked the experience and ability to carry on a conversation. The test required the student to respond to questions such as, "What's happening in this picture?" Obviously, an element of subjectivity entered into the evaluation. If a student was unable or reluctant to say anything more than "this is a boy," "that is a ball," the student was labeled as LES.

In the 1970s millions of dollars of soft money had become a major source of support for new programs in public education. In SFUSD, state and federal grants subsidized the activities and projects of OBED. Indeed, the majority of OBED operating funds in fact proceeded from this vast reserve. Soft money economics and ethnolinguistic minority politics were often mixed together as OBED tried to achieve a semblance of order in the distribution and monitoring of the use of such funds. Ms. Cathy Marconi was the OBED's principle administrator controlling and monitoring these funds. Marconi not only had to keep OBED informed of the status of a multitude of state and federal programs (their deadlines for renewal, specific mechanics of proposal writing, criteria for monitoring compliance, changes in regulations, and massive paperwork), but also had the thankless task of monitoring the fiscal aspects of the programs in the field.

OBED received funds from the federal government under several programs: Title VII (Bilingual Education), the Emergency School Assistance Act (ESAA), and the Comprehensive Employment Training Act (CETA). In addition there were a score of state programs. These programs included: California Assembly Bill 1329, for assistance to LES-NES students (most East Asian immigrant students were in this category); Assembly Bill 2284, Senate Bill 1641, and Sentate Bill 90, initially for educationally disadvantaged students, which included many East Asian immigrant students. All of these programs, each with its own regulations and criteria, involved large sums of money. While OBED dispensed some funds directly, in many cases individual schools had applied for grants from one or more of the programs. Each school had a separate portfolio of state and federal grant monies. Each school requested help from Marconi for help in preparing and submitting proposals, which had to be incorporated into the OBED master proposals, and in monitoring programs to ensure that they complied with governing regulations.

In the basement complex of the director's office at the OBED central office there were a number of key staff members in addition to Ms. Marconi. One of these was the program manager for the ESAA federal program. She was in charge of administering the hundreds of thousands of dollars of funds. In addition, during the course of the year she was assigned to conduct competency tests for Chinese, Spanish, and Philippine bilingual teachers.

In the late 1960s and early 1970s, the SFUSD bilingual education program remained an ad hoc affair. Anybody that was Chinese and possessed a California credential was mobilized as a "bilingual teacher." Many were reluctantly drafted, but eventually came to support the new programs in this initial period. By 1977 a new level of sophistication in bilingual education resulting from large endowments from federal and state agencies required a new level of technical proficiency in the practitioners of the field. Teachers were now required to be biliterate as well as bilingual. The Spanish and Philippine teachers had little problem. Among the Chinese teachers in SFUSD, however, there arose wailings and moans. Most Chinese bilingual teachers were minimally bilingual in the Say-Yup sub-Cantonese dialect.

In the post-1965 era most of the Chinese immigrants were from Hong Kong and spoke the Sam-Yup, or standard Cantonese dialect. As there was a rapid influx of Cantonese immigrant students, the Say-Yup-speaking American-born and educated teachers were increaingly outnumbered, ineffective, and anachronistic. Further complications were evident in the influx of Mandarin-spaking Chinese from Taiwan and much of Southeast Asia. Even if the teachers had been truly bilingual, or in this case tri-lingual, few if any were biliterate. The written and reading exams consisted of elementary Chinese essays and excerpts, which most of the teachers found beyond their capabilities. This situation should not be taken as a criticism of the teachers; indeed, they are to be commended for their dedicated and professional job. Their plight is to be approached with sympathy and understanding. It represents a situation in which there is a conflict between new needs and older practices and precedents.

The third key staff member in the director's basement complex was the liaison between OBED and the community. In 1977-78 this position was occupied first by Mr. J. Gonzales, and then by Mr. Julio Jacamo. This position caught my attention as an anomaly. Few could argue against the need for the director of the bilingual education program to have direct access to the community. The implementation of controversial policies and complex programs clearly demanded this. However, a change might have helped to maximize the benefits from such a position in OBED.

The director of OBED, Mr. Del Portillo, was Spanish speaking, originally from Cuba. His liaison persons were also Spanish speaking, and thus focused their attention and expertise on the Spanish-speaking community. This meant that the director had excellent, intimate, up-to-date communications with the Hispanic community in San Francisco. What about his communications with the East Asian, or, more specifically, with the Chinese community? It might have been more appropriate to have two liaison persons, one for the Spanish and one for the Chinese community. OBED had the services of a number of individuals that were fluent in several languages. Ideally, one of the liaison persons could handle Spanish and Philippine and the other could handle Chinese (Mandarin and Cantonese), Vietnamese, or Japanese. The director often relied upon other staff personnel to perform liaison functions. I suggest that Spanish-speaking staff members could also have done this. There should have been an Asian community liaison person in place of, or at least in addition to, the Spanish-speaking liaison position at OBED. Finally, there was my position. My title and duties reflected the cardinal feature of OBED in an age of soft money. Officially, I was employed by SFUSD, but in reality my position and duties were created in part as a response to the CETA program, which encouraged local government to create "public service employment positions" for the chronically unemployed.

My immediate duties in June 1977 were to administer the CETA bilingual aide program on behalf of and under the supervision of the director of OBED. This meant keeping records and monitoring the work of some fifty bilingual aides that served the needs of Spanish, Chinese, Japanese, Korean, and Philippine students in scores of elementary and secondary schools across the city. CETA employees worked a twelve-month calendar, whereas most employees worked only a nine-month school year. This meant that suitable work had to be "found" for the CETA people during vacation periods (summer, Christmas, and spring). Between reassignments, monitoring, and vacation and pay records there was a great deal of room for maneuvering by the aides. As I entered into the position, I was given the task of creating order from disorder. The program grew from fifty aides to over one hundred when I left. We expanded the program to provide for "pocket languages," which required bilingual aides in the following areas: Hindi, Arabic, Russian, Samoan, French, Portuguese, as well as additional aides in the Korean, Japanese, and Vietnamese language areas.

My position also called for the supervision of the initial screening, testing, and assignment of all new foreign immigrant students entering the system through the central office. Assignments were made according to the student's profile. This profile was based on the following criteria: the student's age, previous education, address, and, most importantly, his or her degree of proficiency in English.

We had in the office a huge computer printout directory of all street addresses in the city of San Francisco. Each specific address had an accompanying list of elementary, junior high, and senior high schools. This was the masterplan integration directory of addresses. In it, certain addresses were listed as being within an "impact area." This might be the Chinatown-North Beach area for the Chinese, the Hunter's point and Bayview area for the Blacks, or the Mission area for the Hispanics. If a new student was of one of these ethnolinguistic minorities residing in an impact area, then he/she would have to be bused to an alternate school also listed in the directory. Thus, if a new immigrant from Hong Kong lived in a designated Chinese impact area, then that student would have to be assigned to the alternate school. It was district policy and federal law that no more than a predetermined percentage (perhaps 30 percent) of a school in any part of the city could be composed of any given ethnic-racial group.

Room 22a handled the processing of immigrant students after they were processed by Room 39 on the fourth floor. In Room 39 Mr. Eddie Sung checked immigration papers and passports to determine the eligibility of the prospective student. In room 22a we then processed the student and ultimately gave an assignment. The student and parent were briefed on why and how the assignment was made. After the situation was explained and an agreement reached, the parents and student proceeded to the school for registration. The assignment forms were sent to the first floor, Room 18, for the district Student Assignment Officer to confirm or make adjustments according to the ever-changing statistics and regulations.

In addition to these two primary responsibilities my position as staff aide afforded me the opportunity to become involved in other aspects of the OBED's many programs. There was a constant stream of meetings and conferences, new projects and continuing projects. For example, there was a component of OBED that was technically part of the central office staff but was housed at various school sites in the field. There were the Title VII programs managers, each of whom had his/her own facilities and staff. They were securely established and funded by a perennial supply of federal monies from the Title VII bilingual program. In addition to the Chinese, Spanish, and Philippine languages, there were also the Korean and Japanese components. In addition to the weekly staff meetings of the whole OBED, the director frequently met with the Title VII program managers. These meetings were necessary, because the program managers were decentralized in the field and also because their work had to be coordinated with the general activites of OBED.

The Indochinese Refugee Assistance Program (IRAP) was a special program established by SFUSD in the OBED, with grants from the Federal government. It was slated to be a temporary program, and it did terminate in June, 1978. When I joined the OBED, IRAP was quartered on the second floor of the OBED central offices with the four resource teachers and Dr. Lum. Mr. Cal Haena, head of the IRAP program, needed larger facilities and consequently received an increase in funds in the 1977-78 year. In addition, he wanted his program established on a basis similar to that of the Title VII program managers, who all had their programs housed on school sites, away from OBED's central offices. IRAP moved from central office to Golden Gate Elementary School. This again represented the centrifugal forces at work in OBED. In the field, IRAP, like the Title VII people, gained a measure of independence.

IRAP was unique in many ways. In 1977-78 it had the largest budget and the most independence. It was not only involved in the immediate task of servicing the needs of Vietnamese and other Indochinese students but was also involved in curriculum, staff, and community work. The program was able to purchase hundreds of thousands of dollars worth of expensive equipment and materials, as well as hire a sizable professional and paraprofessional staff.

In 1977-78 Dr. Lee Mahon, director of the Office of Learning Resources (OLR), moved with her staff from the central office to Parkside School. This development had significance for OBED activities in 1977-78. Parkside had been closed with several other schools in an SFUSD effort to economize. The move provided OBED with two helpful resources. First, Ms. Jennie Louie, the resource teacher in charge of curriculum materials for OBED, was able to secure separate housing for her many materials. OBED had, over the years, developed many innovative materials for the classroom. The *Golden Mountain* series, by Robert Sung, is one of the best in the country. It takes the student from introductory through advanced readings and writing in Chinese, using the Cantonese dialect. At Parkside, Ms. Louie, like the Title VII and the IRAP groups, found more room and more independence. She worked as an adjunct under both Mr. Del Portillo at OBED and Dr. Mahon at OLR.

Public Policy and the Educational Process

Pluralistic public policy was reflected clearly in the mechanics of the management process of OBED, which served as the agency for the implementation of SFUSD policies. But it is in the field, in the classroom, and in the schools of the system that the viability of such policies were most crucial.

The pluralistic public policy of SFUSD, initiated as a defensive response to federal court mandates, was a conservative and cautious effort at first. By 1977-78, however, the efforts were both positive and aggressive. They have not been an unqualified success, but they do represent solid gains upon which further developments can be based. Such achievements are clearly visible in the field, from the entry of the East Asian immigrant students into the system to their graduation from secondary schools and entry into community colleges or adult schools.

In the mid- and late-1970s SFUSD established a series of educational centers. There is a Chinese Education Center (CEC) in the heart of Chinatown. It consists of a new facility, the renovated military police station on Clay Street between Kearny and Montgomery Streets. The new facility consists of several floors of classrooms and a rooftop playground. The building is dwarfed by the Transamerica Pyramid Building and the Chinatown Holiday Inn. There is a Philippine Educational Center at Third and Harrison Streets, south of Market Street, and a Spanish Educational Center in the Mission District. In the 1978-79 year a new educational center was scheduled to open in the Richmond district to serve the Chinese in Chinatown West.

These educational centers fully reflect the pluralism in SFUSD policy concerning the East Asian immigrant minority students. The Korean, Japanese, Vietnamese, and other minority groups could certainly use such facilities, but financial restrictions and their "relatively small numbers" have not made such facilities possible at present.

Educational centers, especially those for Chinese and Filipinos, serve the East Asian community in many ways. First of all, immigrant families go to their respective centers for a wide variety of services. The Chinese Educational Center is most directly related to the subject of this paper. Many would not consider the Filipino group to be East Asian, but their needs, problems, and tasks are certainly closely related.

The Chinese Educational Center is a citywide facility. It will work with Chinese immigrant families from any part of the city. Most of their case work however, comes from the small areas of Chinatown, North Beach, and the area between Nob Hill and Van Ness Avenue. My office provided the same services as did the Chinese Education Center (CEC). Students and their families who lived in distant areas of the city usually came to the central office for assistance.

The CEC gave each student a battery of tests appropriate to his or her age and grade level. It also provided counseling to the families or referred them to appropriate social agencies. The student was either enrolled at the CEC or sent to a school in the system. Any student entering the CEC program could only stay for a maximum of one year before enrolling in a regular school. If the CEC staff thought the student was ready, he or she could be transferred to a regular school before the end of the year. Thus, the student population at CEC changed constantly. The staff was bilingual in Chinese and English. Many of its members could speak both Mandarin and Cantonese (both the Sam-Yup and Say-Yup sub-dialects of Cantonese).

As noted above, any Chinese student from any part of the city could utilize the CEC. There was some busing available, but many parents worked in the area of Chinatown or had other reasons for going there and took their children with them. Not all Chinese immigrant families and their children wished to avail themselves of the CEC facilities. Many wanted to send their children to regular schools near their homes in other parts of the city because they wanted their children to become totally submerged in English.

The Chinese and other East Asian immigrant students had many other opportunities and alternatives open to them besides the educational centers. After each student was screened and tested, a personalized academic program was developed. There were options available for different needs. Primary or elementary children had the option of bilingual classroom experience.

In SFUSD, there were self-contained bilingual classrooms at the elementary level, in accordance with federal and state guidelines. This meant that the child stayed in a single classroom all day. By law, no more than two-thirds of the class could be target language students (Chinese in a Chinese bilingual classroom, Japanese in a Japanese bilingual classroom, etc.). The remaining one-third included whites, Blacks, Hispanics, and anyone else. This was largely an effort to prevent a bilingual class from degenerating into a monolingual class in which the target language was used exclusively.

In the self-contained class, the teacher divided up the curriculum into blocks of instruction, balancing the target language and English as evenly as possible. Instruction in the English blocks was in English, and instruction in Chinese blocks was in Cantonese. This was true for other target languages. SFUSD had Chinese, Philippine, and Spanish bilingual classrooms. In 1977-78 there were also bilingual classrooms in Japanese and Korean. There were none in Vietnamese, Laotian, Cambodian, Tai, Malay, Hindi, Arabic, or Samoan. When there were significant concentrations of such students, OBED assigned bilingual paraprofessional or ESL personnel to assist regular teachers. After February, 1978, OBED had paraprofessional personnel fluent in Burmese, Arabic, Hindi, Russian, Fiji, Samoan, and Vietnamese.

Bilingual, self-contained classrooms existed only at the primary or elementary level. At the secondary level there were bilingual classes offered, but not all of the students' classes were bilingual. There were Chinese bilingual classes offered in senior high schools in biology, math, chemistry, and physics, as well as in some social sciences and humanities. There were Chinese bilingual classes at Galileo and Mission Senior High Schools. In 1977-78 there was a start in Korean, especially at Benjamin Franklin Junior High School in the Western Addition. There was also a Korean teacher hired to teach courses at Presidio Junior High School in the Richmond District. In the latter case, the situation degenerated into a monolingual class. The teacher hired at Presidio had been a former bilingual aide in the CETA program, for which I was responsible. His English was quite poor, and this monolingual Korean class resulted.

At least from the perspective of my office bilingual programs were strongest and most widely applied at the elementary level. ESL was used at both elementary and secondary levels but seemed to be more in use at the secondary level. Eugene MacAteer High School in the Laguna Honda area had an especially large and active program. It had special introductory courses and programs designed to meet the needs of new immigrant students at the secondary level. George Washington and Abraham Lincoln High Schools, in the Richmond and Sunset Districts respectively, provided intermediate and advanced ESL classes. All new students at this level were encouraged to attend MacAteer's introductory program before enrolling at a high school near their home where intermediate and advanced courses were offered. MacAteer had a summer schoool program that got new students off to a good start in the system.

My screening and testing procedures were parallel to those of the various educational centers. All entries into SFUSD sought to provide the best alternatives possible in the light of each student's experience, education, language proficiency in English, and specific family needs. The programs were especially helpful for the Chinese, Korean, Filipino, and Hispanic communitites. IRAP and Title VII helped Japanese, Korean, and Indochinese students were programs were inadequate or nonexistent. In the case of the influx of new ethnolinguistic minorities, the CETA bilingual aide program was the start of a concerted assistance where none had existed before.

In the summer 1978 the Samoan community leaders started a summer school program for secondary-level Samoan students, focusing especially on office skills. The CETA bilingual aide program provided paraprofessional assistance, while SFUSD provided facilities at James Lick Junior High School. At the same time the Southeast Asian refugee program, under Dr. Hunyh started a summer school program for Vietnamese students (elementary through secondary) with some assistance from the CETA bilingual aide program. CETA aides served as teachers (some had credentials) and others served as paraprofessionals. SFUSD could not offer classroom space, so Star of the Sea (a Catholic School for girls) provided facilities in the Richmond area.

Conclusion

My experience with SFUSD certainly cannot be taken as a basis for in-depth study of the mechanics of pluralism in SFUSD public policy, but it offers a view of the operation of one of this country's major school districts as it attempts to serve a large and diverse immigrant student population which includes a sizable East Asian component.

By the mid-1970s SFUSD had developed public policies clearly in support of the pressing needs of the rapidly growing numbers of ethnolinguistic student minorities. This new area of concern added greatly to the already controversial and combative desegregation efforts. In this period the district began to assume a more positive attitude towards minority groups. District programs and activities, from the childcare centers to the education centers to the community colleges and adult schools, all began to consider ethnolinguistic minority needs above and beyond the polarized situation of the white majority versus racial minorities.

Pluralism, the concept underlying new policies and programs, was manifested in many ways. In policy, it was basically the recognition of the serious need to accommodate ethnolinguistic minorities. On a practical level we have seen the designation of thirteen ethnic categories and twenty-two language groups supported by hard and soft money in state and federally funded programs. Pluralism has not only been reflected in the formulation of public policy but has also affected the implementation process. It has been noted that the management process, together with the instructional activities in the classroom, also exhibit an application of pluralism.

In the year prior to my tenure as an OBED administrator, I had served as a paraprofessional employee of SFUSD in Winfield Scott School in the Marina. It was there that I observed first hand the operation of such policies in the school. I immediately became aware of the uphill battle that such new policies and programs faced when confronted by faculty and staff committed to the established educational programs of the past. At a time when economics are at least as influential as politics or educational philosophies, it is clear that the new policies and programs associated with the pluralistic perspective have not been universally embraced in SFUSD. Indeed, many would say that not even the majority of the faculty and staff embrace such notions, because such ideas are often seen as a threat to tenure, promotion, and other interests of the more traditional approaches in education.

As noted at the start of this brief survey, San Francisco has not been completely successful in its efforts. Many in the community, especially the radicals and those of the many other heretofore unrepresented ethnolinguistic minorities, claim that too little has been done. Money, time, and resources are wasted on political battles among the highest echelons of SFUSD leadership.

Pluralism, as it has been applied, has been a political expediency rather than a real revolution in education.

I would say, however, that my year of intensive and intimate association with the OBED has shown me that much has been done. The effort to seek an equitable redistribution of wealth and power in our society will always have its detractors. Some say "too much and too fast," others say "too little and too slow." Such is the case when attempting to provide for ethno-linguistic minority student rights.

SFUSD has not been without its faults, but it has, in my view, demonstrated a commitment to serving all of the students, including the rapidly growing ethnolinguistic student minorities. In spite of complex and paralyzing economic and political developments at the local level, the system has tried to maintain those commitments made when new policies were developed several years ago.

I regret that in the post-Proposition Thirteen era it appears that programs and activities related to the special needs and problems of the ethnolinguistic student minorities are among the most "dispensable," and are thus among the first to receive the most radical cuts in budget and staff. Were it not for the availability of federal and state soft monies Howard Jarvis and Robert Alioto would have destroyed in a single stroke what thousands of people over a period of several years worked to develop. I know that there are many committed professionals that still support the pluralistic public policies and programs reviewed above. I am confident that they will emerge again to recoup the losses suffered in 1978-79, and will move on to expand into new areas. For my part, I am now an outsider as before, but an intensely concerned one. If the necessary changes are to come about, then we so-called outsiders have to become insiders.

Notes

1. Benjamin Tom, "On Politics and Education in San Francisco: Commentary by the President of the Board of Education," *Amerasia Journal* 5, no. 7 (1978): 93.
2. Ibid., p. 95.

George O. Roberts

The Role and Responsibility of Textbooks in Promoting Pluralism

The Inherent Pluralism of the United States: A Myth?

The United States has historically been recognized as a crucible for meaningful pluralism. Even before it attained the status of a sovereign state, America had provided a haven for individuals and groups of various nationalities who suffered persecution in their homelands because of their beliefs or who saw opportunities to advance and prosper that the new nation afforded. The diversified peopling of the continent resulted from "expelling forces which drove people from their homes, and attracting forces which lured them westward. Most important was a large reserve population sufficiently dissatisfied with existing conditions to brave the wilderness."[1] Regrettably, however, the individuals and groups that settled in the United States soon found that success in a milieu of pluralistic egalitarianism was not readily attainable. Differences of race, language, and religion came to be the factors that determined one's place on the national ladder.

American society has been pluralistic, but it has retained a rigid system of stratification based on race and other sociocultural criteria.[2] This reality has, in turn, produced contradictory expectations: on the one hand, it encourages people to believe that, in spite of initial physical and sociocultural differences among individuals and groups, pluralism provides equal opportunity for developing one's capabilities and equal access to the benefits appropriate to such development. On the other hand, for most people pluralism in America merely tolerates initial differences with the expectation that diverse individuals and groups will be absorbed into the "melting pot" as they are inculcated with the dominant values of White Anglo-Saxon America.

Until the second half of the twentieth century, the United States operated as a society based on Anglo-American values and priorities. Until the 1950s, therefore, little was done to ensure that the civil liberties and opportunities guaranteed to all by the American creed were not denied to those individuals and groups whose differences could not be eliminated through immersion in the mythical melting pot. Thus, from the eighteenth to the early twentieth century, pluralism was only an illusion for a significant number of visibly different minority groups and individuals—Blacks, Chicanos, Native Americans, and Asians—and even for those less visible ethnic minorities whose language and other sociocultural manifestations made them different from the dominant group of white Anglo-Saxon Americans.

At the same time, however, a process of enlightened socialization was developing the capacity to force policymakers and wielders of power to put into practice the ideals of egalitarian pluralism. Thus it was that various laws began to affect economic, political, and educational institutions that had once served as instruments for the perpetration of unequal treatment and opportunities. The various civil rights acts from Title I through Title IX are now household words. During the past twenty years efforts have been made to bring ideals in line with practices.

The public school, which became a prominent feature of the American nation in the early nineteenth century, has been a very significant agent of such change.[3] When compulsory education and its programs became the responsibility of the public sector, many disadvantaged citizens were able to gain access to the process which had the power to translate ascriptive limitations and disabilities into achievement benefits and rewards.

Through the legislation and implementation strategies it developed to meet this challenge, California has been a leader in this effort. The education codes of California, for example, have made it quite clear that no citizen can be deemed to be properly educated without adequate exposure to the true nature of American pluralism.

In this regard, the state, through the Superintendent of Public Instruction and the California State Board of Education, has monitored and assessed the adequacy of instructional material being used in the public schools. In the early 1970s, the State Board of Education assumed a significant level of leadership by undertaking to ensure the availability of quality instructional materials, especially in the social sciences, which do so much to shape student attitudes and knowledge about groups and individuals different from the dominant segment of American society. There can be no question that the efforts in this direction, spearheaded by concerned minority educators and community leaders, have brought about a vast improvement in instructional materials related to the various ethnic groups that constitute the totality of American society. The volume in which this essay appears, *Pluralism, Racism, and Public Policy* reflects the efforts of public officials and citizens to eliminate the contradiction between the ideals of equal opportunity and mutual respect and the traditional educational practice of ignoring the existence of minority persons who could not be Americans.[4]

Achievements during the past ten years justify the enthusiasm of a few of California's leaders for the focus on bilingualism and multiculturalism. For instance, Superintendent Wilson Riles concluded that "the philosophy of education implemented through a bilingual-bicultural approach will bring a new spirit of humanism so richly deserved by cultured man, regardless of color, creed, or nationality." Assemblyman Peter Chacon was equally positive in his opinion: "bilingual education is a most exciting and promising trend in education. I am convinced that it promises to provide a means by which the monolingual non-English-speaking or partially bilingual children can reap the full benefits of their scholastic careers." Equally appropriate and enthusiastic is the view of Senator Alan Cranston that

> bilingual education can be a great force in fostering educational change in America. It challenges the assumption that schools need to offer only one curriculum in one language—English—to serve one group of children—Anglos. It will go a long way toward ending the nightmare of educational neglect that has so long plagued Spanish-speaking and other bilingual children in America.

Enough time has elapsed to assess the impact and effectiveness of programs and policies which have been pursued both at the federal and state levels. It is certainly true that the 1960s and 1970s have witnessed a tremendous upsurge in policies and programs whose objective has been to promote a keener awareness and appreciation of the multicultural reality of American society. The activities of various minority pressure groups have been partly responsible. Their efforts which otherwise would have elicited lukewarm or indifferent reactions have ensured that the articulated goals of these pluralistic policies and programs are not diluted or sidetracked. Persons closer to the arena of a disadvantaged existence, and those who have been more directly the victims of denial and unequal access to opportunities and privileges, would argue with vehemence that not much has been accomplished.[5] They would present as evidence the ever-widening gap in socioeconomic attainments between ethnic minorities on the one hand and the dominant majority population on the other. These dissatisfied critics would go further to make a strong case that many of those responsible for implementing pluralistic policies and programs maintain negative attitudes which render them ineffectual.

Although these criticisms cannot be easily dismissed, it is a fact that a significant advance in multiculturalism and pluralism has occurred, and the educational institutions ought to be recognized for having played an important role. Both the majority and ethnic minorities have benefitted from the awareness that differences among people should not be used to rank some as inferior and others as superior. The result has been not only a heightened sense of self-esteem among those previously burdened with a feeling of inferiority and insecurity but also a keener awareness and appreciation among those who have been free to develop a false sense of superiority.

A significant outcome of this development has been the opportunity for effective participation by previously disadvantaged segments of the population, including new immigrants who tended, by and large, to manifest glaring cultural differences. One can say, in conclusion, that a cultural enrichment has developed, befitting the true character of the United States. At long last, the multiplicity of cultures is being recognized as a strength from which this nation has grown and prospered.

The Essential Role and Responsibility of Textbooks in Pluralism

All societies have had to depend upon education as the principal agent by which to inculcate their citizens with the norms, values, and ethos of the society. As has been noted by McCarty and Associates,

> ... the schools, like other social institutions, are primarily self-serving. They exist primarily to meet the economic needs and, to a lesser degree, the psychological needs of those involved in running them; and they obtain the support and resources that permit them to go on existing by serving the more powerful elements of society.... They divide the population into winners and losers, in ways that correspond adequately though imperfectly to the class and ethnic distinctions existing in the society; and they instill in each child throughout childhood and adolescence the expectation as to which of these he or she is to become. By the time most pupils drop out or graduate they have internalized the evaluation that the schools make of their worth and prospects....[7]

They further argue that:

> Schools, and the expectations of society for them, are unlikely to be very different in 1980 from what they are today.... Professionals often overlook the fact that those flaws in the system that they identify either are not recognized at all by the public or are considered popularly to be virtues rather than vices.... The public likes the schools; when it is dissatisfied, it is because the schools are not meeting their agreed-upon objectives, and not because these objectives themselves are dubious or misdirected.[8]

Equally germane is the viewpoint of the Study Commission on Undergraduate Education:

> The goal of the school system is the maintenance of the status quo with respect to cultural, racial, sexual, and economic class, superiority-and-inferiority relations. Too often, America's school systems promulgate the erroneous theory that some people are better than

others, that one sex is superior to the other, is transmitted to the
student body through the selection of curriculum content, books,
texts, and symbols, and school personnel (including administration).
The family, the general environment of the community, TV and
media also disseminate the idea.[9]

While it is true that the overall culture often determines the priorities and the
strategies to be used in such an endeavor, other supportive institutions are
often instrumental in determining whether the educational institution will
approach its responsibility loosely or in a highly structured manner. On the
one hand, there has always been the opportunity for education through
such agents of primary socialization as the family. In other instances, peer
groups, neighborhood groups, and other vested interest groups operating
within the parameters allowed by the society and its culture have also served
as agents of enculturation and education. As noted by Frost and Baily,

> Education is created by the culture to serve its interests and must
> bear the marks of its creator. In the past, state and national cultures
> have produced educational systems to acculturate their young and
> preserve their integrity. While they have been influenced somewhat
> by events and conditions beyond their borders, their character has
> been determined largely by regional factors. . . . As we turn to con-
> sider educational developments in the nations of the twentieth
> century, we must appreciate the fact that they are essentially
> products of one-world events and only secondarily the results of
> internal happenings. . . . A closer study of these events will reveal
> that they are products of conditions and happenings throughout
> the world. This gives emphasis to the fact that if we are to under-
> stand. . . . western education in the twentieth century, we must add
> to the western tradition developments in Russia, China, Japan, India,
> Africa, and other areas of the world. . . . We of the West have be-
> come part of one world, and there is no turning back.[9]

In more recent history, especially since the industrial revolution, societies
have extended to institute a more extensive and formalized procedure through
the establishment of public schools. In this effort, particularly in providing
greater access for its citizenry, the United States has been a leader in developing an extensive and effective system of free public education. Furthermore,
it has been the case particularly in the United States that one finds a profu-
sion of instructional materials at little or no cost. Even though one can argue
that the taxation structure makes it necessary for most working citizens to
contribute towards schools and instructional materials, it is true that citizens
have obtained access to these facilities regardless of their financial or socio-

economic status. One could argue, of course, that the quality of these facilities varies from community to community, and that those who are wealthy can obtain facilities far superior to those available to ordinary citizens.

The point to be emphasized, however, is that the United States, especially since the mid-nineteenth century, has succeeded in providing a vast network of formal educational facilities, thus enabling almost all of its citizens to experience the enculturative and socializating effect of education. Effective citizenship, in turn, has accrued from exposure to the educational provisions and processes to the extent that opportunities for such access were restricted or open. It would seem reasonable to deduce that the successful emphasis on public education has made it possible for American society to enhance the notion of pluralism while emphasizing the values and strategies preferred by the dominant white majority.

Although the social, physical, economic, and political environment is important, no component has proved more essential in pursuing a specifically charted course of socialization, and, in turn, of pluralism, than the school and the teacher. The teacher, with the support of mandated instructional materials, including textbooks, has had the opportunity throughout all levels of the educational system to interpret and to inculcate not only attitudes, but the skills necessary for effective participation in society. Such participation is often influenced by the views held of self and others. Therefore, the teacher, the curriculum, and the textbooks, by projecting superior/inferior images, may leave the student little choice but to develop those attitudes which will reinforce his or her own identity as superior or inferior. If, however, the teacher and textbooks present pluralism as essentially egalitarian and respect the enriching impact of differences and diversity, then the student will most likely develop attitudes and viewpoints consistent with that presentation. After all, teachers are most often the instruments used by school administrators to uphold prevailing values, including being

> prejudiced, uninterested in social change, and uncommitted to reform, particularly the sort of reform in tough areas which draws on the roots and resources of the areas. They are on the contrary increasingly committed to service to and protection of the centralized hierarchical system in which they will 'rise' or 'fall' and not to people in the neighborhoods, particularly if they are minority people.[11]

It should not be forgotten, of course, that textbook presentations can be made consistent with the social world outside of school. Hence, the teacher becomes so important and must assume a great deal of responsibility for seeing that the ideals and expectations of the society are upheld through the execution of his or her socialization function.

The Case of California: Pluralism and Textbooks

In my view, California, by virtue of its clearly articulated education codes, has been at the forefront of the movement to promote egalitarian pluralism in its schools. California is quite clear in its mandated categories of competency for teachers and curricula. Further, the education codes, as implemented and enforced by the State Board of Education, have almost complete control of what textbooks and other instructional materials ought to contain and reflect. According to the California Education Code (sections 8501 through 8576 and 9240 through 9246), instructional materials must also provide a foundation for understanding the "role and contributions of women, American Negroes, American Indians, Asian Americans, Mexican Americans, and other ethnic groups to the economic, political, and social development of California and the United States, with particular emphasis to be placed on the roles of these groups in contemporary society,"[11]

In the early 1970s, under the pressure of educational groups representing the minority segments of the society, the State Board of Education was challenged to exercise its responsibility. The outcome of this pressure was that, in 1972, after over a decade of indifference to prevailing inconsistencies between mandated parameters of textbook content and the real discrepancies, the State Board of Education decided to undertake a more careful review and approval of textbooks to be used in the public schools of California. It is quite possible that other states throughout the nation have been pressured into actions similar to the decision of the California State Board of Education, thereby guaranteeing an end to the dominance of Anglo-Saxon images and values. Only by ending such one-dimensional presentations can we give adequate and appropriate recognition to the existence, contributions, and aspirations of ethnic minorities.

It may be that the pressure by ethnic minorities in California against illegal instructional materials was exacerbated by the renewed and widespread mood of protest which had seized the country by 1968. The fact, however, is that the textbook controversy of 1972 would not have arisen if those responsible for implementing legal mandates had not been consistently remiss. Six months of careful review by an appointed Ethnic Task Force revealed gross abuse of the education codes of California. This review forced the State Board of Education to withdraw the approval which it had irresponsibly granted to scores of textbooks and supplementary instructional materials. One consequence of this "victory" was the formation of numerous curriculum and instructional materials committees, each claiming expertise and responsiblity for its own ethnic or racial group. With one voice, all these groups—independently representing Blacks, Chicanos, Native Americans, Japanese Americans, Chinese Americans, and women—called for the total withdrawal of traditional textbooks and the rejection of the many "racist and sexist" major publishers whose illegal products they deemed contemptible and reprehensible. These groups felt that they alone had the competence and the responsibility to prepare and disseminate appropriate and acceptable instructional materials. Given the lack of capability, if not professional and technical competence, it is fortunate that the responsible legal body, the California State Board of Education, sought another means of resolving the controversy. It appointed a committee to assist the traditional publishers to bring their products into compliance with the education codes, acknowledging that change, however urgent and necessary, can only be a process and not an instant event.

By 1974, the process of change influenced the character and content of instructional materials. Initially, these changes were superficial, entailing peripheral references to ethnic experiences and persons, or the neutralizing of traditional sex and ethnic roles and images. Subsequently, however, serious and deep analysis, along with rational integration into the traditional instructional crucible, was given to previously neglected aspects of the totality of American society. Related developments occurred in the training of teachers and in the upgrading of entrenched personnel through in-service training.

Textbooks today, especially in California, provide the majority of American citizens with the means to appreciate the reality of their plural society. Anglo-Saxon children are being made to recognize that other groups, apparently different because of color or cultural manifestations such as language, have made equally significant contributions to American society. Blacks did come to the country involuntarily; Native Americans did succumb to the incursions of Anglo-Saxon opportunists; Chinese and Japanese did respond to Anglo-Saxon demand for their labor, as well as to the promise of personal enhancement which the new nation presented.[12] Other immigrants with characteristics slightly different from the original settlers did submit to an initial subservience. All these groups suffered to varying degrees. But each in its own way made contributions which the dominant group felt free to acknowledge or to ignore. Those whose "disabilities" were viewed as temporary managed to enter the American melting pot and to assimilate into the dominant society. On the other hand, those with permanent "disabilities," such as Blacks, Asians, and Native Americans, were excluded from the pluralistic "pot" which was based on an ideal of egalitarianism. Such denial has contributed to the type of alienation to which Malcolm X referred in 1964: "I am speaking as what I am: one of twenty-two million black people in this country who are victims of your democratic system. They're the victims of the Democratic politicians, the victims of the Republican politicians. They're actually the victims of what you call democracy."[13] The denial of access and recognition to these "permanently" disabled and disadvantaged groups was to a large extent the result of irresponsible presentations by teachers and the textbooks which served as a means for the interpretation and inculcation of attitudes, skills, and the rewards of American society.

This decade has not only witnessed improvements in the multicultural contents of textbooks (particularly in the social sciences and humanities) but has also seen appreciable progress in the pluralistic awareness of teachers. Even teachers of natural sciences and related subjects have shown an inclination toward seeking out approaches and constructs different from traditional Anglo-Saxon usages. Aside from increasing recognition of the viewpoints and theories of previously ignored minority philosophers and chemists, for example, efforts are being made to include the traditional constructs and experiences of ethnic minorities in the formulation and implementation of learning, teaching, and evaluative procedures and principles. It is thus that *Soul on Ice* appears in class book lists along with *Pride and Prejudice*, as does George Washington Carver along with Albert Einstein. Regrettably, of course, there are still many teachers who have retained professional callousness and have earned the label of retreatists: "The retreatist not only is no longer concerned with the goals of the system; he really has no concern with the means toward achieving those goals either. . . . He goes through the motions of the job, but he could not care less about any aspects of it beyond his own personal comforts and his paycheck."[14]

Highlighting this development has been the attention to bicultural and bilingual education from the federal through the local level. While there is clear recognition of the magnitude of such a project, which entails constant vigilance against powers seeking its demise or stagnation, a process of adequacy and relevance has been initiated which is consonant with the pluralistic ideal of America.[15] Clearly stipulated competencies for bilingual and bicultural teachers—language proficiency, multicultural awareness, professional subject matter preparation, and knowledge of community differences—can only sustain the pace of achieving realistic pluralism. What these competencies ensure is that a tradition of imputed superiority resulting from ignorance will be corrected through cultural relativism and a resultant appreciation of personal and group achievement.

In the area of language proficiency, for example, it is now widely acknowledged that those for whom the primary language of communication and instruction is secondary need not be judged inferior. To enhance the learning and teaching process, teachers are required not only to recognize the inherent diversity and plurality of languages but also to gain access to those that are relevant through self-acquisition or the availability of intermediaries. Indeed, bilingual competencies have become a common expectation in arenas of instruction that are clearly multicultural. It is in this same vein of responsible enculturation that the 1970s have witnessed the proliferation of programmatic support for preparation in subject matter pertaining to cultural diversity and the peculiar character of ethic communities. The concern expressed repeatedly by a few diligent educators is finally being heeded:

> Over the years we have subscribed to the time-honored principle that teaching materials are only as good as the teachers using them. The principle, coupled with the inescapable fact that educators, like most other Americans, are likely to harbor negative attitudes toward racial and ethnic minorities, suggests that before the classroom teacher can present his pupils with the accurate, realistic image of minority group relations that is so desperately needed, he will need to re-examine, clarify, and modify his own attitudes and predispositions toward minorities. In these times he can ill afford to do less.[16]

But more competence would not suffice to create the atmosphere essential to dignified pluralism. The persistent influence of generations past must be met with teachers and such supportive instructional materials as would increase the available pool of humane and creative professionals. Do you remember the fine old story about the two bricklayers? They were asked, "What are you doing?" One replied, "I am laying bricks." The other said, "I am building a cathedral." The first is a tradesman; the second has the soul of an artist or professional. The difference is in the meaning of the activity. It is not in how expertly or skillfully the bricklayers daub mortar onto each brick; it is not in the number of hours of supervised practice they had; it is not in how much information they have about the job; it is not in their loyalty to the boss; it is not in their familiarity with other constructions. It is how they feel about what they are doing, in their sense of the relationship between their work and that of others, in their appreciation of potentialities, in their sense of form, in their need for and enjoyment of significance, in their identification of self with civilized aspirations, and in their whole outlook on life. A similar distinction can be made between teachers who hold class or teach school and teachers who educate children, between training programs that turn out manpower and those that turn out professionals.

The tradesman-teacher operates by scanning his memory of various courses for specific examples or instructions to follow or emulate. By contrast, the professional-teacher, who reflects his internalized sense of education in the specific situation, spontaneously creates appropriate structures of response. Putting it another way, the first teacher looks for the particular weapon or tool to use, while the other teacher mobilizes his entire being in a holistic response to the situation. The first teacher is unidimensional, responding to an idea, feeling, performance, or attitude as if it existed by itself; the second teacher responds, usually without conscious analysis at the time, to the pattern of these components, to his apprehension of meanings in the various ways of life in the situation.[17]

Conclusions and Recommendations

The promise of attaining realistic pluralism through current programs of bicultural education must not create a blindness to certain inherent limitations. Despite its ideals of egalitarianism, the United States can be no different from other societies and nations based on the inevitable social stratification of its citizens. Equity and equal access, no matter how genuinely cherished and propagated, will always succumb to the pressure of unavoidable ranking and inequity. In short, while attempts to promote better opportunities for personal and group advancement are to be lauded, the reality of societal existence demands a recognition that inequities will continue to exist, and that white Anglo-Saxon values and strategies will retain their place of dominance. One would be well-advised, therefore, to consider multicultural activities as a necessary and valuable means by which ethnic minorities can gain access to the power structure, and thus participate much more effectively in that structure. It is also the case that multicultural activities ought to be perceived as an enrichment of the sector that maintains control in a plurality.

The following recommendations address the role and responsibility of textbooks in promoting realistic pluralism:

1. Tighten the existing flexibility in the choice of textbooks and monitor the use of alternative or substitute materials.
2. "Retool" traditional teachers and administrators so as to improve their limited knowledge of, and respect for, materials which highlight ethnic minorities.
3. Place more sensitive and knowledgeable minorities in senior administrative positions responsible for public policy formulation and implementation.
4. Improve the quality of life for those ethnic minorities who are the victims of deliberate inequity and discrimination.
5. Develop and strengthen community schools in terms of instructional and physical plant facilities. "Bus" teachers and equipment of quality, rather than children who need the security of familiar surroundings.
6. Develop inter-community programs and experiences in neutral facilities or sequential locations. The comprehensive and centralized facilities serving a variety of feeder communities are a good example, as are specialized schools in music, drama, or science, which serve a wide range of communities and ethnic groups.
7. Ensure that key teachers, whose numbers need to be increased, are at least bicultural, if not multicultural, in orientation, sensitivity, and pedagogical style.

8. Reexamine the structure, content, and transmitting agents of teacher training institutions, and encourage the removal of those deficiencies which obstruct the acquisition of pluralistic awareness, appreciation, and knowledge.

9. Finally, inculcate the recognition that a pluralistic posture does not entail absolute equality among the segments comprising the plurality. Either because of numbers or the locus of effective power, one of these segments will always be paramount, thereby putting itself in a position to influence, if not to determine, the degree of tolerance, empathy, compromise, and accommodation which will guide the nature of interaction among the various segments.

As has been noted by the Study Commission on Undergraduate Education of Teachers:

> Meaningful pluralism requires a situation in society . . . where no one race, sex, culture, or class is preferred over another. . . . Opportunities must be created for "preferred groups" to confront their illusions of "being better" and to realize the evil of their arrogance. They must learn to deal with their prejudices and acquire a healthier self image. They, as members of the majority, must behave in congruence with American declarations of "democracy," "law," and "justice" for everybody.[18]

Notes

1. Ray A. Billington, *Westward Expansion* (New York: Macmillan Co., 1960), p. 43.
2. See Charles Madden and Gladys Meyer, *Minorities in American Society* (New York: D. Van Nostrand, 1973).
3. S. E. Frost, Jr., and Kenneth P. Bailey, *Historical and Philosophical Foundations of Western Education* (Columbus, Ohio: A. Bell & Howell Co., 1973), pp. 412–478.
4. Cf. Peter Rose, *Through Different Eyes* (London: Oxford University Press, 1973).
5. See, for example, Gary T. Marx, *Protest and Prejudice* (New York: Harper & Row, 1969).
6. Donald J. McCarty and Associates, *New Perspectives on Teacher Education* (San Francisco, Cal.: Jossey-Bass, 1973), p. 26.
7. Ibid., pp. 40–41.
8. Study Commission on Undergraduate Education of Teachers, *Teacher Education in the United States* (Lincoln, Neb.: University of Nebraska Press, 1975), p. 219.

9. Frost and Bailey, p. 505.
10. Study Commission, p. 51.
11. Kenneth P. Bailey, et al., *Social Sciences Education Framework* (Sacramento, Cal.: State Department of Education, 1975), pp. 1–2.
12. Cf. Louis Schneider and Charles Bonjean, *The Idea of Culture in the Social Sciences* (London: Cambridge University Press, 1973).
13. Archie Epps, *The Speeches of Malcolm X at Harvard* (New York: William Morrow, 1969), p. 134.
14. Richard Wisniewski, *New Teachers in Urban Schools* (New York: Random House, 1968), pp. 59–60.
15. See, for example, Douglas M. Knight, et al., *The Federal Government and Higher Education* (Englewood Cliffs, N.J.: Prentice-Hall, 1960), and U. S. Congress, *Elementary and Secondary Education Amendments of 1973* (Washington, 1973).
16. James A. Banks and William W. Joyce, *Teaching Social Studies to Culturally Different Children* (Reading, Mass.: Addison-Wesley Publishing Co., 1971), p. 359.
17. McCarty and Associates, pp. 198–199.
18. Study Commission, pp. 221–222.

Part III

The Present and Future:
Criticisms and Suggestions

Introduction

This concluding section presents a dim view of the results of current public policy enacted for the purpose of developing cultural pluralism in the United States. The essays confirm the deep-rooted racism in America and, they collectively demonstrate the fundamental weakness of public policy essentially predicated upon an assumption of an unchanged institutional framework. Without basic structural changes and specific, concise laws there is little chance to implement new policies that offer real opportunity for and are sensitive to the needs of minorities. Power relationships play a key role in this analysis of ethnicity, while class issues provide additional insights.

Jim Baron discusses economic and social mobility in America for racial minorities. He examines the relative importance of a person's total socioeconomic environment and ethnic and cultural heritage in assessing social mobility. Within this context Baron argues that legislative and judicial victories have not provided increased economic opportunities for minorities. Without such opportunities, current policy must be viewed with skepticism.

Samuel Gaertner and John Dovidio discuss the attitudes and self-conceptions of "tested non-racists." Their research shows that in certain situations these people display racist behavior similar to that of people who acknowledge their prejudice. They suggest the implications involved for both the formulation and implementation of public policy. They conclude by assessing the meaning of "liberal" values for racism and pluralism.

Finally, M. R. Karenga assesses the myth or reality of the existence of cultural pluralism in American society in terms of power and its relation to liberalism, racism, and Marxism. Dr. Karenga looks to ethnic studies programs and their development of sensitive research methodologies that seek to promote solutions enabling minorities to overcome their powerlessness.

James N. Baron

The Promise of Racial Equality: A Skeptic's View

"It is important to know what you can do before you learn to measure how well you seem to have done it."
— JOHN TUKEY

This year marks the twenty-fifth anniversary of the Supreme Court's historic ruling in *Brown* v. *Board of Education*, and the fifteen-year commemorative of the pathbreaking civil rights act enacted by Congress. Lest the mere passage of time give the impression that progress towards racial equality has been cumulative and linear, it seems worthwhile to examine our successes and failures in the arenas to which these two landmarks applied—education and the workplace, respectively.

While the popular media have continued to convey a sense of boundless optimism regarding the future, I remain decidedly skeptical. Nowhere is this egalitarian euphoria more conspicuous, than in the case of the revamped Equal Employment Opportunity Commission (EEOC) under the management of its new commissioner, Eleanor Norton. I recently talked over the phone with a rather "well-situated" individual who works at EEOC. Always the skeptic, I asked whether the glowing news reports were true in their claims of a reduced backlog of cases and innovative antidiscriminatory strategies. The response was a terse "no way in hell." After a little probing, my confidant opened up to provide a sobering portrait of the agency's current "holding pattern." It does not want to rock the boat which carries the congressmen who oversee the agency and pay lip service to it in order to exploit its political appeal. This employee told me about having quit a previous job to come to EEOC, believing that they were "on the right track." Now, overwhelmed by a feeling of desperation, this same idealist finds it hard to come to work. Many others at EEOC, I was assured, share these perceptions. It occurred to me afterwards that I had been talking to a total stranger, whose personal and political frustrations must be quite intense to warrant such candor.

Taken alone, this conversation is certainly an inadequate basis for indicting current equal opportunity programs. Hence, a critical overview of the track record of egalitarian policy in education and employment should help place recent events (most notably, the *Bakke* decision) in context and suggest some important implications of curent controversies for the future of anti-discriminatory policy.

Education and Equality: "The Road Not Taken"

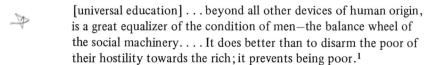

> [universal education] . . . beyond all other devices of human origin, is a great equalizer of the condition of men—the balance wheel of the social machinery. . . . It does better than to disarm the poor of their hostility towards the rich; it prevents being poor.[1]

What we now know about the effects of schooling on social and economic achievement indicates that Horace Mann's pronouncement is seriously in error. The last fifteen years of educational research have driven home three primary points:

1. Differences in school resources do not significantly affect the educational attainment and ideals of students, after the social, racial, and economic composition of the school is taken into account.[2]
2. While school integration slightly improves the performance of black school children, its effects are negligible above and beyond the impact of students' family backgrounds. As David Armor of the Rand Corporation has written, "programs which stress financial aid to disadvantaged black families may be just as important, if not more so, than programs aimed at integrating blacks into white neighborhoods and schools."[3]
3. Finally, even if education were equalized among racial and ethnic groups, the effects on social and economic equality would be minimal. Christopher Jencks asserts that attending a school which emphasizes the "appropriate" attitudes and values (whatever these might in fact be) is of greater importance for one's eventual success than attending a school that boosts measurable cognitive outcomes. In short, his view is that "educational inequality is of marginal importance for either good or ill. Such things as control over capital, occupational specialization, and the traditions of American politics . . . turn out to be far more important than schooling."[4]

Thus, despite a drastic narrowing of the racial gap in educational attainment, equalization of educational opportunity has not fulfilled its mission. Furthermore, the increase in relative educational attainment by minorities cannot be attributed solely to recent egalitarian educational policies—we should have expected the gap in educational attainment between the races to decrease even without egalitarian interventions simply because there is little room for "improvement" in the distribution of schooling among whites.

The legacy of the last fifteen years of educational reforms thus appears to be a tragic paradox. Confronted with the huge influx of baby boom school-age children (especially among minorites) who would be at best marginally employable and at worst a political nuisance, the "Great Society" funnelled its energies and resources into education as never before. The result was a mind-boggling mass of educational theory, research, and experimentation which claimed to balance "relevance" with the mandate of equal opportunity. In retrospect, however, it appears that those groups which benefitted most from the era of educational smorgasbord were the very ones who needed it the least. Because educational reforms, including desegregation, never reflected a coherent vision of what "should be," they have merely accentuated what "already is." And, as usual, the ones who have suffered the most are the ones with the most to gain.

Without impugning the motives of the framers of current egalitarian policies, the civil rights legislation of the mid-60s makes sense when set against the backdrop of the relative prosperity of the late 50s and early 60s. Equal opportunity seem more palatable when one's own future has been safeguarded; at the same time, liberal educational reforms served as palliatives, guaranteeing that the newly established claims to affluence of the white middle class would not be undermined by fundamental conflicts. I still recall that during the Watts riots my parents were afraid to let us go out and play in our upper-middle-class white neighborhood in the suburban San Fernando Valley, some thirty to forty miles from the violence. Television brought the threat right into our living rooms, and an accession to ideological egalitarianism must have seemed like a small price to pay to protect that TV set.

Of course, in recent years the economic and political commitment to education has waned as the waves of inflation and recession have undermined the vision of civil rights advocates. Governmental expenditures on education as a proportion of the gross national product have actually declined slightly in the last several years, reflecting the increasing conservatism which has accompanied fiscal austerity.[5] As the historian J. R. Pole noted recently, "the increasing economic depression of the late 1960s and 1970s did not seem like a propitious time for the kind of government spending that would have been required by effective [egalitarian] policies that looked beyond relief to a reordering of the entire scale of government subsidies and supports. In any case, the structure of political power made such programs unlikely."[6] Because the precipitous declines in fertility which have recently alarmed educators are occurring more slowly among minority populations, there are relatively more disadvantaged minority children in school than ever before.

Thus, with an irony so often characteristic of political change, the post-affluence backlash will cause disproportionate harm to the very social groups for whose benefit those changes supposedly were instituted.

Confronted with the conspicuous failure of educational reform to effect economic equality, few egalitarians would contend that equalizing schooling "doesn't matter," but rather would claim that the justification for doing so must be to improve individual lives rather than individual incomes.[7] The pathbreaking *Brown* decision in 1954 inspired the hope that schools' liberating potential could be unleashed to eradicate the cultural bases of discrimination. The Court's ruling relied heavily on sociological and psychological research demonstrating the ways in which discrimination operates in schools. Subsequently, countless studies have demonstrated the importance of the informal social arrangements within schools (clubs, cliques, faculty role models, dating practices, and the like) as determinants of eventual achievements.[8] In recognizing the significance of the inner workings of schools, the Court seemed to be saying: If schools cannot be made more "relevant" to the world of work, then perhaps the same egalitarian ends can be achieved by remolding the social arrangements within schools and other institutions which breed discrimination.

Indeed, the justices had set the stage for such an approach even prior to the *Brown* decision. For example, in the 1950 case of *McLaurin* v. *Oklahoma State Regents for Higher Education* (339 U. S. 637), the Court held that a black doctoral student was being denied his constitutional right of "commingling" with his fellow students by formal and informal circumstances which isolated him socially, thereby depriving him of an integral part of graduate training. And on the same day, in the case of *Sweatt* v. *Painter* (339 U. S. 629), the Court upheld the right of a Negro to attend a "white" law school (even though the plaintiff's state of residence offered him legal training in a "black" school) since the former institution not only was objectively superior, but also

> possessed to a far greater degree those qualities which were incapable of objective measurement, but which made for greatness in a law school, including reputation of the faculty, experience of the administration, position and influence of the alumni, standing in the community, and traditions and prestige. . . .[9]

Over the last 25 years, similar thinking has figured prominently in the Court's reasoning which, until recently, has reflected two major principles:

1. The interests of the federal government in equality transcend the rights of specific states to protect their own interests.
2. The Constitution requires an attack against the substance of discrimination, not just the form. Thus, the Court has a responsibility

to undermine the foundations of historical and societal discrimination, and not merely to redress specific instances of bad faith. Not only must the formal inequality of statuses be abolished, but also the informal inequality of roles.[10]

Unfortunately, these two principles have been eroded in the last few years by landmark judicial decisions regarding schooling. The relative primacy of federal over state powers has been threatened, for example, in adjudicating the constitutionality of local property taxes as a basis for financing education. In the battle of *San Antonio School District* v. *Rodriguez* (411 U. S. 959, 1973), the Court upheld the validity of educational funding based on property tax, arguing that the right to education was not explicitly or implicitly guaranteed by the Constitution. Yet in its reassessment of the widely publicized *Serrano* case (*Serrano* v. *Priest*, 135 CalRptr 34, 1977; petition for writ of certiorari denied in *Clowes* v. *Serrano* [432 U. S. 907, 1977]), the California high court was not deterred by the Federal *Rodriguez* decision, ruling that "(1) discrimination in educational opportunity on the basis of [school] district wealth involves a suspect classification, and (2) education is a fundamental interest."[11] By refusing to hear the *Serrano* appeal, the Supreme Court in effect abdicated its authority in the matter. While egalitarians might prefer the outcome in this instance, the precedent signals an increasing timidity at the federal level in espousing Constitutional guarantees, thereby in effect empowering states to arrive at their own determinations.

The Court's recent wavering in its assault on invidious "societal" discrimination in education is equally conspicuous. As recently as 1971, in *Lau* v. *Nichols* (414 U. S. 563), the Court reaffirmed its commitment to reversing historical discrimination by upholding the right of Chinese school children in San Francisco to receive compensatory English language instruction. The significance of the *Bakke* decision lies in the completeness of the judicial "about face" in this regard. By abandoning an emphasis on substantive discrimination in favor of an exclusive focus on formal inequality, the Court has frozen affirmative action programs by imposing a weak and static conception of equality on educational institutions. The complete and disturbing regression in the Court's thinking (even since the *Lau* case) was noted by several of the dissenting justices in the *Bakke* case,[12] who rejected the contention that constitutional principles such as equality can be "immutable." They emphasized, once again, a sociological conception of discrimination, arguing that the presence of a social stigma—that is, some significant interpersonal result—must be the decisive element in determining whether prior maltreatment has occurred. In effect, the *Bakke* case has lifted the problem of racial discrimination out of its social and historical context, ignoring, as Justice Marshall observed in his dissent, the fact that "the position of the Negro today in America is the tragic but inevitable consequence of centuries of unequal treatment."[13] Thus, the Court has effectively bound the wrists of egalitarian reform, allowing only the most minute and harmless movements of the extremities.

Employment and Earnings: "Good Fences Make Good Neighbors . . ."

> "[Work] . . . is the open sesame to every portal, the great equalizer in the world. . . ."
>
> —SIR WILLIAM OSLER, 1903

Are recent judicial interpretations of equal employment legislation and the achievements of affirmative action programs in the workplace any more encouraging? Many social critics have lauded the "awe-inspiring" accomplishments in the era of "equal opportunity," though some have seen egalitarian policies as antimeritocratic forms of "affirmative discrimination."[14] However, the evidence for improvement in the economic standing of racial minorities must be interpreted cautiously.

While absolute differentials in status and income persist between the races, there has been an indisputably impressive reduction recently in *relative* inequality, especially among the youngest and most highly educated individuals. The economic returns due to schooling have increased substantially for Blacks, though only from higher education. In essence, Blacks have become more like whites in all aspects of socioeconomic attainment over the last few decades. The Black population is characterized by an increasingly varied set of social background experiences, indicating that the families into which Black boys and girls are born are becoming more socially and economically heterogeneous. So are the families to which these children are destined. However, Blacks are still much more similar in their family backgrounds and eventual attainments than are whites.[15]

In recent years the relationship linking social background and schooling to success has become stronger for Blacks and more like the process of achievement among whites. Of course, this is a mixed blessing. Although it indicates a greater level of opportunity and attainment among Blacks, it also suggests that Black families are becoming increasingly unequal. As Featherman and Hauser note, "it is ironic that parity between Black and white men in the achievement process may occur as a consequence of greater socioeconomic ascription within the Black population."[16] As the process of stratification converges across racial groups, Black families will come to resemble more and more their white counterparts in the extent to which inequality is reproduced across generations.

However, even granting the impressive relative economic gains of Blacks, there is cause for considerable skepticism. Much of the overall economic improvement of Black families is concentrated within households headed by young Black males. Meanwhile, the proportion of female-headed Black households has increased dramatically—from 21.7 percent of all Black families in 1960 to 39.2 percent in 1978.[17] Not surprisingly, the economic position of these households has improved far less dramatically than has the standing of husband-wife families.[18] Furthermore, much of the supposed gain in the standing of Blacks seems to reflect the increasing ability of Black *households* (especially male-headed ones) to close the gap vis-à-vis white ones, no doubt primarily because of the prevalence of two-earner Black families as against one-earner white families.[19] In absolute terms, for example, minority families experienced an increase of 140 percent in real median income from 1947 ($3,563) to 1975 ($8,540), and for unrelated minority individuals the increase was 83 percent, from $1,647 to $3,012 in the same period. However, compared to white families similarly situated, the ratio of Black to white median income rose from .51 to 1.65 during the same years for *families*, but declined from .72 to .64 for unrelated individuals.[20] Thus, minority *individuals* have actually lost ground (relatively) within the economic arena.

A number of studies also indicate, rather surprisingly, that the greatest degree of egalitarian progress has been achieved in the areas of the economy least affected by affirmative employment legislation. For example, Smith and Welch recently concluded "that the most dramatic increases in Black relative wages of the 1960s were realized in the most private parts of the private economy," rather than in industries most severely affected by governmental affirmative action legislation and policies.[21]

Admittedly, several more optimistic accounts of the impact of equal employment legislation have been offered by researchers of income inequality.[22] However, a number of these could be criticized—as Burstein has done— for not having adequately specified models to capture the effects of EEO legislation accurately. Meanwhile, Burstein's recent research is not without its own methodological and statistical shortcomings. However, two aspects of Burstein's generally favorable evaluation of EEO legislation as a force contributing to racial and sexual income equality warrant brief mention here. First, the author presents a very interesting graph (his Figure 5) showing temporal changes in the number of court decisions concerning race or sex discrimination rendered under EEO laws between 1968 and 1976, as well as the number of judgments issued which were favorable to the relevant minority group. Burstein's figures indicate an absolute growth over time in the amount of court-related activity (and egalitarian "successes") stemming from EEO legislation. However, while Burstein does not attend to this feature of his graph, his data also indicate that while more and more litigation has developed based on the EEO mandate, an ever-smaller *proportion* of judgments have favored the vanquished group (women or Blacks). Perhaps out-of-court settlements are becoming increasingly commonplace; Burstein's data do not address this issue. However, even if this is the case, an increase in non-adjudicated settlements is not necessarily a trend to be applauded by egalitarians. Conversely (and prehaps more realistically), it may be that the sea of court actions within which antidiscriminatory agencies are increasingly drowning is stifling the latters' ability to obtain favorable judgments for the victims of discrimination.

The second aspect of Burstein's analysis to be underscored is his suggestion that

> the [income] gains [obtained] thus far may have been the easy
> ones, involving the elimination of especially crude and blatant forms
> of discrimination. As discrimination becomes more subtle . . . [and]
> as structural discrimination becomes a more important part of total
> discrimination, and as the legal system is confronted more and more
> often with conflicts between fundamental values—such as non-
> discrimination and affirmative action—further gains may become
> more difficult to achieve.[23]

This last point should be borne in mind when evaluating the effects of any egalitarian intervention—including mass education—on processes of socio-economic achievement.[24]

Gintis[25] has cogently summarized a number of reasons (including several discussed above) for questioning the results of recent research which purports to verify the "thesis of industrialism."[26] Gintis suggests that some of the apparent relative improvement of minorities may actually reflect an increase in downward mobility, especially among the young, due to the ever-growing pool of "overeducated Americans"—most of whom, of course, are white.[27] In other words, the socioeconomic returns from education have declined for an appreciable portion of the working population (especially among whites), a trend which is more suggestive of a "homogenization" of the labor force as a result of "surplus educational production," rather than economic "upgrading" through meritocratic sorting based on educational criteria. Gintis also contends that "the observed improvement in the 1960s [of Blacks cannot] be divorced from the acute dislocation and social pressure induced by a highly self-conscious and explosive black community." He concludes that economic gains among minorities are likely to be undercut as a consequence of renascent recessions and as the "massive upgrading in economic activity in the South" in recent years—which has helped to narrow the racial gap—begins to taper off.[28]

Finally, all these findings which are supposed to evoke egalitarian optimism apply to those members of disadvantaged groups fortunate enough to

be in the labor force. But the consequences of unemployment (and underemployment) for minority advancement must not be overlooked. Table 1
shows rates of unemployment by race and sex in 1965, one year after the
passage of the Civil Rights Act, and in 1978, and gives the ratio of minority
group unemployment to white male unemployment in each period.

Apparently the well-intentioned policies of the Great Society era have not
altered the structural conditions which systematically exclude women and
minorities from employment. Why not? Some compelling answers are provided by asking those very individuals who have been excluded from the
labor force. According to the Bureau of Labor Statistics (spring quarter,
1979), only 9.3 percent of the white males and 7.4 percent of the white
females in this group actually want a job, whereas 15.9 percent of the black
men and 17.4 percent of the black women do.[29] It is interesting to note in
this regard that 15.9 percent and 16.1 percent of white men and women not
in the labor force (respectively) and currently in school would like a job,
while the corresponding figures for black males and females are 22.6 percent
and 23.5 percent. These findings run contrary to some common myths about
the desire for work among minorities (including women). Persons who want
work but think they cannot obtain employment constitute 15.6% of the unemployed white males, 11.9 percent of the white females, 16.9 percent of
the black males, and 12.8 percent of the black females.

Why don't these individuals think they can find employment? Table 2
provides some suggestive evidence, distinguishing job seekers by race and sex

Table 1. Unemployment rates by race and sex: 1965 and 1978.

| | **Year** | | | |
| | 1965 | | 1978 | |
Group	Rate	Ratio of minority group employ- ment to white male unemploy- ment	Rate	Ratio of minority group employ- ment to white male unemploy- ment
White males	3.6%	—	4.5%	—
White females	5.0%	1.39	6.2%	1.38
Black males	7.6%	2.11	10.9%	2.42
Black females	9.3%	2.58	13.1%	2.91

Source: U. S. Bureau of the Census, *Statistical Abstract of the United States: 1966,*
(87th edition), Washington, D.C.: U. S. Government Printing Office, p. 220; Bureau of
Labor Statistics, *Employment and Earnings,* vol. 26, no. 1, Washington, D.C.: U. S.
Government Printing Office, January, 1979, p. 167.

Table 2. Reasons given for believing that one cannot get a job by individuals not currently in the labor force, by race and sex (Spring quarter, 1979).

Group	Personal Factors	Job-Market Factors	
		Could Not Find a Job	Thinks No Job Available
White males	29.6%	29.6%	39.8%
White females	38.0%	31.2%	30.9%
Black males	31.4%	52.9%	15.7%
Black females	24.6%	52.6%	22.8%
WHITES	35.0%	30.6%	34.4%
BLACKS	27.2%	52.7%	20.1%
MALES	30.8%	35.3%	33.9%
FEMALES	34.4%	36.8%	28.8%

Source: Bureau of Labor Statistics, *Employment and Earnings*, vol. 26, no. 4, Washington, D.C.: U. S. Government Printing Office, April, 1979, p. 62.

and breaking down their responses into "personal" and "job-market" factors (according to the Bureau of Labor Statistics). There appear to be only slight differences *overall* between men and women in the reasons adduced for unwanted joblessness. However, the data disaggregated by race and sex reveal some interesting patterns. Among whites, the "human capital" *weltanschauung* seems to prevail, reflecting the thinking of conventional economics which relates inequality to differences among individuals in "job-relevant" characteristics. Blacks, however, seem to attribute their plight to the structure of the labor market itself. About 53 percent of the blacks (as opposed to about three-tenths of the whites) blame their situation on the fact that they simply could not find a job—that is, not that a job doesn't exist for them (which is perhaps more a "personal" than "structural" factor), but rather that they are somehow segregated from the employment opportunities. Unlike their white counterparts, blacks seeking work are much less likely to ascribe their misfortunes to "personal factors"—that is, the unavailability of jobs, their age, or a lack of education or training.

These voices from the margin are apparently corroborating a view to which social scientists are becoming increasingly sensitive, namely, that the source of inequality is in the demand side, not the supply side, of the labor picture.[30] It is employers who dole out jobs with particular requirements and rewards, hiring individuals based on the anticipated costs of on-the-job training and their own sociological theories (e.g., "statistical discrimination") which are used to impute the relevance of individuals' personal characteristics to the demands of the job. According to this line of reasoning, the disadvantaged position of minority workers is not due to inadequate training or ability, since these are developed for the most part after an individual lands a job; rather, it is a consequence of the restriction of employment opportunities for minorities to segments of the economy which are least unionized, most labor intensive, which offer the fewest possibilities of promotion within the firm, require the least skill and most supervision, and provide the smallest degree of job security.[31] Trapped within this "secondary" labor market, disadvantaged and minority workers experience little opportunity for social and economic mobility. In contrast to the more skilled and unionized work force (much of which is white and male) in the capital intensive "primary" sector, they remain subject to the vicissitudes of the economy and their employers. The alternative is unemployment or underemployment, rather than advancement.[32]

Nonetheless, egalitarian policies have customarily focused on changing the composition of labor supply rather than the structure of labor demand. As Thurow and Lucas have argued,

> Our experience with large investments in higher education should
> at least raise questions about the impact of supply oriented programs
> to alter the distribution of market incomes. Such investments may
> be capable of altering the distribution of income, but post-War
> experience is not encouraging.[33]

Furthermore, despite the compelling empirical evidence which substantiates such a structural perspective, the propriety of programs which incorporate this view in attacking discrimination is being challenged in the Supreme Court, where recent decisions regarding equal employment inspire no more optimism than the rulings pertaining to educational equality.

As in the case of education, the Court had reaffirmed, until recently, its commitment to reversing historical discrimination in its fullest sense. In so doing, the Court appeared to adopt a perspective quite similar to the one outlined above, recognizing and attempting to redress the structural and institutional bases of labor force stratification and inequality.[34] As recently as 1971, in the case of *Griggs* v. *Duke Power Company* (401 U.S. 424), the Court required "the removal of artificial, arbitrary, and unnecessary barriers to employment when the barriers operate invidiously to discriminate on the basis of racial or other impermissible classifications."[35] By questioning the screening devices used by employers to allocate individuals to jobs, the *Griggs* decision offered the promise of a judicial precedent with which to overturn the subtle workings of discriminatory labor practices. Yet by 1976, in *Washington* v. *Davis* (426 U.S. 229), the Court had already turned back from that commitment, declaring the primacy of *intent* (rather than consequences) in determining racial discrimination. And in the aftermath of *Bakke*, the Court's retreat in matters of employment policy seems likely to continue unabated.

The most serious challenge involves the *Weber* case. Kaiser Aluminum, along with the Steelworkers' union, instituted a training program which sets quotas for Blacks in craft positions. Since these jobs monopolize skill, promotional and training opportunities, supervisorial functions, and other characteristics related to advancement and success, Kaiser has argued that the internal job structure of the firm must be racially reorganized (through numerical goals) if current practices are not to perpetuate past discrimination. If the Court upholds the claims of Weber, a white employee who is alleging "reverse discrimination," not only will the future of voluntary remedies be jeopardized, but so will the validity of approaches which seek to grapple with the systemic causes of inequality rather than its individual manifestations.[36]

Future Prospects: Neither Black Nor White

"The best way out is always through."
    –ROBERT FROST, 1914

The foregoing account suggests that current programs for achieving equality in education and work are somewhat like feeding chicken soup to a cancer patient. Indeed, the soup does help. It is soothing, and, more importantly, we *think* it helps, and it reminds us of the illness and the need to take our other medicines too. However, current affirmative action programs, like chicken soup, are not, after all, a cure, especially when the strain of judicial rulings and popular sentiment has left us with nothing but a very weak broth. But lest we throw out the baby with the bouillon, let me sketch out a few implications of this overview for the future of egalitarian policy.

We must first discard the view that inequality has its origins (and thus its solution) in the attributes of individuals. Since most job skills are learned on the job, and since an individual's success will depend in large part on possessing habits, attitudes, and social skills which are right for that job in that firm, we cannot hope to eradicate discrimination merely by increasing measurable cognitive abilities or years of schooling among the disadvantaged. Rather, schools must impart marketable packages of competence, both vocational and interpersonal. They must also "enlighten" students about the different social settings within which any occupation is performed, since these exercise a profound influence on the eventual economic and psychological outcomes of work. Such a program was initiated with apparent success in Michigan in 1975, combining instruction in occupational skills with the development of "proper worker attitudes" in 170 different job training programs leading to certificates of competence recognized throughout the state.[37]

Further, we cannot ignore the well-documented effects of informal social interactions within schools on the ultimate attainments of students. Achieving "racially balanced" educational institutions cannot be an end in itself. Tacit discrimination in student activities, clubs, committees, governing bodies, teams, and facilities must be vigorously attacked, for these are some of the principal arenas where racism, sexism, and the erosion of self-esteem are reproduced each generation.

In the work setting, we must remove the structural barriers to equality which are built into firms and industries.[38] By allowing informal arrangements to persist which effectively discriminate—social contacts among workers; memberships in work related voluntary associations; access to services which the firms plays a role in providing, such as credit, insurance, and health care; opportunities for "enrichment," either cultural or job related—employers and unions undo whatever gains are made by changing recruitment and promotion policies.

One possible strategy for tackling the "structural" bases of labor market discrimination involves reorganizing and redistributing work in accordance with the implicit "prices" of various job characteristics in order to equalize the returns achieved by performing certain kinds of tasks. Thurow and Lucas, for example, have shown how various detailed occupational attributes are rewarded differentially by race and sex. For example, all other job traits and personal characteristics being equal, a minority male who has to take instructions from and/or help others on the job forgoes a nickel per hour in wages, while white women lose thirteen cents and white men about a dollar an hour; meanwhile, minority women actually gain nineteen cents an hour for their dutifulness. "Equal pay for equal work" must be interpreted broadly enough to redress such glaring inequities in how individuals with the same endowments of "human capital" are rewarded for utilizing comparable technical and social skills on the job.[39]

We must also develop policies to counter the implications of the Court's recent ruling in *Bakke* which precludes the use of quota schemes to ensure the delivery of services (health care, in this case) to minority communities. Affirmative action programs have virtually disregarded the complex relationship between work, community, and quality of life. For example, while newer American communities exhibit some decline in racial residential segregation, overall segregation levels have changed very little.[40] Segregated neighborhoods reflect the segregation of jobs in the community, each reinforcing the other. Recent evidence also indicates that the larger the minority population in a community, the more social and eocnomic inequality exists, irrespective of the demography, social composition, and industrial structure of the area; moreover, competing minorities in an area merely exacerbate this discrimination, worsening the socioeconomic attainments of members in the other group.[41]

The geographer Allan Pred has recently demonstrated how firms' locational decision-making strategies—including implicit and explicit policies of sales and purchases—serve as critical determinants of inter-regional inequality of income and employment.[42] His major contribution is to document the tendency for spatial biases of information, opportunities, and rewards to perpetuate and exacerbate existing regional inequities. Thus, Pred argues, corporate locational decisions should be central concerns of development policies aimed at effecting regional equalization. One presumes that the same arguments apply to markets for "human capital."[43] Admittedly, there is little evidence to support conclusively the claim that minority doctors provide more (and/or better) health care to disadvantaged minorities than would white males. Nonetheless, we must accept the fact that "free markets" for education, health care, legal services, and other crucial needs seldom work to the advantage of vanquished groups. Furthermore, a number of studies *do* indicate that minority recipients of social services (e.g., medical care) are more likely to utilize and be satisfied with available resources when those services are performed by individuals from the same minority group.[44] Policies which stimulate *opportunities* for minorities to become teachers, doctors, or lawyers—or which even increase the actual *supply* of such individuals but leave unexamined the question of how *demand* for such services is likely to mediate their delivery—are likely merely to transplant institutional racism into some other arena or locale, rather than retard its growth.

In short, egalitarian programs for schooling and work should reflect explicit objectives for the quantity and quality of a community's population. Demographers have learned a great deal about the relationship between occupational and economic achievements on the one hand, and geographic mobility and community formation on the other. Yet this knowledge has not been incorporated into programs designed to achieve racial equality. Educational and employment policies must give due regard to the impact of schools and work on the supply of and demand for minority individuals. Strong incentives should be developed to attract minorities (or whites) into neighborhoods whose schools are racially imbalanced. Similarly, housing policy and economic incentives can be valuable tools in regulating the flow of certain categories of job-seekers into and out of an area, encouraging an equalization of employment opportunities.

Employment policies which promote racially segregated neighborhoods and communities—whether intentionally or not—are no less reprehensible than production techniques which pollute the environment, thereby degrading the quality of life in a different fashion. It is within the neighborhoods to which employees return each evening that the drama of racial inequality is reproduced (or eliminated) in the next generation. Firms have always exercised implicit or explicit control over the living circumstances of employees and their families; it seems prudent to take advantage of that fact by linking affirmative action in the workplace to affirmative action in the community. Full environmental impact disclosures currently allow communities to evaluate the anticipated effects of local corporate activity. Perhaps comparable reports detailing the impact of firms on their economic, educational, and cultural "environments" are now in order.

If this review seems overly critical of past achievements and too stringent in defining "success," this is because I share the view expressed recently by the historian J. R. Pole that Americans have always seemed to want "a society run on egalitarian principles without wanting a society of equals."[45] Moreover, economic scarcity, renewed political conservatism, the rise of sociobiology, and an increasingly individuated language and culture symbolized by the new interpersonal technologies for "getting clear" all signal a frightening revival of age-old ideologies of equality grounded in Social Darwinism. If we are to pursue a "society of equals"—and I believe we must— then there can be no compromise or delays. I trust, however, that there will always be room for skeptics.

Notes

1. Horace Mann, "Education and Prosperity" (from Twelfth Annual Report as Secretary of Massachusetts State Board of Education), reprinted in *Old South Works*, vol. 6, no. 144 (Boston, 1848), p. 7.
2. For representative summaries and examples of the pertinent empirical literature, see Robert M. Hauser, *Socioeconomic Background and Educational Performance* (Washington, D.C.: American Sociological Association, 1971); John W. Meyer, "High School Effects on College Intentions," *American Journal of Sociology* 76 (1970): 59–70; Christopher S. Jencks, et al., *Inequality: A Reassessment of the Effect of Family and Schooling in America* (New York: Harper & Row, 1972); Harvey A. Averch, et al., *How Effective is Schooling?: A Critical Review and Synthesis of Research Findings* (prepared for the President's Commission on School Finance) (Santa Monica, Cal.: Rand Corporation [R–956–PCSF/RC], 1972); Edward L. McDill, et al., "Institutional Effects on the Academic Behavior of High School Students," *Sociology of Education* 40 (1967): 181–199; Richard P. Boyle, "The Effect of the High School on Students' Aspirations," *American Journal of Sociology* 77 (1971): 628–639. See also the essays which appear in Frederick Mosteller and Daniel P. Moynihan, eds., *On Equality of Educational Opportunity* (New York: Vintage Books, 1972), and the review symposium in the *American Journal of Sociology* 78 (May 1973).

3. David J. Armor, "School and Family Effects on Black and White Achievement: A Reexamination of the USOE Data," in Mosteller and Moynihan, p. 226.

4. Christopher S. Jencks, "The Coleman Report and the Conventional Wisdom," in Mosteller and Moynihan, p. 105.

5. See U. S. Bureau of the Census, *Statistical Abstract of the United States: 1978*, 99th ed. (Washington, D.C.: U. S. Government Printing Office, 1978), p. 135; National Center for Educational Statistics, *Digest of Educational Statistics 1977–78* (Washington, D. C.: U. S. Government Printing Office, 1978), p. 23. Moreover, the picture may in fact be even worse, insofar as the redirection of educational priorities in recent years appears to have shifted these reduced funds away from those educational programs most likely to have an appreciable impact on *socioeconomic* minorities. For example, Office of Education (OE) expenditures on "emergency school aid," which include services and training mandated under the Civil Rights Act, constituted 4.01 percent of all OE expenditures in 1974, but have since dwindled to an estimated 2.82 percent for 1978. OE funds transferred from other federal sources, such as the Manpower Development and Training Act and the Office of Economic Opportunity, have tapered off entirely in recent years. Within higher education, allocations to "special programs for the disadvantaged" have declined absolutely and relatively, from almost 2 percent of total OE expenditures in 1976 to less than 1 percent (estimated) in 1977 and 1978. Meanwhile, funds earmarked for "education for the handicapped," which one suspects do not disproportionately favor minority students, constituted 0.01 percent of total OE expenditures in 1960, 1.16 percent in 1970, 1.80 percent in 1975, and an estimated 4.88 percent in 1978. Note that these funds are distinct from those used for "educationally deprived children" in elementary and secondary schools, from which *educably* handicapped minority children might be more likely to benefit; expenditures for this purpose decreased from 36.89 percent to an estimated 23.09 percent of the OE total between 1966 and 1977, although the estimate for 1978 shows a relative increase to 28.21 percent of the total budget. (It will be extremely interesting to see how the recent unanimous Supreme Court decision in *Southeastern* v. *Davis*—which absolves schools and colleges from responsibility for changing their curricular standards in order to accommodate handicapped individuals—will affect the funding of various types of educational programs.) The calculations reported above are based on Table 158 in National Center for Educational Statistics, *Digest*, pp. 163–166.

6. J. R. Pole, *The Pursuit of Equality in American History* (Berkeley, Cal.: University of California Press, 1978), p. 329.

7. See, for example, the essay by William Sewell in the *American Journal of Sociology* review symposium; Jencks, et al., *Inequality*; Pole, *The Pursuit of Equality*.

8. For example, James S. Coleman, *The Adolescent Society* (New York: Free Press, 1961); C. N. Alexander, Jr., and Ernest Q. Campbell, "Peer Influences on Adolescent Educational Aspirations and Attainments," *American Sociological Review* 29 (1964): 568–575; Otis D. Duncan, et al., "Peer Influence on Aspirations: A Reinterpretation," *American Journal of Sociology* 74 (1968): 119–137; Otis D. Duncan, et al., *Socioeconomic; Background and Achievement* (New York: Seminar Press, 1972); C. Wayne Gordon, *The Social System of the High School* (Glencoe, Ill.: Free Press of Glencoe, 1957); Robert A. Rehberg and W. E. Schaefer, "Participation in Interscholastic Athletics and College Expectations," *American Journal of Sociology* 73 (1968): 732–740; Robert M. Hauser, *Socioeconomic Background*; Karl Alexander and Bruce K. Eckland, "Contextual Effects in the High School Attainment Process," *American Sociological Review* 40 (1975): 402–416; Kenneth L. Wilson and Alejandro Portes, "The Educational Attainment Process: Results from a National Sample," *American Journal of Sociology* 81 (1975): 343–363; see also the results presented recently by Peter Mueser in Chapter 5 of Christopher S. Jencks, et al., *Who Gets Ahead?* (New York: Basic Books, 1979).

9. Sheldon R. Shapiro, "Annotation: Racial Discrimination in Education—Supreme Court Cases" in *United States Supreme Court Reports* (24 L Ed 2d 765, 1969), p. 783.

10. Similar portraits of the Court's stance on discrimination in the last quarter-century are provided by Pole, *The Pursuit of Equality*, and Marjorie Heins, "The Fourteen-Year Furor Over Equal Employment," *Working Papers for a New Society* (July/August 1978) pp. 61–71.

11. *West's California Reporter* 135: 367.

12. *Regents of the University of California* v. *Bakke* (57 L Ed 2d 750, 980 S Ct).

13. Ibid., p. 837.

14. Nathan Glazer, *Affirmative Discrimination: Ethnic Inequality and Public Policy* (New York: Basic Books, 1975). (And "Introduction: 1978" in the paperback edition.)

15. For example, see David L. Featherman and Robert M. Hauser, "Changes in the Socioeconomic Stratification of the Races, 1962–73," *American Journal of Sociology* 82 (1976): 621–651, and *Opportunity and Change* (New York, 1978).

16. Featherman and Hauser, "Changes," p. 639.

17. U. S. Bureau of the Census, *The Social and Economic Status of the Black Population in the United States: An Historical View, 1790–1978*, Current Population Reports, series P–23, no. 80 (Washington, D.C.: U. S. Government Printing Office, 1979), Tables 74 and 125.

18. The ratio of black to white median income among husband-wife families increased from 0.62 to 0.80 between 1964 and 1976, while the corresponding ratio among female-headed households changed only slightly (from 0.57 to 0.62) over the same period; see Tables 22 and 136, ibid.

19. See, for example, Tables 22, 23, 26, 136, and 140 ibid. Table 26 indicates that Black families in the North and West in which both husband (under 35 years old) and wife are employed actually earned 7 percent *more* than comparable white families.

20. U. S. Bureau of the Census, *Social Indicators 1976* (Washington, D.C.: U. S. Government Printing Office): p. 453. The figures for unrelated minority individuals pertain to Blacks only in 1975, but refer to "Black and other races" in all other years.

21. James P. Smith and Finis R. Welch, "Black-White Male Wage Ratios: 1960–70," *American Economic Review* 67 (1977): 333.

22. E.g., Richard B. Freeman, "Changes in the Labor Market for Black Americans, 1948–72," *Brookings Papers on Economic Activity* 1 (1973): 67–120; Stanley Masters, *Black-White Income Differentials* (New York: Academic Press, 1975); and Paul Burstein, "Equal Employment Opportunity Legislation and the Income of Women and Nonwhites," *American Sociological Review* 44 (1979): 367–391.

23. Burstein, "Equal employment," p. 388.

24. Interestingly, a similar argument regarding the equalizing effects of educational opportunity was advanced by Nathan Keyfitz six years ago in "Can Inequality Be Cured," *Public Interest* 31 (1973): 91–101. Keyfitz suggests that education could have actually effected an increased standard of living and narrower income distribution in America over the last several decades, but that as variation in the amount of schooling has gradually decreased in the U. S., the influence of education on income and equality has been "exhausted" (see p. 92).

25. Herbert Gintis, "The American Occupational Structure Eleven Years Later: An Essay Review of David L. Featherman and Robert M. Hauser's *Opportunity and Change*," forthcoming in *Contemporary Sociology*.

26. This view regards "industrialization" as the central evolutionary force which propels societal transformation toward increasingly meritocratic principles and practices for distributing rewards. See, for example, Donald J. Treiman, "Industrialization and Social Stratification," pp. 207–34, in *Social Stratification: Research and Theory for the 1970s*, ed. Edward O. Laumann (Indianapolis, Ind.: Bobbs-Merill, 1970); Clark Kerr, et al., *Industrialism and Industrial Man* (New York: Oxford University Press, 1964).

27. See Richard B. Freeman, *The Overeducated American* (New York: Academic Press, 1976); Ivar Berg, *Education and Jobs: The Great Training Robbery* (Boston, Mass.: Beacon Press, 1971).

28. Gintis cites research by Donald J. McCrone and Richard J. Hardy which demonstrates that socioeconomic improvement among Blacks is concentrated in the South and in the post-1963 period; see their "Civil Rights Policies and the Achievement of Racial Economic Equality, 1947–1975," *American Journal of Political Science* 22 (1978): 3–17.

29. The calculations presented in this section are based on data reported in Bureau of Labor Statistics, *Employment and Earnings* 26, no. 4

(April 1979): 62. These data are subject to some seasonal fluctuations; the same computations based on data for the winter quarter, 1978 provide even *stronger* support for the interpretations offered here.

30. Cf. Lester C. Thurow, *Generating Inequality* (New York: Basic Books, 1975).

31. The most comprehensive "dualist" account of work organization and labor force discrimination is provided by Peter J. Doeringer and Michael J. Piore, *Internal Labor Markets and Manpower Analysis* (Lexington, Mass.: D. C. Heath & Co., 1971).

32. For empirical evidence of the salience of economic "segments" and labor market structures for racial discrimination in employment, see ibid.; Barry Bluestone, "The Tripartite Economy: Labor Markets and the Working Poor," *Poverty and Human Resources Abstract* (Supplement) 5 (1970): 15–35; Doeringer and Piore, *Internal Labor Markets*, especially chapter 8; Marcia K. Freedman, *Labor Markets: Segments and Shelters* (Montclair, N.J.: Allenheld, Osmun & Co., 1976); Randy PL Hodson, "Labor in the Monopoly, Competitive, and State Sectors of Production," forthcoming in *Politics and Society*; E. M. Beck, Patrick M. Horan, and Charles M. Tolbert, II, "Stratification in a Dual Economy: A Sectoral Model of Earnings Determination," *American Sociological Review* 43 (1978): 704–720, and "Labor Market Discrimination Against Minorities: A Dual Economy Approach," unpublished manuscript, Department of Sociology, University of Georgia, Athens; Robert Bibb and William H. Form, "The Effects of Industrial, Occupational, and Sex Stratification on Wages in Blue-collar Markets," *Social Forces* 55 (1977): 974–996.

33. Lester C. Thurow and Robert E. B. Lucas, "The American Distribution of Income: A Structural Problem," Study prepared for the Joint Economic Committee (Washington, D.C., 1972), p. 19.

34. A similar interpretation of the "dualist" orientation of the Supreme Court's equal employment rulings in the early 70s has been offered by Michael Wachter, neoclassical economist who is certainly no great fan of such an orientation; see his "Primary and Secondary Labor Markets: A Critique of the Dual Approach," *Brookings Papers on Economic Activity* 3 (1974): 637–680. Wachter writes: "This [stance by the Court] may be good social policy—or at least it is aimed at achieving a desirable social end—but its economic underpinning is open to controversy" (n. 43).

35. Jerald L. Director, "Annotation—Racial Discrimination in Labor and Employment—Supreme Court Cases," in *United States Supreme Court Reports* (28 L Ed 2d 928, 1971), p. 938.

36. The Court has of course upheld the propriety of Kaiser's and the Steelworkers' efforts since I first drafted this essay (in February 1979). Even skeptics are surprised every once in a while. However, the *Weber* decision does not appear to signal a revived judicial fervor against structural discrimination, but rather reaffirms a commitment to protecting the rights of corporations—as legal "individuals"—from state interven-

tion. Many optimists have regarded the *Weber* ruling, in conjunction with recent decisions upholding busing in Ohio, as an indication of the Court's renewed affirmation of affirmative action. Perhaps the Burger Court is indeed becoming more vigorous in championing minority rights. However, the 1978–79 session serves to demonstrate how particularistic the Court's reasoning has been of late, depending upon the specifics of each case rather than *any* broader vision. As *Time* recently observed, "the Court is without an identity, and at times, unpredictable," *Time*, 16 July, 1979, p. 72.

37. See Sheila Huff, "Education, Work, and Competence," *Society* 13 (1976): 44–51.

38. Some economists who advocate a "dualist" perspective (e.g., Doeringer and Piore, *Internal Labor Markets*) argue that these arrangements which systematically allocate minority group members to "secondary" and/or less lucrative and promising jobs are "functional" from the point of view of employers (and, perhaps, employees). Others (e.g., Richard C. Edwards, *Contested Terrain* [New York, 1979]) regard these arrangements as part of the process through which capitalists (and their managers) regulate and control their labor force, a view which I find more compelling. In any event, presumably what is "functional" is by no means inevitable; certainly one could alter the potential costs (benefits) to firms and unions for perpetuation (eliminating) such practices, as has been attempted, for example, in the case of federal contractors.

39. Thurow and Lucas, "The American Distribution of Income," Tables 16 and 17.

40. Thomas L. Van Valey, et al., "Trends in Residential Segregation: 1960–1970," *American Journal of Sociology* 82 (1977): 826–844.

41. W. Parker Frisbie and Lisa Neidert, "Inequality and the Relative Size of Minority Populations: A Comparative Analysis," *American Journal of Sociology* 82 (1977): 1077–1130.

42. Allan Pred, *City Systems in Advanced Economies* (New York: Halsted Press, 1977).

43. For instance, spatial biases in community production and recruitment of health care professionals is well documented; see, for example, William A. Rushing, *Communities, Physicians, and Inequality* (Lexington, Mass.: D. C. Heath & Co., 1974), especially Chapter 4.

44. Illustrative arguments regarding the importance of minority group status (of physicians and patients) in the perception and delivery of medical care—and pertinent empirical evidence—are provided by Bonnie Bullough and Vern L. Bullough, *Poverty, Ethnic Identity, and Health Care* (New York: Appleton-Century-Crofts, 1972), Chapter 8; Leon S. Robertson, et al., *Changing the Medical Care System: A Controlled Experiment in Comprehensive Care* (New York: Praeger, 1974), Chapters 6 and 8; Robert R. Carkhuft and Richard Pierce, "Differential Effects of Therapist Race and Social Class upon Patient Depth of

Self-exploration," *Journal of Consulting Psychology* 31 (1967): 632–634; Ronald Andersen, Joanna Kravits, and Odin W. Anderson, eds., *Equity in Health Services: Empirical Analyses in Social Policy* (Cambridge, Mass.: Ballinger, 1974). See especially Chapter 10, which shows that Blacks and/or those with low incomes are less likely to perceive themselves as ill or to seek medical care—all other things being equal— even though when such individuals *do* seek such care, their physicians actually judge them as sicker than whites and/or the affluent; Lloyd C. Elam, "What Does the Ghetto Want from Medicine,"pp. 33–42, in *Medicine in the Ghetto*, ed. John C. Norman (New York: Appleton-Century-Crofts, 1969); Nathan Hare, who vehemently argues for complete racial separatism in health care in "Does Separatism in Medical Care Offer Advantages for the Ghetto," pp. 43–49, ibid.; Victor W. Sidel, "Can More Physicians be Attracted to Ghetto Practice," pp. 171–180, ibid.

45. Pole, *The Pursuit of Equality*, p. 333.

Samuel L. Gaertner and John F. Dovidio[1]

Racism Among the Well-Intentioned

We have grown up in a society with racist traditions. In a country that is over 200 years old, founded on the principle of equality, it took 188 years to adopt a law proclaiming that Blacks are equal and should be so treated. We are still trying to decide about women. What we hope to do in this chapter is convince you that we must no longer attribute the racial inequalities in our country only to an overt, redneck brand of bigotry. We believe that we have reached the point where discrimination against Blacks and other minorities is no longer moral or legal. Consequently, overt prejudice may indeed be decreasing.[2] However, we caution you that the overt form may be replaced with a more subtle, insidious type of bigotry.

Recently, researchers have accumulated evidence supportive of Gunnar Myrdal's[3] conclusions regarding the complex and conflicting nature of white America's attitudes toward Blacks and other minorities.[4] These investigators have characterized the racial attitudes of most whites as neither uniformly favorable nor negative but ambivalent.

Our work has focused on those white Americans, who, in terms of racism and public policy, seem "well-intentioned." That is, they genuinely profess egalitarianism, as well as the desire to ameliorate the consequences of racism and poverty. However, we believe that the racial attitudes of many of these well-intentioned people may be characterized by a special type of ambivalence: aversiveness.[5]

Among aversive racists there seems to be a conflict between negative feelings towards Blacks or other minorities, which are not always conscious, and a conscience that seeks to repudiate or disassociate these feelings from a nonprejudiced self-image. Nevertheless, the magnitude of negative feelings among aversive types may be equivalent to that of people who are also ambivalent but who are more aware of the negative portion of their attitude.

The negativity of the aversive attitude does not seek a destructive end. Emotionally, there is a sense of discomfort, uneasiness and aversion which may motivate early disengagement from interracial interactions. Furthermore, aversives may harbor a sense of superiority (after all, *they* are not culturally deprived) in which positive rather than negative characteristics are differentially ascribed to themselves and to the targets of these attitudes. For example, aversives may not believe that Blacks are lazier than whites, yet they may suspect that whites are somewhat more ambitious than Blacks. Aversive types may also occasionally exhibit "epi-superstitious" rationalizations, that is, there seems to be a similarity between the manner in which many people deal with familiar superstitions and the occasional way in which aversive types compartmentalize belief and behavioral components of their racial attitudes. For example, many people who choose to walk around ladders do not really believe that walking under them would necessarily instigate a series of unfortunate, unlucky events. At the critical decision point, however, a "Why take a chance?" mentality seems to prevail. Thus, individuals who truly do not regard themselves as superstitious may consistently exhibit superstitious behavior. Analogously, an aversive-type individual may sincerely believe that Blacks are no more aggressive than whites but may consistently cross the street to avoid the Black stranger at night. At the decision point, they, too, may be overwhelmed by the "Why take a chance?" mentality. Afterwards, however, they continue to maintain that they are not prejudiced, proclaiming, perhaps, that, "The Black stranger was particularly unsavory anyhow." Thus the racial attitudes of many of these well-intentioned are highly complex and marked by ambivalence. However, because of their egalitarian, liberal value system the maintenance of a nonprejudiced self-image is important and unduly influences many of their interracial interactions.

Instead of responding spontaneously and naturally in interracial situations, the well-intentioned are motivated primarily to avoid acting inappropriately. Acting inappropriately in interracial situations would be very costly because of the obvious threat to the nonprejudiced self-image. Unfortunately, this motivation may change the tone and quality of their interactions and also limit their overall effectiveness in these situations. Hoping to disengage themselves quickly from interracial interactions, they may settle for behavior or policy decisions that may indeed be appropriate; however, they may cease to consider more effective or more appropriate alternatives once their primary motive is satisfied.

This presumed motivation to avoid acting inappropriately in minority related matters suggests two intertwined propositions which lead to specific predictions of when the positive and negative components of aversive racial attitudes would be observable:

1. In situations containing normative directives, i.e., those social rules that instruct people how they ought to feel, behave, or think, so as to be socially desirable, aversive racists would not intentionally behave inappropriately with regard to minorities. In fact, in these situations they may bend over backwards, responding even more favorably to Blacks than to whites, given the additional threat to their egalitarianism. However, in situations in

which normative prescriptions are weak or ambiguous (i.e., when the concepts of right or wrong are not applicable) minorities may be treated differently, perhaps in ways ultimately to their disadvantage, because here wrongdoing would not be obvious.

2. Although aversive types would not usually act unfavorably or inappropriately toward minorities in situations with strong normative prescriptions (as stated in proposition I above), they are motivated, perhaps unwittingly, to seek out reasons unrelated to race, which could be used, in lieu of race or ethnicity, to justify or rationalize negative response. Negative response toward Blacks or other minorities can then occur while the nonprejudiced self-image is preserved because negative response can be attributed to the rationale unrelated to race.

In previous papers we have proposed the existence of an indirect attitudinal process. This process perpetuates a nonracist self-image among many whites by unwittingly enhancing the salience and potency of elements unrelated to race in a situation that would justify or rationalize responding negatively, even if a white were involved. When a Black is involved, however, he/she is more likely to perceive the situation as one in which favorable response is either unnecessary, unwarranted, or precluded by other priorities. For example, millions of children had been bused to public and private schools for many years without very much vocal opposition from white parents. However, when busing became a tool to implement desegregation, suddenly there was strong opposition, not to desegregation per se, but to the nonracial element—busing.

Although our description of aversive racism among the well-intentioned may seem quite accurate to some or far from the mark to others, our discipline of experimental social psychology assesses the validity of "apparent understandings" through the process of empirical inquiry. For the past several years our research has focused on the subtlety of white racism, particularly among aversive types who appear well-intentioned. We will now begin to describe some of this work and thereby provide some empirical verification of our theoretical framework. Given the varied interests of our intended audience we have tried to present the findings of our research in the most accessible fashion, without direct reference to statistical analyses. However, all major effects, and especially the interactions reported, are reliable beyond at least the .05 level of statistical significance.

Earlier, aversive racists were described as well-intentioned liberals who maintain an egalitarian nonprejudiced self-image. Proposition I stated that in situations with clearcut norms, they would not usually discriminate against minorities because wrongdoing would be obvious and thereby threaten the nonprejudiced self-image. However, when norms are weak or ambiguous, differential behavior toward in-groups and out-groups may occur without threatening the egalitarian self-image because wrongdoing would not be obvious. To date we have three studies which specifically address Proposition I.

The first study to arouse our interest in the racial attitudes among the well-intentioned was a field experiment[6] which examined the likelihood of Black and white persons eliciting humanitarian actions from people at different ends of the liberal-conservative spectrum of political and economic attitudes. Previous research, using paper and pencil procedures primarily, had consistently revealed that political ideology is related to a complex network of other attitudes and values, including racial prejudice, general ethnocentrism, and authoritarianism.[7] Liberals have tended to score reliably lower than conservatives on all three dimensions. Scoring high on authoritarianism, which is measured by the "F" test (F = susceptibility to Fascist propaganda) indicates endorsement of such statements as:

1. Most of our social problems could be solved if we could somehow get rid of the immoral, crooked, and feeble-minded people.
2. Obedience and respect for authority are the most important virtues children should learn.
3. What the youth needs most is strict discipline, rugged determination, and the will to work and fight for family and country.

Given the previous findings relating political ideology to authoritarianism, ethnocentrism, and prejudice, the major prediction for this field experiment was derived easily, if not somewhat naively: Black victims would be helped less frequently than white victims by conservatives than by liberals. In this study, registered members of the liberal and conservative parties of New York State, residing in Brooklyn, New York, constituted the sample of liberals and conservatives. A follow-up telephone interview, conducted at least a year later, confirmed the assumption that members of these political parties endorsed the traditional characterizations of liberal and conservative, respectively, and also that liberals scored lower on a questionnaire concerning prejudice toward Blacks than did conservatives.

Utilizing a method devised earlier by Gaertner and Bicman, liberal and conservative households received an apparent wrong number telephone call which quickly developed into a request for assistance.[8] The caller, clearly identifiable by his or her voice characteristics as being Black or white, explained that he or she was attempting to reach a mechanic from a public phone located on a parkway. The caller further claimed that he/she had no more change with which to make another phone call to the garage. The Liberal or Conservative Party member could help by calling the garage on behalf of the stranded motorist.

If the person answering the phone agreed to help, the victim gave him/her a telephone number to call. If this person refused to help or hung up after the caller stated, "And that was my last dime," a "No-Help" response was recorded. However, if the person hung up prior to the word "dime," a "Premature Hang-Up" response was scored and grouped separately from the Help/No-Help categories. In the case of the Premature Hang-Up, it was assumed that people did not have ample opportunity to learn that *their* help was needed.

The results, excluding consideration of Premature Hang-Ups for a moment, indicated that Conservatives discriminated against the Black victim (92 percent helped the white victim, while 65 percent helped the Black victim) to a greater extent than Liberals (85 percent helped the white victim and 76 percent helped the Black victim). Thus, in a situation in which help has been solicited, the results supported the traditional findings regarding political ideology and antiblack attitudes. However, the data supported these traditional findings only when people obtained sufficient information to recognize that their personal assistance was required. A number of people hung up prematurely, prior to the delivery of the full appeal for help. As compared to Conservatives, Liberals hung up prematurely more frequently on the Black than on the white victim. The Liberals discriminated against the Black male in particular; the Black and white male victims received Premature Hang-Ups from Liberals 27.5 percent and 9.5 percent of the time, respectively. Conservatives, however, hung up prematurely only 8.3 percent of the time on the Black male and 4.7 percent of the time on the white male victim. Thus, the usual claim that Liberals harbor less antiblack sentiment than Conservatives was not wholly supported.

Consistent with the concept of aversive racism, it seemed that the antiblack attitudes of Liberals differ qualitatively rather than quantitatively from the racial attitudes of conservatives, who perhaps are more aware of their ambivalent racial attitudes. These findings suggested that antiblack attitudes of well-intentioned Liberals may be revealed more readily in situations in which there are few, if any, clearly definable principles or norms to guide behavior. In these situations the Liberals need not be concerned with the egalitarian application of a general principle. In these types of situations wrongdoing would not be obvious since concepts of right and wrong are not applicable. Therefore, Liberals in such situations may behave differently toward Blacks and whites and yet maintain an unprejudiced self-image. For example, the question of the morality of hanging up on a person reaching the wrong number after informing him of his error has no prescribed answer. Thus, Liberals who hung up prematurely on the Black victim did not behave inappropriately in the sense that they violated normative prescriptions. Consistent with the style of the aversive racist, Liberals avoided further contact with Blacks when further contact was not prescribed. White callers, however, did not elicit a desire to terminate the encounter so readily.

To further support Proposition I, a simulated jury study conducted in our laboratory by Joseph Faranda indicated that the well-intentioned may avoid wrongdoing with regard to Blacks, but cease their search for more effective or more appropriate alternatives earlier than when whites are involved.[9] In this study, university students scoring either high or low on the "F" test were presented with a court transcript of a ficticious criminal case involving a Black or white defendant accused of murdering a storekeeper and his grandchild during the commission of a robbery. After reading one of the prepared transcripts, which included summaries of the prosecution and defense testimony, each student juror was asked to indicate his or her certainty that the defendant was guilty, using a seven-point scale (1 = certain defendant is not guilty; 7 = certain defendant is guilty). Half of the high and low authoritarian students received a transcript in which the prosecution's case, in terms of the evidence introduced, was very weak. Earlier testing demonstrated that with this weak prosecution case it was unlikely for student jurors to be very certain of the defendant's guilt. The other jurors, however, received a transcript presenting the same weak prosecution case except that in addition it contained a segment in which the prosecution introduced extremely damaging evidence involving the defendant's alleged confession to a third party. The defense attorney objected to this testimony as hearsay, given that the prosecution was not able to present the third party in court. The judge then sustained the defense's objection and ordered the jurors to ignore this inadmissible evidence introduced by the prosecution.

Faranda's critical question concerned the ability of the high and low authoritarian students to ignore the inadmissible prosecution testimony against the Black and white defendants. If student jurors exposed to the inadmissible evidence followed the judge's instructions appropriately, they would be equally uncertain of the defendant's guilt as were the jurors whose transcripts never mentioned this damaging testimony.

The results indicated that both high and low authoritarian jurors discriminated against the Black defendant in dealing with the inadmissible testimony, but in different ways (see Figure 1). As you might have expected, high authoritarians were unable to ignore the inadmissible testimony when the defendant was Black. That is, they were more certain of the Black defendant's guilt after exposure to the inadmissible evidence. For the white defendant, however, high authoritarians followed the judge's instructions perfectly. On the other hand, low authoritarians, apparently with good intentions, followed the judge's instructions to the letter, and thus avoided acting inappropriately on behalf of the Black defendant; that is, the presence of the inadmissible testimony did not influence their certainty of guilt ratings of the Black defendant. However, these low authoritarians became *less* certain of the white defendant's guilt when the inadmissible evidence was presented.

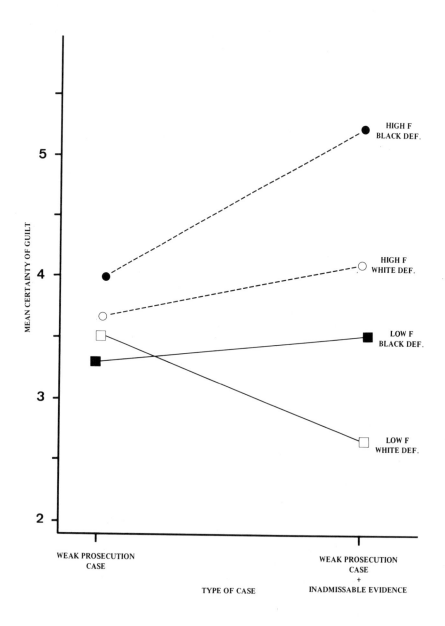

Figure 1.

Later they admitted that they were angry with the prosecution for trying unfairly to introduce this hearsay testimony. They did not mention responding angrily when the defendant was Black, however. When the defendant was Black, low authoritarians responded in a manner that was not inappropriate in assessing the defendant's guilt and then seemed to cease their search for additional options. On behalf of a white defendant though, an alternative other than ignoring the inadmissible prosecution evidence occurred to these well-intentioned people.

A third study supporting Proposition I investigated the willingness of students scoring high and low prejudice to obtain assistance and thus subordinate themselves to a Black or white partner.[10] We began with the assumption that most whites would seek to avoid situations in which they would be subordinate to or dependent on a Black partner, given their familiarity and relative comfort with the traditional role relationship between Blacks and whites. In the context of Proposition I, we first administered a survey which revealed that students believed that in nonemergency situations the act of refusing assistance spontaneously offered by a partner was normatively inappropriate, so long as working together was sanctioned by the powers that be. In addition, they believed that the appropriateness of actively soliciting assistance not spontaneously offered was considerably less clear.

The experiment arranged for students scoring high and low prejudice to have the opportunity either to accept assistance or to solicit assistance from a Black or white partner. It was expected that students scoring both high and low prejudice would accept assistance spontaneously offered more frequently from a Black than from a white partner because they would be especially sensitive about acting inappropriately with regard to Blacks. However, participants in the experimental treatment which required them actively to solicit assistance if help was desired, were expected to solicit help more frequently from a white than from a Black partner. In this way they could avoid an uncomfortable situation without acting inappropriately.

The results supported the hypothesis derived from Proposition I. Participants, regardless of prejudice score, who received the spontaneous offer of assistance in a task relating to abstract thinking, accepted help more often from a Black partner (80 percent) than from a white partner (55 percent). However, participants were less likely to solicit help actively from a Black (40 percent) than from a white (60 percent) partner when help was not spontaneously offered.

In general, the pattern of asking for help was consistent with the theoretical framework provided by the concepts of ambivalence and aversive racism. As predicted, when the partner actively offered assistance, high- and low-scoring people accepted help more from Black partners than from white partners. Nevertheless, when the partner was available but did not spontaneously offer assistance, subjects solicited help less from Black partners than from white partners. In this situation, participants could justifiably choose to work alone since the norms governing active solicitation of assistance are relatively ambiguous.

To summarize: the previous three investigations seem to offer strong and consistent support of the proposition that aversive well-intentioned types tend not to act inappropriately towards Blacks when normative directives are salient and unambiguous. However, in situations in which the concepts of right and wrong are not so clearly applicable, Blacks and other minorities may be treated differently than fellow whites in a manner which serves to cause further disadvantage or to perpetuate racist traditions.

Proposition II returns us to the situation in which normative directives are present. It proposes that well-intentioned types may discriminate here, too, if they can find a reason unrelated to race to justify or rationalize negative response to Blacks. Here, the nonprejudiced self-image can be maintained because negative response can be attributed to the rationale which would justify responding negatively even if whites were involved. In addition, we have proposed the operation of an indirect attitudinal process which differentially increases the influence of these rationales on the behavior of the well-intentioned when Blacks are involved.

A study which relates directly to Proposition II concerns the likelihood that white well-intentioned bystanders will avoid responsibility for helping in an emergency more readily for Black than for white victims.[11] In 1968 Darley and Latane demonstrated that the mere presence of other bystanders decreases the likelihood of intervention relative to the rate of intervention obtained when people witness emergencies alone. Theoretically, the bystander who is alone has total responsibility for the victim's well-being, which impels him/her to action. However, when three other bystanders are present, the same bystander has only 25 percent of the responsibility for helping, as do each of the other three. As the degree of responsibility for helping becomes diffused, the pressure on any one of the bystanders to help is thereby reduced, given that one of the other bystanders may intervene.

In the present study, the presence of other bystanders is assumed, so as to present the participant white bystanders with a nonracial reason to remain inactive (i.e., the belief that one of the other bystanders may intervene and help). Thus, it was expected that those who score either high or low prejudice would help white victims more readily than Black victims when they believe other capable bystanders are available. However, they would not discriminate against Blacks when they believe that they are the sole witness of a serious emergency. When alone, they bear total responsibility for helping, and the search for justifiable reasons to avoid intervention is more likely to be unsuccessful. Even those scoring high prejudice, particularly those tested on university campuses, were expected to help without regard to the victim's race when they were alone. They, too, are considered to have ambivalent racial attitudes and would probably not regard themselves as bigoted to the extent that they would fail to help a Black victim in a serious emergency. To provide information relevant to the relationship between psychophysiological arousal and bystander responsiveness as a function of the victim's race, each participant's heart rate was monitored continuously via biotelemetry, which would not inhibit the delivering of assistance, as would more traditional apparatus requiring that subjects be directly wired to the physiograph.

White students scoring both high and low prejudice received a description of an experiment in extra-sensory perception in which they were told that they would be attempting to receive telepathic messages from a sender (another student) in a cubicle across a narrow hall. Actually, the sender, who was to become the victim, was a tape-recorded voice sent over the intercom system. The purpose of the experiment, as explained to the participant, was to test the "physiological synchrony" theory of ESP. This "theory" proposed that when a participant successfully received a message from a sender, their autonomic nervous system (i.e., heart rates) would be in greater synchrony than when the message was not successfully transmitted.

The race of the victim was established by the picture on a college I.D. presented to the subject to determine if the participants were strangers. The voice of the sender was also identifiable as Black or white. Half the participants were informed that they would be the only receiver, while half were told that two other receivers located near the sender would be participating also. The latter group of subjects were also shown two additional I.D. cards of the other white "participants." The experimenter then left the bystander alone to begin the ESP task.

After the first seventeen trials, the sender interrupted the ESP task explaining that it looked as though a stack of chairs piled to the ceiling of the sending cubicle was about to fall. In a few moments the emergency occurred: the sound of falling chairs accompanied the victim's calling out, "They're falling on me. . . ." People who emerged from their cubicles moving in the victim's direction within three minutes after the emergency and those who did not intervene were immediately assured of the sender's well-being.

Did subject bystanders discriminate against Black victims only in the apparent presence of other bystanders? Yes. The findings strongly supported this expectation. When bystanders believed that they were the only witness, Black victims (93.8 percent) were helped slightly more often than white victims (81.3 percent). However, when the bystander believed that two other witnesses existed, Black victims were helped less often than white victims (37.5 percent v. 75 percent). Furthermore, there were absolutely no differences in the behavior of bystanders scoring high and low prejudice. Furthermore, when bystanders believed that they were the only witness, Black victims elicited slightly greater levels of heart rate escalation (14.52 bpm) than white victims (11.39 bpm). However, when they believed that two other bystanders existed, white victims elicited greater levels of escalation (10.84 bpm) than black victims (2.40 bpm).

In this study, when white bystanders (regardless of prejudice score) believed themselves to be the only witness to an emergency, their helping behavior and psychophysiological responsiveness were quite high for both Black and white victims. The presence of other apparent bystanders, however, radically altered this pattern in a manner which was of particular disadvantage to the Black victims. With a sufficient, nonracial justification for avoiding involvement, high proportions of bystanders no longer intervened on behalf of Black victims, as they did when they were alone.

The finding that helping behavior and cardiac response were lower for Black victims only when high- and low-prejudiced bystanders were together with others seems to support the indirect attitudinal process framework, Proposition II, and the underlying assumption regarding the ambivalence of racial attitudes among whites. That is, even when well-intentioned whites are totally responsible for the well-being of Blacks, they seem genuinely concerned both psychophysiologically and behaviorally; however, when this responsibility can be shared, there is no longer the same evidence of personal concern.

Given over 200 years of racism, white America is apparently accustomed to the dependency, subordination, and assumed inferiority of Blacks and other minorities. Furthermore, public policy attempts to remedy the consequences of racism seem only to have perpetuated this dependency and subordination. Recently, however, affirmative action seems to have initiated Black/white relationships which may not be bound by stereotype role expectations. Increasingly, whites are finding themselves in school, job, or other situations in which they are subordinate to minorities. Nevertheless, vocal protests by whites seem to articulate only the concern that qualified whites will be subordinated to less qualified minorities. Consistent with Proposition II, the issue of competence may represent a nonracial rationalization for resisting the changing pattern of role relationships. This strategy would then allow for the continued subordination of minorities, while insulating even well-intentioned whites from the specter of bigotry.

Since it is believed that one of the major causes of racism at the individual level of analysis relates to needs for self-esteem and relative status, any attempt to reverse stereotypic role relationships would present a threat to many whites, who would then be expected to respond negatively to even highly competent blacks in these nontraditional roles. In addition, whites interacting with Black subordinates, particularly those of lower task-related competence than themselves, may initially be expected to respond quite favorably to this relationship because it serves to reinforce traditional relative status expectations from which whites have benefitted.

To examine this issue, which relates to Proposition II, we conducted an experiment to investigate the manner in which whites initially confront these nontraditional and traditional role relationships with Black and white supervisors and subordinates, respectively.[12] Given the rationale presented above, it was expected that in a nonemergency helping situation, whites would respond less favorably to Black than to white supervisors described as having relatively high task-related competence. In addition, whites were expected to respond more favorably to Black than to white subordinates described as having relatively low task-related competence, because these Black subordinates reinforce stereotypic expectations.

In this study, white male university students scoring high or low prejudice were introduced to a Black or white male partner (actually a confederate of the experimenter) and informed that the purpose of the experiment was to study the effects of the intellectual composition and group structure on group task performance. Consequently, one person would be a supervisor and the other a worker.

In addition, each participant was led to believe that he scored above average on a test of abstract intelligence, a capacity related to performance on the group tasks. Furthermore, their Black or white partner was described as scoring well above average when the partner was to become the supervisor, while he was described as scoring well below average when he was to become the worker.

After completing a brief questionnaire while the experimenter was not present, the confederate, while reaching to replace his pencil, apparently by accident, knocked a container of seventy-five pencils to the floor. He leaned over, mumbled, and proceeded around the table to pick up the pencils at a constant rate. This provided the participant with an unsolicited opportunity to offer assistance in the form of a friendly gesture.

The results supported the hypotheses derived from Proposition II. Specifically, black supervisors (58 percent) were helped less frequently than white supervisors (75 percent), while subordinate Blacks (83.3 percent) received help more often than did white subordinates (25 percent). Again, the prejudice score of the participant was not related to his behavior in this study. It appears, then, that even well-intentioned whites may respond negatively even to competent Black supervisors, while they seem to show great favoritism toward less competent Black subordinates. But how could these people have justified negative response to the competent Black supervisor? Actually, the participants' ratings of their partner's intelligence and their ratings of their own intelligence indicated that "competence" may indeed have been the rationale. The participants' rating indicated that in spite of the experimenter's "objective" feedback relating to relative abstract cognitive abilities, the competent Black supervisor was perceived to be intelligent, but less intelligent than the participant himself. Competent white supervisors, however, were perceived to be relatively more intelligent than the participants. In addition, using a subtle relative-to-self rating, Black supervisors, as compared to white supervisors, were described not only as less intelligent but also as less kind, less important, less good, less reputable, less reliable, and less responsible. When the partner was the subordinate, Black and white workers were evaluated no differently on any of these dimensions.

If, in the face of objective evidence to the contrary, whites typically misperceive the competence of Blacks or other minorities moving into relatively higher status positions, then the resistance to affirmative action programs seems quite legitimate and justifiable to such whites and also makes this resistance difficult to change. In addition, if deficiencies in qualifications of Blacks (relative to one's own) are routinely assumed, then even the well-intentioned may be participating in the continued restriction of the educational and professional advancement of blacks and other minorities, even though racist historical antecedents may have initially produced social inequities.

Conclusions and Implications

We hope that we have alerted you to the possibility that reduction in overt forms of bigotry may not necessarily signal the beginning of a more egalitarian era. Instead, overt bigotry may be in the process of becoming a more subtle, insidious form. We have raised the possibility that liberal, well-intentioned whites, believing themselves to be unprejudiced, may under specifiable circumstances behave no differently toward minorities than those who acknowledge their racial antagonism.

It seems likely that this insidious, subtle, aversive form of racism is likely to manifest itself, perhaps disproportionately, among the ranks of educated whites who influence the formulation and administration of programs designed to ameliorate the consequences of racism. We do not necessarily mean to imply that all or most of those involved in public policy are necessarily racist. However, when racism does exist among educated, well-intentioned, liberal whites, we believe that it often takes the aversive form.

Given the subtle nature of aversive racism, the most appropriate strategy for dealing with the issue as it relates to public policy may simply be to caution ourselves about the possibility of its potential existence. In addition, public policy should be written and administered with little room for subjective idiosyncratic interpretation which could result in differential treatment without the commission of an obviously inappropriate act. Also, further attempts to change racial and ethnic attitudes may most profitably focus on the affective (i.e., emotional) as well as on the cognitive components of these attitudes. To some extent, cognitively, aversive types may already be close to a nonracist level, yet they continue to experience a sense of aversion and discomfort with regard to the targets of their attitudes. Furthermore, these feelings seem to result in discriminatory behavior when circumstances permit unfavorable response without the self-attribution of bigoted intent.

We would like to remind you of William Ryan's powerful book, *Blaming the Victim*, which argues that public policy solutions to racism and poverty represent a subconscious compromise between policy formulators' humanitarian values and their own self-interests.[13] Ryan argues that victim blamers sympathetically focus their attention on the consequences of racism and poverty rather than on the more troublesome causal agents. The consequences (e.g., cultural deprivation or other victim deficiencies) resulting from racism and poverty are then treated as the causal agents in the continuing cycle of oppression. The defect to be remedied is perceived to reside within the victim (i.e., his cultural deprivation), rather than within the socioeconomic structure responsible for the defect in the first place.

Victim blamers, as described by Ryan, include sympathetic social workers, social scientists, and liberal politicians with a genuine commitment to help the disadvantaged. Furthermore, they tend to be middle-class individuals who are relatively well-off. Thus public policy solutions to racism and poverty involving more drastic social reform, such as redistribution of income and wealth, are a threat to the victim blamer's own sense of well-being. Out of self-interest and humanitarian concern, they perhaps unwittingly perceive deficiencies to be remedied as existing within the victim. Victim blamers then identify totally with the solution rather than with the problem of racism. Evidence which supports the concepts of aversive racism and ambivalence suggests that their identification may be misplaced.

Notes

This essay is copyrighted by Samuel L. Gaertner and John F. Dovidio.

1. Much of the research reported in this essay was funded by the Office of Naval Research, Organizational Effectiveness Research Programs, under Contract Numbers N00014–70–A–0003 and N00014–76–C–0062.
2. *Newsweek*, 26 February 1979.
3. Gunnar Myrdal, *An American Dilemma: The Negro Problem and Modern Democracy* (New York: Harper & Row, 1944).
4. I. Katz, "Experimental Studies of Negro-white Relationships," ed. L. Berkowitz, *Advances in Experimental Psychology* 5 (New York, 1970); I. Katz, S. Cohen, and D. C. Glass, "Ambivalence, Guilt, and the Scapegoating of Minority Group Victims," *Journal of Experimental Psychol-*

ogy 9 (1973): 423–436; and I. Katz, S. Cohen, and D. C. Glass, "Some Determinants of Cross-racial Helping Behavior," *Journal of Personality and Social Psychology* 32 (1975): 964–970.

5. J. Kovel, *White Racism: A Psychohistory* (New York: Pantheon, 1970); S. L. Gaertner, "Nonreactive Measures in Racial Attitudes Research: A Focus on 'Liberals'", in *Toward the Elimination of Racism*, ed. P. A. Katz (New York: Pergamon, 1976); and S. L. Gaertner and J. L. Dovidio, "The Subtlety of White Racism, Arousal, and Helping Behavior," *Journal of Personality and Social Psychology* 35 (1977): 691–707.

6. S. L. Gaertner, "Helping Behavior and Racial Discrimination Among Liberals and Conservatives," *Journal of Personality and Social Psychology* 25 (1973): 335–341.

7. T. W. Adorno, et al., *The Authoritarian Personality* (New York, 1950).

8. S. L. Gaertner and L. Bickman, "Effects of Race on the Elicitation of Helping Behavior: The Wrong Number Technique," *Journal of Personality and Social Psychology* 20 (1971): 218–222.

9. Joseph Faranda, "The Effects of Inadmissible Evidence Introduced by the Prosecution and the Defense, and the Defendant's Race on the Verdicts of High and Low Authoritarians," (M.A. Thesis, University of Delaware, 1979).

10. J. F. Dovidio and S. L. Gaertner, "The Subtlety of White Racism: The Likelihood of Whites to Request Help from a Black or White Fellow Worker" (Office of Naval Research, Organizational Effectiveness Programs, 1977).

11. Ibid.

12. J. F. Dovidio and S. L. Gaertner, "The Subtlety of White Racism: Helping Behavior and Stereotyping by Whites Toward Black and White Supervisors and Subordinates" (Office of Naval Research, Organizational Effectiveness Programs, 1977).

13. W. Ryan, *Blaming the Victim* (New York: Vintage Books, 1972).

M. R. Karenga

The Problematic Aspects of Pluralism: Ideological and Political Dimensions

Introduction

The early advancement of cultural pluralism as an ideological approach to ethnic diversity in the United States has its roots in two main developments: (1) the work of idealistic middle-class immigrants; and (2) the intellectual response of self-conscious ethnics as well as thinkers like John Dewey, who argued that diversity enriches culture. As Milton Gordon notes, the idealistic members of the middle class "followed the example of their English predecessors and 'settled' in the slums to 'learn to sup sorrow with the poor.'" In the "settlement houses" in which they lived and worked, these idealists "were forced to come to grips with the realities of immigrant life and adjustment;" i.e., the coercive and damaging aspects of the Americanization process.[1] Gordon states that although reaction to these stark realities varied, "on the whole the settlements developed an approach to the immigrant which was sympathetic to his native cultural heritage and to his newly created ethnic institutions."[2]

The damage done to the beleaguered and bewildered immigrants by "those forces which impelled rapid Americanization" contributed to ethnic alienation, family disorganization, and other forms of social disorientation. American intellectuals thus saw a need to respect diverse cultures, to appreciate the distinctiveness of each culture and its contributions to the country as a whole.

Undoubtedly, the most significant early assessment of cultural pluralism was an article published in 1915 by Horace Kallen, entitled "Democracy Versus the Melting Pot."[3] Kallen, like subsequent advocates of cultural pluralism, was gravely concerned about the severity of the Americanization process, which compelled compliance and self-denial in the interests of the melting pot. He argued that the melting pot theory was an expectation, not a fact, and that the loss of a group's identity within the society as a whole was neither completely possible nor desirable. "All is not, however, fact, because it is hope," he stated, "nor is the biography of an individual ... the history of a group."[4] As other cultural pluralists would later argue, he observed with some sarcasm, that those who have tried to lose themselves have, in fact, not entirely succeeded. He contended that they "protest too much; they are too self-conscious and self-centered, their 'Americanization' appears too much like achievement, a tour de force, too little like growth."

Kallen further argued that no human being can cut him/herself off from sociohistorical circumstances that shaped him/her. "Behind him in time and tremendously in him in quality are his ancestors," Kallen states. Moreover, "around the him in space are his relatives and kin, carrying in common with him the inherited organic set from a remoter ancestry."[5] "In all theses, he lives and moves and has his being." The need then, Kallen concludes, is not a program of coerced unity, for "the notion that the program might be realized by radical and even forced miscegenation, by the creation of the melting pot by law, and thus by the development of the new 'American race' is . . . as mystically optimistic as it is ignorant."[6]

Democracy, if it is to be real, must protect each ethnic or national group's right to be. Amalgamation proposals challenge that right and do damage to "the selfhood which is inalienable in them."[7] A real solution must evolve a "truly democratic commonwealth" whose

> . . . form would be that of a federal republic; its substance a democ-
> racy of nationalities, corporation voluntarily and autonomously
> through common institutions in the enterprise of self-realization
> through the perjection of men according to their own kind.[8]

This arrangement would truly allow each ethnic group its inalienable identity and provide it with the freedom to make its own unique and valuable contribution to American society as a whole.

As Gordon points out, the doctrine of cultural pluralism was advanced "to oppose the assumptions and demands of the "Americanization" of Anglo-conformity viewpoint and in the process was to reject, also, the more kindly intended blueprint of the melting-pot enthusiasts."[9] Given this focus, the goal of cultural pluralism projected

> . . . a society where ethnic groups would be encouraged to maintain
> their own community social structure and identity and preserve
> certain values and behavior patterns which are not in conflict with
> broader values, patterns and legal norms common to the entire
> society.[10]

Subsequent definitions and projected goals of cultural pluralism have concurred with these original concerns. An example of this focus is the definition of cultural pluralism by Antonio Pantoja et al. They point out that:

> The cultural pluralism movement has, at its core, the aspiration
> and value to create a new society, where culturally different groups

that exist within our country can fully experience both the positive and distinctive attributes of their given and ascribed differences without penalties of loss of status [or] educational, social or political disenfranchisement.[11]

This aspiration and value, however, met opposition at the movement's inception and produced a social and ideological struggle which continues even today.

The key emphasis in the cultural pluralist theory is ethnic self-determination and appreciation of the unique contribution of each culture. But practice has proved that in reality it is a limited self-determination, permitted only insofar as it does not challenge the goals and values of the established order. The thrust of politics urged—even compelled—minorities to "melt into the dominant ethnic culture (white Protestant) rather than contribute to a new amalgam composed of equal or proportionate contributions from each group."[12] It is this contradiction which challenges the aspirations and values of cultural pluralism and raises essential questions about its viability as a theory of social construction. The essential problem of cultural pluralism, then, is that its goals, both as an ideology and movement, conflict with values and behavior patterns of the dominant society, creating obstacles to effective implementation.

Three alternative ideological thrusts or conceptual models raise questions about the validity, relevance, and possibilities of development of cultural pluralism. These ideologies and models are liberalism, racism, and Marxism. As conceptual and goal models, they challenge the cultural pluralist assertions of the rights and equality of the various American cultural entities. For "if politics is seen as a process in which men reconcile, sometimes violently, value conflicts and make decisions as to who gets what, how and why, it is obvious that bias-competing ways of looking at and evaluating the world are at the very center of politics."[13] Moreover, the struggle over value conflicts is not simply an ideological battle, but a practical project marked by disparities in power and social resources. Therefore, cultural pluralism as a desire and program of cultural minorities is defined and made practicable by the power and resources its advocates can bring to bear at any given time in the realization of their goals.

Liberalism and Pluralism

Liberalism poses as a nondoctrinaire social theory defined by its emphasis on tolerance and rationality. In fact, however, it is a political ideology in a battle with other ideologies for the support of the masses and the right to define and construct reality. Thus, as Groth contends:

> Whether radical or conservative, innovative or rigidly tradition-
> alist, political ideologies are, above all, belief systems with which
> social institutions and processes may be manipulated toward what
> David Easton calls authoritative allocation of values.[14]

Thus, liberalism, like racism, Marxism, and cultural pluralism is a political ideology which seeks to establish and maintain its version of the best possible world.

A definitive example of liberalism's political character and tendency to impose its own social vision at the expense of other ideologies is its approach to Afro-American ethnicity or ethnic nationalism. Although cultural pluralism presupposes and allegedly respects ethnicity, in practice the liberal proponents of this theory often reject ethnicity as a viable and useful social concept. In fact, the American liberal's position on Afro-American ethnicity reflects an attitude of cultural hegemony and social hypocrisy. Within the liberal framework, Afro-American ethnicity is considered alternately as unimportant as a social force, pathological in its origin, and dysfunctional in its purpose. It is viewed as reactive rather than proactive, primeval rather than progressive and doomed to a timely death by superior secondary associations. Liberalism's social and ideological approach to Afro-American ethnicity is essentially rooted in and reflective of its basic two-pronged approach to the solution of the Black question in general: assimilation and psychological reductionism.

Assimilation as a liberal theory and policy is a curious mixture of cultural chauvinism, social hypocrisy, and disdain for diversity. There is inherent in the assumptions of assimilation an "optimistic liberal faith" that nationalism—or ethnicity, as it is referred to in liberal literature—is a primordial attachment at best and that "With more faith in science, with more experience in political democracy, with more of the advantages of economic progress," people will forsake their ethnic ties and sentiments.[15]

The chauvinistic assumptions of assimilation are clearly reflected in Nathan Glazer's description of the Americanization of European nationality groups, which argues that there is no justification for a differentiation of cultures. He argues that "Their justification for existence might be called on one level nostalgia, on another ideology."[16] These arrogant assumptions about European nationalities are expressed with greater social insensitivity with regard to Afro-Americans. As Nathan Hare points out, liberals

> ... have persistently sought to superimpose the interpretations
> and tendencies of white European immigrants (and the patterns
> of their conflict or/and assimilation) on the study of the kidnapped
> and enslaved Black Africans in America.[17]

By fitting Blacks in the European formula, "The assimilationist bias assumes that Black Americans as a group should 'escape' from their habitat as an alternative to cohesively renewing and developing it." Such assumptions imply and express a thrust toward coercive homogenization and stand in stark contradiction to liberalism's announced concern for liberty and self-determination as well as the proposed values of cultural pluralism.

In 1926 Robert E. Parks made a statement which still informs and encourages liberal assimilationist assumptions. He argued that assimilation was an inevitable, cosmic, and irreversible process.[18] Supportive of this pseudo-scientific theorizing is the equally unfounded assertion of Will Herberg, who contends that "the perpetuation of ethnic differences is altogether out of line with the logic of American reality."[19] Lloyd Warner and Leo Srole also argue the melting pot myth, contending that "The future of American ethnic groups seem to be quite limited; it is likely that they will be quickly absorbed."[20]

Glazer and Moynihan are more chauvinistic and contemptuous in their approach to Black consciousness and culture. They dismiss Black historical origin and thousands of years of cultural achievements with a facile and clearly racist contention. "It is not possible," they assert, "for [Blacks] to view themselves as other ethnic groups viewed themselves . . . because the [Black] is only an American and nothing else. He has no values and culture to guard and protect."[21] Given the Glazer-Moynihan contention, the insistence on assimilation reveals itself as essentially a demand for cultural genocide. It is a Hegelian demand that Blacks recognize their historical irrelevance and accept their ultimate historical death at the hands of a greater, more historically effective people.

Sartre summarized this hypocritical and inhuman liberal view in discussing the democratic-assimilationist attitude toward the Jew. The democratic-assimilationists, Sartre observed

> . . . like the scientist, failed to see the particular case; to him the
> individual is only an ensemble of universal traits. It follows that his
> defense of the Jew saves the latter as a man and annihilates him as
> a Jew. . . . he fears that the Jew will acquire a consciousness of
> Jewish collectivity. . . . 'There are no Jews,' he says, 'there is no
> Jewish question.' This means that he wants to separate the Jew
> from his religion, from his ethnic community, in order to plunge
> him into the democratic crucible whence he will emerge naked and
> alone, an individual and solitary particle like all other particles.[22]

The problem, however, is that the crucible is often less than democratic for Blacks, and it has not yet proved capable of absorbing and transforming them into bona fide individual Americans. Thus, they suffer both social and racial alienation in the wake of these assimilationist failures.

Moreover, assimilation's callous call for the surrender of Black identity does not automatically and unconditionally insure Black absorption into the mainstream. Gordon makes a crucial distinction between structural assimilation (participation in the power structures of the dominant society) and acculturation (submission to the cultural hegemony of the dominant group). This distinction clearly points out the hypocrisy of the liberal homogenization approach and outlines the requirements for realistic intergroup harmony. As Gordon contends, "Behavioral assimilation [acculturation] has taken place in America to a considerable degree. . . . Structural assimilation, then, has turned out to be the rock on which the ships of Anglo-conformity and the melting pot have foundered."[23] Failure to perceive this distinction is to obscure the issue rather than treat it critically.

Moreover, the desirability of assimilation of Blacks is cogently questioned by Harold Cruse and Ralph Ellison in terms of its deceptiveness as a solution and its damage to the unique contribution of Blacks to American culture. Cruse observes that:

> Although the three main power groups—Protestants, Catholics, and Jews—neither want nor need to become integrated with each other, the existence of a great body of homogenized, interassimilated, white Americans is the premise for racial integration. Thus the [Black] integrationist runs afoul of reality in pursuit of an illusion, the 'open society'—a false front that hides several doors to several different worlds of hyphenated Americans.[24]

And Ellison, arguing the validity and value of the Black experience, points out that "in [Black] culture, there is much of value for America as a whole. What is needed are [Blacks] to take it and create of it the uncreated consciousness of their race."[25] Such a position is often criticized by liberals as narrow, although few, if any, would use the label for Jews resistant to absorption.

Social harmony and human homogenization are two drastically different phenomena. Diversity does not insure or necessarily imply division. It is more proactively conceived as human richness rather than an inevitable symbol and source of antagonistic division. As Andrew Greeley proposes:

> . . . ethnicity is far from being a divisive force in society. It can be viewed as a constructive one; at the last, it is an inevitable one. Men will necessarily differentiate themselves. What is important is whether the differentiations that take place can become socially constructive.[26]

In the final analysis, Greeley concludes, "Diversity may lead to hellish miseries in the world, but without the power to diversify and to locate himself somewhere in the midst of the diversity, man may not be able to cope with the world at all."[27]

Finally, it is important to note that the liberal assumption that ethnicity or nationalism will disappear with increased contact, mobility, and opportunity is more assimilationist hope than hard social fact. Fredrik Barth discovered that such an assumption is erroneous and that, in fact, the opposite appears to be true. His findings show ". . . that boundaries persist despite a flow of personnel across them. In other words, categorical ethnic distinctions do not depend on an absence of mobility, contact, and information. . . ." What is true, however, is that "one finds that stable, persisting, and often vitally important social relations are maintained across such boundaries and are frequently based precisely on the dichotomized ethnic statuses." In other words, Barth concludes, ethnic distinction does not depend on a group's interaction and acceptance; on the contrary, these distinctions are often "the very foundations on which embracing social systems are built."[28]

Another approach of liberalism to ethnicity is the psychological-reductive approach of moralism concerning racism, which it defines as essentially prejudice. If prejudice is the central problem, as liberalism argues, then the "race problem" is in essence a moral problem and it "logically" follows that a little (or lot) of moral rectification, as Gunnar Myrdal argues, is all the "social self-healing" America needs.[29] The argument contends that there is no structural obstacle to equality or assimilation, only a moral one. And this will pass away eventually, for "the conquering of the color caste in America is America's own innermost desire" and "the main trend in its history is the gradual realization of the American creed."[30] Thus, what we have here, Myrdal would have us believe, is not objective structural and practical impediments to groups mingling and melting in the mainstream, but a moral dilemma.

Put another way, as John Horton contends, the moral dilemma school argues that the so-called racial problem in the United States can be reduced to

> . . . a moral crisis arising from an incongruity between legitimate and
> ethical social goals (for example, success and equality of oppor-
> tunity) and socially available opportunities to achieve these goals.
> American society is good and ethical, but anomic because the
> American Creed of equality has not been fully institutionalized;
> the ethic is widely accepted in theory but not in practice.[31]

Such an assumption implies patience and adjustment, not nationalistic-ethnic demands that the American dilemma give way to the American dream and that patience and adjustment yield to the realization that only structural change can end the conditions that create social consciousness and conduct and give rise to mutually respectful and beneficial relations among the people who belong and contribute to this experiment called America. Hence, the negative liberal attitude toward ethnicity stems from the concrete demands that challenge the moralistic and psychologistic solutions liberalism proposes.

Finally, the liberal model of society often poses the Blacks as pathological both in acceptance and rejection of American society. Myrdal[32] considers all Blacks to be pathological. Glazer and Moynihan[33] concur but attach the label especially to Afro-American nationalists, whom they designate as extremists. Myrdal reeks of paternalistic racism when he contends that Afro-American culture "is not something independent of general American culture. It is a distorted development, or a pathological condition of the general American culture."[34] As Nathan Hare observes:

> The main failure of the pathological approach is that only the minority ('deviant'—exhibiting a particular form of behavior different from most other persons) is regarded as sick. This makes the victim responsible beyond reality for his own malaise or, more importantly, neglects the sickness of the general society, relieving the status quo of its responsibility for producing epidemics of social pathology, such as racial conflict. Sociology thus becomes victimology.[35]

Moreover, the liberal tendency is to see Blacks as totally reactive, never proactive. Thus, even Afro-American nationalism becomes a reaction-formation—anger arising from paternal rejection. Ralph Ellison, in reviewing Myrdal's proposition, takes issue with Myrdal's argument that Blacks live by reactions to white people. He raises the pertinent question of how "can a people . . . live and develop for over three hundred years simply by reacting." Ellison argues that Blacks are not simply products of white men but of their own self-conscious and self-constructive efforts. After all, he asks, "Men have made a life in caves and upon cliffs, why cannot [Blacks] have made a life on the horns of the white man's dilemma?"[36]

Ellison notes that Myrdal's racist assumption that Black culture and personality are simply reactive products of social pathology leads to two other equally erroneous assumptions. The first is that true American culture is a white product and that Blacks should assimilate it, for it is in fact the highest culture. American culture is not a simple construction of whites, Ellison points out, and there is some question as to why Blacks should regard everything whites do as "higher culture," even though evidence screams the opposite. After all, Ellison concludes, "lynching and Hollywood, fadism and radio advertising are products of [this so-called] 'higher' culture, and the [Black] might ask, 'why if my culture is pathological, must I exchange it for these?'" It is obvious, then, that pathology is not a single race phenomenon. Thus, "What is needed in our country," Ellison asserts, "is not an exchange of pathologies, but a change of the basis of society." After all, social conditions create social consciousness and conduct, and change in the former lays the basis for change in the latter.

It is again clear that liberalism is full of contradictions in regard to cultural pluralism, and its position on ethnicity among Blacks is a case in point. On one hand, it argues for their freedom, equality, and access, but on the other hand it attacks their self-consciousness and capacity for historical and social construction. Moreover, it argues for cultural pluralism and denies the value and validity of Black culture and its maintenance which is a *sine qua non* of contributions to the cooperative plurality of cultures. Such contradictions make a mockery of cultural pluralist projections and call for a sober reassessment of liberalism's core principles and practice.

Racism and Pluralism

Cultural pluralism confronts an even more intractable opposition in racism. In fact, it is a safe and elemental assumption that racism as an ideology conditions or affects in varying degrees both liberalism and Marxism. For if social conditions create social consciousness, and American society is marked by racism, then liberalism and Marxism, as ideological products of American society, are necessarily affected by the racist conditions under which they evolve. Racism, as a competing construction of reality, challenges cultural pluralism by denying the value of Third World cultures and by establishing structures to insure their deformation and ultimate destruction. It is obviously impossible to practice cultural pluralism if the dominant culture and people impose their will, values, views, and structures at the expense of all others. The uniformity sought by liberalism applies also to the racist program, which suggests the confluence of the two ideological systems.

Racism here is viewed as more than racial prejudice, which is simply an attitude. It is more definitively a system of denial and deformation of a people's history and humanity and right to freedom, based exclusively or primarily on the concept of race. Racism must not be confused with prejudice and other negative sentiments about physical appearances. As a system of thought and practice, it involves at a minimum "a violent imposition, an ideology, and an institutional arrangement."[37] In other words, "To divide the world into races, to violently impose on other peoples the views, values, and rule of one's race, to develop an ideology to justify this imposition, and to construct institutions that consolidate and insure this imposition is racism, regardless of its variations."[38] Thus, racism expresses itself on three basic levels: as a violent imposition, as ideology, and as an institutional arrangement. And it is in these areas that nationalism seeks to negate and transcend it through a nationalist redefinition and reconstruction of reality.

Racism is first and foremost an act of violent imposition—of conquest, appropriation and control along racial lines. It is a physical, psychological, and cultural act of violence against a people's history and humanity in racial terms. Without the key factor of imposition, racism as a social process and phenomenon is reduced to an attitude or belief which is more precisely defined as racial prejudice. To dislike or hate someone because she/he has defiant Black hair and bold features instead of yellow hair and weak features is racial prejudice, but to divide and rule society and the world along racial lines and develop an ideology to justify these racial divisions and rule is racism.

Stokely Carmichael and Charles Hamilton recognized imposition as a fundamental aspect of racism, defining it as "...the predication of decisions and policies on considerations of race for the purpose of *subordinating* a racial group and maintaining control over that group."[39] Hodge, et al., also posed domination as key to the definition of racism, thus defining it as "the belief in and practice of the domination of one social group identified as a 'race' over another social group, identified as another 'race'."[40] Robert Blauner also notes the ideological and practical aspects of racism, pointing to: (1) "the conquest of people of color by white Westerners"; (2) "the establishment of slavery as an institution along color lines"; (3) "the consolidation of the racial principle of economic exploitation"; and (4) "the elaboration and solidification of the racist potential of earlier modes of thought."[41]

As an act of imposition, racism also means the interruption, destruction, and appropriation of a people's history. It involves the combining of their history—both as written legacy and daily life—with the conqueror's history, such that it has no independent existence and appears as a mere appendage of the conqueror's. Closely and unavoidably linked to the appropriation of history is racism's appropriation of the labor of the conquered people. Labor, like struggle, is a motive of history because it is a self-creating, self-defining, self-developing, and self-confirming life activity. As the essential process through which a people creates, defines, develops, and confirms itself, it is the essential act of history. Peoples are introduced and honored in the world by what they have done, by the images of themselves which they have raised above earth. Once their labor has been appropriated, so has their history, for the two are unavoidably linked. A subjugated people works, but it works for the conqueror's history and society, for his honor and in his name. Without control of its labor, it has no control or real sense of history. Without control of its own labor, without control of its productive capacity—mental, manual, and material—a conquered people loses the capacity to create, define, develop, and confirm itself—in a word, the capacity to make history.

It is for this reason that Amilcar Cabral and other freedom fighters argue that until the productive forces (labor, land, and resources) are free, there is no liberation. Speaking directly to this question, Cabral contends that:

> The principle characteristic, common to every kind of imperialist domination, is the negation of the *historical process* of the dominated people by means of violently usurping the free operation of the process of the development of the *productive forces.*[42]

He links labor to history and identifies the sociopolitical task of rescuing them from foreign hands as the essential act of liberation.

Racism, as an act of imposition, as an act of conquest, not only involved the appropriation of Black labor, but also the racial divison of labor for society. As Blauner states:

> Modern race relations owe their origins to the exploitative dynamic and expansionist thrust of Western Europe that exploded in the late fifteenth century, ushering in the so-called 'Age of Discovery'.[43]

In this process of economic expansion, racism played a fundamental role in the enslavement and perversion of African labor. Capitalism—the organized, armed, and ceaseless search for profits—turned to slavery for cheap and mindless labor with a brutal and unrestrained ferocity. African slavery, as Eric Williams observes, played a vital role in the expansion of Western economies.[44] C. L. R. James corroborates this view when he observes that

> Nearly all the industries which developed in France during the eighteenth century had their origin in goods or commodities destined for either the coast of Guinea or America. The capital from the slave trade fertilized them. Though the bourgeois traded in other things than slaves, upon the success or failure of the [slave] traffic, everything else depends.[45]

With African slavery, an ideology developed to justify and perpetuate it along racial lines.

Racism as ideology, practice, and structure was a fundamental part of the capitalist and slave systems in America. As ideology, racism evolved from three fundamental factors: (1) the need to justify conquest, enslavement, and exploitation of Third World peoples, especially Africans; (2) the existence of cultural propensities in Europe conducive to racist theorizing; and (3) acquired contempt that logically followed from the conquest, deculturalization, and dehumanization of Third World peoples.

Even though Walter Rodney argues that it is a mistake to hold that "Europeans enslaved Africans for racist reasons," he nevertheless states that "it can be affirmed without reservations that the white racism which came to pervade the world was an integral part of the capitalist mode of production."[46] Moreover, he contends that, given the dialectical interrelationship and interaction of race, labor needs, and the need to rationalize the exploitation of African labor, "oppression of African people on purely racial grounds accompanied, strengthened, and became indistinguishable from oppression for economic reasons."[47]

Given these contentions, it is difficult to deny, as many dogmatic Marxists do, that racism is an exclusive product or function of class division and struggle. In fact, racism as an ideology has shown itself capable of lasting and living even when the so-called material basis for it is gone. Socialist societies, whose rule ended capitalism's pimping and promotion of racism, still have a white ruling group in a multiracial society and the problem of racist attitudes and activities among the ruling class—i.e., the numerical majority.

The second component and expression of racism is an ideology—an elaborate pseudointellectual system of racially negative categories, assumptions, and contentions that tend to justify the imposition and reinforce the institutional arrangements. Thus, racism is not satisfied with its violent appropriation of Africa's historical personality and initiative; it seeks also to reinforce and justify its hold on Black humanity by denying its reality and creative richness. Frantz Fanon correctly points out that "it is not enough for settler to delimit physically, that is to say with the help of the army and the police force, the place of the native. As if to show the totalitarian character of colonial exploitation the settler paints the native as a sort of quintessence of evil."[48] To the white conqueror and racist, Africans are not just a people without values; according to Fanon, they are the negation of values.

It is through slavery that this redefinition and denial of Black humanity took place to the greatest degree. As John Henrik Clarke argues, "The tragic and distinguishing feature of the slave trade introduced by the Europeans was that it totally dehumanized the slave and denied his basic personality."[49] The need to justify slavery is well documented. The need was to create a marginal human or subhuman, devoid of redeeming qualities and in need of white intervention for salvation from him/herself. Furthermore, this being had to be deprived of possible allies, based on his/her alleged human marginality, as well as deprived of historical memory and reduced to a pliant, pathetic creature for which there was periodic sympathy but no real salvation. The first deprivation was to prevent outcry and intervention by opponents of slavery; the second deprivation was to cultivate adjustment and minimize rebellion. To accomplish this task, the ideology of racism assumed three basic forms: 1) religious absurdities; 2) biological absurdities; and 3) cultural chauvinist absurdities.

The first dimension of ideological racism is religious absurdities. It is a reflection of an age-old attempt to get God to authorize and underwrite an action to give it a sacred and unchallengeable legitimacy. Africans were children of darkness; whites were the children of light. It is written, for the racist, that light will triumph over darkness, which justifies the conquest of the Third World by Europe. It is also written, for the racist, that the

Judeo-Christian must smite the heathen hip and thigh and make him a hewer of wood and drawer of water. Such is the lot of the sons and daughters of cursed Ham. It is this Judeo-Christian mystification which, as Aimé Césaire argues, is the most hypocritical, vicious, and effective lie because of its highly emotive power and character, its decisive ability to dismiss the demand for evidence. Cesaire condemns the "slavering apologists," the Christian pedants who

> . . . laid down the dishonest equations *Christianity-civilization*,
> *paganism-savagery*, from which there could not but ensure abomin-
> able colonialist and racist consequences whose victims were to be
> the Indians, the yellow peoples and Blacks.[50]

Thus, the heathen is pictured not only as biologically and spiritually deficient but also an offense to God—a sin for which there had to be the redemptive shedding of blood.

This thrust to conquer and Christianize was seen and projected as a great white mission—as Rudyard Kipling put it, the white man's burden. Europe's conquest and the disappearance of "heathen hordes" was, according to Thomas Gosset, seen as God's will—although it was obvious that the responsibility for mass murder and subjugation resided with His chosen, the whites. Gosset notes that at the height of America imperialist expansion, one Senator Albert Beveridge, a chief apologist for racism, argued that the United States' growth was a race movement, that whites were the most masterful race, that their race movement was an answer to a Divine Command, and that American leaders were therefore not just statesmen but "prophets of God."[51] Thus, the chief justification for slavery and imperialism became the Bible and, as E. Franklin Frazier notes, "Ministers all over the South searched the scriptures to prove that [Blacks] had been cursed by God to serve other races or that Jesus had either approved slavery or at least had not condemned it."[52]

The second ideological dimension of racism is biological absurdities. Through religious absurdities, the white Christians "heathenized" Third World peoples. Through biological absurdities they dehumanized those peoples, pushing them further to the edge of humanity and leaving them with little basis to claim and defend their human worth, equality, and right to freedom. As Cesaire contends, it is in this context that there is "no human contact, but relations of domination and submission," with the whites as rulers and slave drivers "and the indigenous man . . . [as] an instrument of production." Thus, he concluded "colonization = thingification."[53]

The first biological absurdity is the concept of race itself, based primarily on skin color and the size and shape of features like noses and lips.[54] Europe must be given credit for developing the concept of race during its imperialistic expansion giving each of us varying degrees of humanity according to how closely we resembled the white man. It is clear now, and perhaps was clear even to its originators, that race as a concept is neither scientific nor strictly biological. The concept of race is not just a classification of features; it includes the fundamental assumption that physical features determine the degree of humanity, the quality of thought and behavior, and the role one can and should play in society and history as a result of this brutal logic. Naturally, whites who created this mystification placed themselves at the top and Blacks, their opposites, at the bottom—both in theory and practice.

Thus, race is more precisely and correctly defined as a social construction which employs biological differences for the facilitation and justification of the oppression and exploitation of Third World peoples. Race was and is an ideological weapon in the struggle of Europe to conquer the world and to justify and perpetuate its conquest. Its unscientific quality is thus exposed by its social motive; it is not a means of understanding humanity and its rich diversity but rather of dividing and controling it. Regardless of the biological emphasis, the absurdity was employed to set the African apart, to put him/her outside civilization and humanity and thus insure the absence of restraints and the reinforcement and perpetuation of the racist system. Neither racism nor slavery could survive if Blacks were not so defined. As Winthrop Jordan states, "Slavery could survive only if the [Black] were a man set apart; he simply had to be different if slavery were to exist at all."[55]

The third dimension of ideological racism is cultural chauvinist absurdities. This ideological form included two basic theoretical aspects: Social Darwinism and the linkage of genes and culture. Social Darwinism borrowed from biological Darwinism basic concepts of natural evolution, characterized by struggle and conflict and the natural triumph of the strong and superior over the weak and inferior. As Gosset contends:

> . . . the idea of natural selection was translated into a struggle
> between individual members of society; between different nations
> and between different races. This conflict, far from being an evil
> thing, was nature's indispensible method of producing superior
> men, superior nations and superior races.[56]

Thus, the assumptions were that the strong would and *should* survive for the good of the species and the advancement of civilization.

Closely related to Social Darwinists' assumptions is the linking of genes and culture. This aspect of cultural chauvinism promotes the myth that Europeans are genetically unique and that this has produced a greater material advancement of Europe and North America compared with the Third World. This assumption treats industrial advancement as a natural product of a superior genetic-cultural combination with which Europeans were divinely blessed. The argument is that the superior cultural achievement of Europe is directly related to and a product of European genetic superiority. If Third World people are equal to Europeans, why, historically, have they not proved it through equal cultural achievement? As Robert Allen correctly contends, such assumptions and loaded questions conveniently obscure "the fact that it was capitalist exploitation of the colonial world that contributed to rapid and continuing material progress in Europe and North America. . . . [Thus] by separating culture from economics and history, cultural chauvinism regards culture as a metaphysical attribute of a people or nation."[57]

Rodney agrees with this analysis and posits that Third World underdevelopment is in dialectical relation to Western overdevelopment, that Western advancement was based on imposed Third World backwardness, and that Third World poverty is directly and undebateably linked to Western wealth.[58] Moreover, it is clear that those cultural chauvinist assumptions are essentially ahistorical and sociological generalizations that also obscure the fact that white achievement is uneven and not evidenced among all whites or even among all Western Europeans. There is ample evidence of Third World cultural achievement in different historical periods: the world and human civilization are not a white product.

The third and final component of racism is the institutional arrangements that were made to consolidate and perpetuate both the imposition and the ideology which justifies it. This component of racism is essentially a system of political, economic, and social structures which insure the power and privilege of whites over Third World peoples. The impact of the racist imposition would diminish and the absurdity of its ideology would eventually be exposed if it were not for the established structure, procedures, and practices which give social reality and permanence to its power and propositions. Thus, in court, Afro-Americans are proven to be more criminal because they receive more convictions and publicity. In school systems, Afro-American Studies were not taught with any seriousness in white colleges before the Black studies movement because of the racist assumption that Blacks had no history or relevance except in marginal relation to whites. Banks cannot loan to Blacks because of the risks of irresponsible racial behavior. Neighborhoods are closed to them because they will bring down property values. These structures, procedures and practices limit or deny access and equal treatment to Afro-Americans and other Third World peoples and at the same time prove their social and historical incompetence by structuring and insuring it.

Institutional racism belies the social myth of assimilation and integration and reveals that cultural pluralism is less than workable, because "the logic of racial oppression denies members of a subjugated group the full range of human possibility that exist within a society."[59] This full range of human possibility is impossible to achieve outside institutions which structure behavior, control, rewards and punishments. Thus, Gordon's distinction between structural assimilation (participation in the power structures) and acculturation (cultural absorption and hegemony by the dominant group) is clearly instructive,[60] and Kallen's dream of a commonwealth of equally contributive cultures evaporates. Afro-Americans are refused entrance to power positions or critical social space but are encouraged to forget their own culture, to deny their African roots except as a commercial venture, and to become happily homogenized in the dominant Anglo cultural matrix. The structural option offers power and self-determination; the acculturation option offers powerlessness, dependency, and resultant pathology. No wonder racism supports the latter and violently objects to the former.

Marxism and Pluralism

Marxism projects itself as a humanistic and necessary alternative to both the vulgarity and violence of racism and the sterility and hypocrisy of liberalism. Its positon on cultural pluralism, however, reflects some of the negative aspects of liberalism and racism. Especially significant is Marxism's theoretical resistance to racial, ethnic, and national projects in favor of the panacea of international solidarity. Thus, its appreciation of cultural pluralism is limited, for the ultimate aim is one socialist culture, not a plethora of potentially competing ethnic or national units.

As an ideology whose basic scope and direction are international, Marxism cannot help but be hostile to nationalism, which exalts what is immediate and local. From the beginning Marx fought national allegiances while maintaining his own ties to Germany. However, it is a basic contradiction of Marxism that in spite of its advocacy of internationalism, it proceeds from definite national contexts, from definite conditions that create a definite consciousness. Thus, Marx and Engels called for internationalism while asserting the superiority and civilizing mission of Germany.[61] German socialists spoke piously about internationalism, but turned German socialism into German nationalism.[62] Likewise, Lenin and Stalin argued self-determination but conducted programs of Russification and suppressed nationalism when it became "expedient."[63] Moreover, the Internationals have always been dominated by one main national group (Germans or Russians) and divided by national rivalries and struggles.[64] Nevertheless, Marxism continues to uphold its internationalist principles and resist internal nationalist tendencies.

Another source of Marxism's resistance to nationalism is its Eurocentrism, especially as it applies to the Third World. Edward Shils is correct when he contends that "... every ideology—however great the originality of its creators—arises in the midst of an ongoing culture."[65] However passionate its reaction against that culture, it cannot entirely divest itself of important elements of that culture. This is true of Marx and Marxists, as well as of other Europeans who defined and dealt with the national question. They were never quite able to accept the entry of the African, Asian and Latin

American nations into the world community and arrogantly glorified Europe, especially Western Europe, as the hope of humankind.[66]

Marx's world and personal views conditioned his attitude toward nationalities. He supported the Irish, Polish, and Austrian struggles for independence but detested the Pan-Slavic movement.[67] He thought Germany to be, in Hegelian terms, the most historically effective nation and argued that China and India were outside the pale of history because they had no modern state formation. In fact, as Joseph Petrus observes, Marx and Engels "viewed the non-West with suspicion and declared Asia to be without history—an 'Oriental Despotism.'"[68] Marx argued that nationalism was linked to democracy when defending the Poles and that it was linked to internationalism when defending the Irish.[69] But he argued with equal passion that some nations, like Turkey, had "neither the temperament nor disposition for the capitalist enterprise."[70]

Lenin turned to the East only after being disappointed in the West. Revolution, it seemed, had to be made somewhere besides downtown London, Berlin, or Paris. Imperialism was first debated in terms of the viability of European capitalism if it had to search for markets. But Lenin raised a political question that considered imperialism as the means by which socialists could obtain needed allies.[71] He devoted little attention to the conditions of the colonial masses. M. N. Roy, appearing at the Comintern Congress of 1920, found Lenin embarrassingly ignorant of the Third World and was asked by Lenin for advice and assistance in developing a landmark document on the national and colonial question.[72]

Shades of economic determinism and related theoretical assumptions in Marxism also resist the nationalism and ethnicity which cultural pluralism demands and assumes. The nation for Marx, Lenin[73] and Stalin[74] is a capitalist category, an economic category, a context for the bourgeoisie's control of its market. Its subjective and cultural content are reduced to formulations by the bourgeoisie, mere mystification to hide the real economic content and concern. The problem with this one-dimensional interpretation was dealt with brilliantly by Antonio Gramsci with his concept of cultural hegemony, which sought to identify the force of culture as a fundamental shaper of human practice and method of rule.[75]

Giving such great and exclusive weight to economic forces not only resists cultural interpretations of nation and society but also brings about an embarrassing convergence of Marxists and imperialists. They both believe religiously in the value of economic progress, regardless of human costs, and the constructive, civilizing role of capitalist exploitation.[76] James Joll observes that the French, Germans, and Italians all had different historical and cultural experiences to draw on at the beginning of World War I. Thus, the Marxist assertion that the workers and socialists had no nationality and belonged to the international working class was less than realistic and rational.[77]

Marxism's emphasis on economic factors, then, often ends up in a kind of class reductionism. It becomes at that point a materialism that ironically resembles the liberals' hope to eliminate race by movement into the middle class. As Blauner states, "This tendency to reduce race to class has been practiced by radical theorists and liberal policy-makers." The similarity of approach is reflected in the fact that:

> Marxists have expected that a developing class consciousness
> cutting across ethnic and racial lines would eliminate national and
> racial considerations and lead to the collective solidarity of
> oppressed groups. [Likewise] Liberal sociologists expected race
> and ethnic concerns to recede as large numbers of individuals from
> the minority groups began to move into the middle class.[78]

However, in a racist society, class level at best diminishes racial oppresssion of middle-class Blacks on personal levels; it does not eliminate it for them as a people. Secondly, it is, as Marxists admit, the middle class or petty bourgeois elements who form the leadership and driving force of the nationalist movement. Finally, the Marxist expectation of working class unity across racial and ethnic lines is complicated by the racial ideology, privileges, status and access which the white working class possess and treasure.

Class reductionism, however, refuses to see, as Fanon pointed out, that in a racist context the world is divided not only into the classic Marxian haves and have-nots, but also into Black and white. Those two aspects—economic and racial—complement and reinforce each other and place the Black in a special position of dual alienation within this world. Fanon argues cogently that the colonial world:

> . . . divided into compartments, this world cut in two is inhabited by
> two different species. The originality of the colonial context is that
> economic reality, inequality, and the immense differences of ways
> of life never come to mask the human realities. When you examine
> at close quarters the colonial context, it is evident that what parcels
> out the world is to begin with the fact of belonging to a given
> race, a given species.[79]

In such a context where race is primary, the economic structure and the superstructure merge. "The cause is the consequence. You are rich because you are white, and white because you are rich." Marxism which posits an unavoidable primacy of economic base has found itself incapable of recognizing and responding to this fact or Rodney's[80] contention that at one level and time, racial oppression of Africans became indistinguishable from and more fundamental than their economic oppression of whites. "This is why," Fanon tells us, "Marxist analysis should always be slightly stretched every time we have to do with [such a] problem." And in expanding the analysis, "everything up to and including the very nature of pre-capitalist society, so well explained by Marx, must here be thought out again."[81]

Fanon is arguing here that race is a major factor in the evolution and structure of a racist society and is not simply an automatic and reducible function of economic structure. On the contrary, critical analysis will reveal that these factors are interdependent and require an approach which admits this fundamental fact. The concept which links economic structure (class) and race is the concept of alienation. The Afro-American as a conquered worker is alienated through class and race relations. With the conquest of the African and the appropriation of his/her labor, the capitalist or slavocrat also appropriates his/her *productive capacity* and his/her *self-expressive capacity*. As Renate Zahar notes, "Work is . . . the human quality which, over and above the economic sphere, defines the essence of man. . . ."[82] Thus, appropriation of it by another is appropriation of the human capacity for self-development, self-definition and self-confirmation.

Herbert Marcuse agrees and posits that:

> The worker alienated from his product is at the same time alienated from himself. His labor itself becomes no longer his own, and the fact that it becomes the property of another bespeaks an appropriation that touches the very essence of man. Labor in its true form is a medium for man's true self-fulfillment, for the full development of his potentialities: the conscious utilization of the forces of nature should take place for his satisfaction and enjoyment.[83]

However, enslaved labor is a perverted labor which "cripples all human faculties and enjoins satisfaction." But a critical analysis shows that alienation is not simply an economic phenomenon. "As the absolute inability of the individual to recognize and develop himself and his own potentialities, alienation always has both economic and intellectual aspects. . . ."[84] In the racist context, this means that racism adds to economic alienation a cultural alienation. To the dehumanization of a conquered worker racism adds dehumanization and depersonalization on the basis of race. As Sekou Toure observed, ". . . the aggression Africa was victim [of] expressed itself in all fields of existence of our peoples: cultural, spiritual, military aggression . . . going from biocide to genocide."[85]

For the dogmatic Marxist, then, it is class or nothing, and all other factors affecting and shaping the social process must be reduced to that dimension, regardless of the theoretical deformities this mechanical materialism produces. The need, however, is clearly one of a new theoretical model that recognizes and responds critically and creatively to the reality of both the class and racial-ethnic structure of society. Such a model would logically lead to an analysis of ethnicity and racial consciousness not as prehistoric hangovers, but as fundamental factors in the social process—sociohistorical forms of consciousness which have played and will continue to play a major role in human history. Once this is accomplished, cultural pluralism will receive a more critical appreciation among Marxists, for it will then become clear through a more critical Marxist analysis that human diversity is not the source of human division, but the basis of human richness.

Conclusion

Cultural pluralism, it has been argued, is a social construction of reality, a vision of social organization which is forced to compete with other ideological systems in society. Likewise, in practice, it becomes a political project which also faces political opposition. Thus, its success will depend on the ideological clarity and structural capacity it demonstrates in defining, defending, and developing its interests. Put another way, cultural pluralism must develop its political counterpart, political pluralism, if it is to prevail. Political pluralism essentially means developing and defending polycentric circles of power. Power is defined here as the structural capacity to realize one's will even in opposition to others. Without such structural capacity, the advocates of cultural pluralism will be reduced to discussions of the desirable and deprived of the realization of their goals.

In addition to the development of a structural capacity to introduce and establish its principles and practices, the cultural pluralism movement, if it is to succeed, must be a core motivating factor in a cultural revolution. This cultural revolution must have as its goal the broad and profound change of the views and values of the dominant society. This change must include among other things: (1) a rejection of race as a social and biological category; (2) a political socialization of the masses of Americans which includes respect for cultural and ethnic differences; (3) the wholesale rewriting of textbooks to include the rich contributions of Third World people to U.S. and human history; (4) the creation of alternative educational systems among Third World peoples; and (5) a creation of alternative media among Third World peoples.

Essential to the cultural revolutionary process is the consolidation and continuous expansion of the ethnic studies thrust. From this thrust must come the core concepts, research, and other intellectual products of cultural pluralism and the cultural revolution. Ethnic studies programs represent in their essence the rescue and reconstruction of Third World peoples' history and humanity and thus are pivotal in reshaping the self-concept of Third World peoples, as well as their conception of society and the world. They also give society and the world a more realistic picture of Third World people.

To fulfill their sociohistorical mission, ethnic studies, as culturally pluralistic disciplines, must develop a new body of literature which reflects audaciousness and initiative in both research and intellectual production. They must defy established disciplines, develop their own socially conscious methodology and form the core of a new social science for human society. By achieving this, their contribution will benefit not only the particular peoples, but society as a whole. They will enhance humanity's conception and appreciation of its diversity, which, in the final analysis, is the source of its richness.

Notes

1. Milton Gordon, *Human Nature, Class and Ethnicity* (New York: Oxford University Press, 1978), p. 197.
2. Ibid, p. 199.
3. Horace Kallen, *Culture and Democracy in the United States* (New York: Boni & Liveright, 1970).
4. Ibid., p. 86.
5. Ibid., p. 94.
6. Ibid., p. 119.
7. Ibid., p. 123.
8. Ibid., p. 124.
9. Milton Gordon, "Assimilation in America: Theory and Reality," *Daedalus* 90 (Spring 1961): 137.
10. Gordon, *Human Nature*, p. 160.
11. Antonio Pantoja, et al., "Towards the Development of Theory: Cultural Pluralism Redefined," *Journal of Sociology and Social Welfare* 4, no. 1 (September 1976): 126.
12. Gordon, *Human Nature*, p. 157.
13. Alexander Groth, *Major Ideologies: An Interpretive Survey of Democracy, Socialism and Nationalism* (New York: John Wiley & Sons, 1971), p. 2.
14. Ibid., p. 2.
15. Andrew Greeley, *Ethnicity in the United States: A Preliminary Reconnaissance* (New York: John Wiley & Sons, 1974), p. 14.
16. Nathan Glazer, "Ethnic Culture in America: From National Culture to Ideology," in *Freedom and Control in Modern Society*, ed. Wilbert F. Moore (New York: D. Van Nostrand Co., 1954), p. 172.
17. Nathan Hare, "The Sociological Study of Racial Conflict," *Phylon* 33 (Spring 1972): 27.
18. Robert E. Parks, *Race and Culture* (Glencoe, Ill.: Free Press of Glencoe, 1950).
19. Will Herberg, *Protestant, Catholic and Jew* (New York: Doubleday, 1955), p. 23.

20. Lloyd Warner and Leo Srole, *The Social Systems of the American Ethnic Groups* (New Haven, Conn.: Yale University Press, 1945), p. 295.
21. Nathan Glazer and Daniel Moynihan, *Beyond the Melting Pot* (Cambridge, Mass.: MIT Press, 1963), p. 52.
22. Jean Paul Sartre, *Anti-Semite and Jew*, trans. George J. Becker (New York: Grove Press, 1962), pp. 56–57.
23. Gordon, "Assimilation."
24. Harold Cruse, *The Crisis of the Negro Intellectual* (New York: William Morrow, 1967), p. 24.
25. Ralph Ellison, *Shadow and Act* (New York: New American Library, 1966), p. 302.
26. Greeley, p. 24.
27. Ibid., p. 15.
28. Fredrik Barth, ed., *Ethnic Groups and Boundaries: The Social Organization of Culture Difference* (Boston, Mass.: Little, Brown & Co., 1969), pp. 9–10.
29. Gunnar Myrdal, *An American Dilemma* (New York: Harper & Row, 1944), p. 80.
30. Ibid., p. 1021.
31. John Horton, "Order and Conflict Theories of Social Problems as Competing Ideologies," *American Journal of Sociology* 71 (May 1966): 710.
32. Myrdal, *An American Dilemma.*
33. Glazer and Moynihan, *Beyond.*
34. Myrdal, p. 928.
35. Hare, "The Sociological Study," p. 31.
36. Ellison, pp. 316–337.
37. M. Ron Karenga, *Essays on Struggle: Position and Analysis* (San Diego, Cal.: Kawaida Publications, 1978), pp. 56–57.
38. Ibid.
39. Stokely Carmichael and Charles Hamilton, *Black Power* (New York: Random House, 1967), p. 3.
40. John Hodge, et al., *Cultural Bases of Racism and Group Oppression* (Berkeley, Cal.: Riders Press, 1975), p. 10.
41. Robert Blauner, *Racial Oppression in America* (New York: Harper & Row, 1972), p. 21.
42. Amilcar Cabral, *Revolution in Guinea* (New York: Monthly Review Press, 1969), p. 78.
43. Blauner, p. 29.
44. Eric Williams, *Capitalism and Slavery* (Chapel Hill, N.C.: Capricorn Press, 1944), pp. 50–84.
45. C. L. R. James, *The Black Jacobins* (New York: Vantage Press, 1963), p. 48.

46. Walter Rodney, *How Europe Underdeveloped Africa* (Washington, D.C.: Howard University Press, 1974), p. 88.

47. Ibid., p. 89.

48. Frantz Fanon, *The Wretched of the Earth* (New York: Grove Press, 1968), p. 41.

49. John Henrik Clarke, "Black Americans: Immigrants Against Their Will," *Presence Africaine* 105/106 (1979): 94.

50. Aime Cesaire, *Discourse on Colonialism* (New York: Monthly Review Press, 1972), p. 11.

51. Thomas Gossett, *Race: The History of An Idea in America* (Dallas, Tex.: Southern Methodist University Press, 1963), p. 318.

52. E. Franklin Frazier, *The Negro in the United States* (New York: Macmillan Co., 1957), p. 42.

53. Cesaire, p. 21.

54. Ashley Montague, *Man's Most Dangerous Myth: The Fallacy of Race* (New York: World, 1964).

55. Winthrop Jordan, *White Over Black* (Chapel Hill, N.C.: University of North Carolina Press, 1968), p. 164.

56. Gossett, p. 145.

57. Robert Allen, *Reluctant Reformers* (Washington, D.C.: Howard University Press, 1974), pp. 272–273.

58. Rodney, *How Europe*.

59. Blauner, p. 41.

60. Gordon, "Assimiliation."

61. Horace Davis, *Nationalism and Socialism* (New York: Monthly Review Press, 1967), p. 36.

62. Ibid., pp. 83–102.

63. Alfred Low, *Lenin on the Question of Nationality* (New York: Bookman Associates, 1958), pp. 131–132.

64. Milorad Drackovitch, *The Revolutionary Internationals, 1864–1943* (Stanford, Conn.: Stanford University Press, 1966).

65. Edward Shils, "The Concept and Function of Ideology," *The International Encyclopedia of Social Science* 7 (1968): 69.

66. Shlomo Avineri, *Karl Marx on Colonialism and Modernization* (Garden City, N.Y.: Anchor Books, 1969).

67. Solomon Bloom, *The World of Nations* (New York: AMS Press, 1967).

68. Joseph Petrus, "Marx and Engels on the National Question," *Journal of Politics* 33 (August 1971): 802.

69. Saul Padover, *Karl Marx on the First International* (New York: McGraw-Hill, 1972), p. 39.

70. Davis, p. 66.

71. Low, *Lenin*.

72. Bhabani Gupta, *Communism in Indian Politics* (New York: Columbia University Press, 1972), p. 10.

73. V. I. Lenin, *The Right of Nations to Self-Determination* (Moscow: Progress Publishers, 1973).
74. Joseph Stalin, *Marxism and the National Question* (Calcutta, 1971).
75. Antonio Gramsci, *Selections from the Prison Notebooks* (New York: International Publishers, 1971); and Carl Boggs, *Gramsci's Prison Notebooks* Part I and II, vol. 2, no. 11 & 12 (September-October, November-December, 1972).
76. Davis, p. 69; Avineri, *Karl Marx*.
77. James Joll, *The Second International* (London: Weidenfeld & Nicolson, 1955), p. 108.
78. Blauner, p. 11.
79. Fanon, pp. 39–40.
80. Rodney, p. 89.
81. Fanon, p. 40.
82. Renate Zahar, *Frantz Fanon: Colonialism and Alienation* (New York: Monthly Review Press, 1974), p. 3.
83. Herbert Marcuse, *Reason and Revolution* (Boston: Beacon Press, 1969), p. 277.
84. Zahar, p. 4.
85. Sekou Toure, *Revolution, Culture and Pan-Africanism* (Conakry: Government Press, 1976), p. 169.

Select Bibliography

1. Allen, Robert. *Reluctant Reformers*. Washington, D.C.: Howard University Press, 1974.
2. Allport, Gordon W. *The Nature of Prejudice*. New York: Doubleday, 1958.
3. Banton, Michael. *Race Relations*. New York: Basic Books, 1967.
4. Barth, Gunther. *Bitter Strength: A History of the Chinese in the United States, 1850–1870*. Boston, Mass.: Harvard University Press, 1964.
5. Barzum, Jacques. *Race: A Study in Superstition*. New York: Harper & Row, 1965.
6. Blauner, Robert. *Racial Oppression in America*. New York: Harper & Row, 1972.
7. Book, Susan. *The Chinese in Butte County, California, 1860–1920*. San Francisco, Cal.: R&E Research Associates, 1976.
8. Casso, Henry. *Bilingual/Bicultural Education and Teacher Training*. Washington, D.C.: National Education Association, 1976.
9. Cattel, Stuart H. *Health, Welfare, and Social Organization*. New York: Department of Public Affairs, Community Service Society, 1962.
10. Chase, Allan. *The Legacy of Malthus: The Social Costs of the New Scientific Racism*. New York: Alfred A. Knopf, 1977.
11. Chin, Frank. *Chicken Coop Chinaman*. Washington, D.C.: Howard University Press, 1972.
12. Chinese Historical Society of America. *The Life, Influence and the Role of the Chinese in the United States, 1776–1960*. San Francisco, Cal.: Chinese Historical Society of America, 1976.
13. Chinn, Thomas, ed. *A History of the Chinese in California: A Syllabus*. San Francisco, Cal.: Chinese Historical Society of America, 1969.
14. Chiu, Ping. *Chinese Labor in California, 1850–1880: An Economic Study*. Madison, Wisc.: University of Wisconsin Press, 1963.
15. Cox, O. *Caste, Class and Race*. New York: Monthly Review Press, 1959.
16. Cruse, Harole. *The Crisis of the Negro Intellectual*. New York: Morrow, 1967.
17. Daniels, Roger and Harry H. L. Kitano. *American Racism: Exploration of the Nature of Prejudice*. Englewood Cliffs, N.J.: Prentice-Hall, 1970.

18. de Lone, Richard. *Small Futures: Children, Inequality, and the Limits of Liberal Reform*. New York: Harcourt Brace Jovanovich, 1979.
19. Dinnerstein, Leonard and Jaker, Frederic, eds. *The Aliens: A History of Ethnic Minorities in America*. New York: Appleton-Century-Crofts, 1970.
20. Essien-Udom, E. U. *Black Nationalism: A Search for Identity in America*. Chicago, Ill.: University of Chicago Press, 1962.
21. Fantini, Mario. *Public Schools of Choice: A Plan for the Reform of American Education*. New York: Simon & Schuster, 1973.
22. Franklin, John Hope; Pettigrew, Thomas F., and Mack, Raymound W. *Ethnicity in American Life*. New York: Anti-Defamation League of B'nai-B'rith, 1971.
23. Glock, Charles and Siegelman, Ellen, eds. *Prejudice USA*. New York: Praeger Publishers, 1969.
24. Gomez, Rudlph, ed. *The Social Reality of Ethnic America*. Lexington, Mass.: D. C. Heath & Co., 1974.
25. Gordon, Milton. *Human Nature, Class, and Ethnicity*. New York: Oxford University Press, 1978.
26. Greeley, Andrew. *Ethnicity in the United States: A Preliminary Reconnaissance*. New York: John Wiley & Sons, 1974.
27. Green, R., ed. *Racial Crisis in American Education*. Chicago, Ill.: Follett Publishing Co., 1969.
28. Greer, Colin. *The Great School Legend: A Revisionist Interpretation of American Public Education*. New York: Penguin, 1972.
29. Griggs, Veta, *Chinaman's Chance: The Life Story of Elmer Wok Wai*. New York: Exposition Press, 1969.
30. Hawkins, Brett and Lorinskas, Robert, eds. *The Ethnic Factor in American Politics*. Columbus, Ohio: University of Ohio Press, 1970.
31. Higham, John. *Strangers in the Land: Patterns of American Nativism, 1860–1925*. New York: Atheneum, 1972.
32. Hom, Gloria Sun, ed. *Chinese Argonauts: An Anthology of the Chinese Contributions to the Historical Development of Santa Clara County*. Los Altos, Cal.: Foothill Community College, 1971.
33. Hsu, Francis L. K. *Americans and Chinese*. Garden City, N.Y.: Natural History Press, 1970.
34. _____ *The Challenge of the American Dream*. Belmont, Cal.: Wadsworth Publishing Co., 1971.
35. Jacobs, Paul, ed. *To Serve the Devil*, 2 vols. New York: Random House, 1971.
36. Karenga, M. R. *Essays on Struggle: Position and Analysis*. San Diego, Cal: Kawaida Publications, 1978.
37. Katz, Phyllis A., ed. *Towards the Elimination of Racism*. New York: Pergamon Press, 1976.
38. Kiefer, Christie, *Changing Cultures, Changing Times*. San Francisco, Cal.: Jossey-Bass, 1974.

39. Kitano, H., comp. *Asians in America: A Selected Bibliography for Use in Social Work Education*. New York: Council on Social Work Education, 1971.
40. Knowles, L. L. and Prewitt, K., eds. *Institutional Racism in America*. Englewood Cliffs, N. J.: Prentice-Hall, 1969.
41. Konvitz, Milton. *The Alien and the Asiatic in American Law*. Ithaca, N.Y.: Cornell University Press, 1946.
42. Lan, Dean. *Prestige with Limitations: Realities of the Chinese American Elite*. San Francisco, Cal.: R&E Research Associates, 1976.
43. Levy, Mark and Kramer, Michael S. *The Ethnic Factor: How America's Minorities Decide Elections*. New York: Simon & Schuster, Touchstone Books, 1973.
44. Lieberson, Stanley. *Ethnic Patterns in American Cities*. Glencoe, Ill.: Free Press of Glencoe, 1963.
45. Light, Ivan. *Ethnic Enterprise in America: Business and Welfare Among Chinese, Japanese, and Blacks*. Berkeley, Cal.: University of California Press, 1972.
46. Lincoln, C. Eric. *The Black Muslims in America*. Boston, Beacon Press, 1961.
47. Litt, Edgar. *Beyond Pluralism: Ethnic Politics in America*. Glenview: Scott, Foresman, 1970.
48. Liu, William. *Asian American Research: View of a Sociologist*. Temple, Ariz.: Center for Asian Studies, Arizona State University, 1976.
49. Lyman, Stanford. *Chinese Americans*. New York: Random House, 1974.
50. Mapp, E. *Blacks in American Films: Today and Yesterday*. Metuchen, N.J.: Scarecrow Press, 1972.
51. Meister, Richard, ed. *Race and Ethnicity in Modern America*. Lexington, Mass.: D. C. Heath & Co., 1974.
52. Melendy, H. Brett. *Asians in America: Filipinos, Koreans, and East Asians*. Boston, Mass.: Twayne Publishers, 1977.
53. Miller, Stuart Creighton. *The Unwelcome Immigrant: The American Image of the Chinese, 1785–1882*. Berkeley, Cal.: University of California Press, 1969.
54. Montagu, Ashley. *Man's Most Dangerous Myth: The Fallacy of Race*. Cleveland, Ohio: World Publishing Co., 1964.
55. Morison, Samuel Eliot. *The Maritime History of Massachusetts, 1783–1860*. Boston, Mass.: Northeastern University Press, 1961.
56. Myrdal, Gunnar. *An American Dilemma: The Negro Problem and Modern Democracy*. New York: Harper Torchbooks, 1944.
57. Ogbu, John. *Minority Education and Caste: The American System in Cross-Cultural Perspective*. New York: Academic Press, 1978.
58. Peng, Ming-min. *A Taste of Freedom*. New York: Holt, Rinehart & Winston, 1972.
59. Ryan, W. *Blaming the Victim*. New York: Pantheon, 1972.

60. Schermerhorn, R. A. *Comparative Ethnic Relations*. New York: Random House, 1970.
61. Shibutani, Tamotsu and Kwan, Kian M. *Ethnic Stratification: A Comparative Approach*. New York: Macmillan Co., 1965.
62. Stanton, William. *The Leopard's Spots: Scientific Attitudes Toward Race in America, 1815-1859*. Chicago, Ill.: University of Chicago Press, 1966.
63. Stent, M. D.; Hazard, W.; and Ravlin, H., eds. *Cultural Pluralism in Education: A Mandate for Change*. Englewood Cliffs, N.J.: Prentice-Hall, 1973.
64. Tan, Mely Giok-lan. *The Chinese in the United States: Social Mobility and Assimilation*. Taipei: Orient Cultural Service, 1971.
65. Weiss, Melford. *Valley City: A Chinese Community in America*. Cambridge, Mass.: Schenkman Publishing Co., 1974.
66. Walsh, John. *Intercultural Education in the Community of Man*. Honolulu: University of Hawaii Press, 1973.
67. Wollenberg, Charles. *All Deliberate Speed: Segregation and Exclusion in California Schools, 1855-1875*. Berkeley, Cal.: University of California Press, 1976.
68. ____. ed., *Ethnic Conflict in California History*. Los Angeles, Cal.: University of California Press, 1970.
69. Wu, Cheng-tsu. *"Chink!" A Documentary History of Anti-Chinese Prejudice in America*. New York: Harper & Row, 1972.
70. Wong, Jade Snow. *No Chinese Stranger*. New York: World, 1975.
71. Yung Wing. *My Life in China and America*. New York: Arno Press, 1909.

Contributors

James N. Baron
Research Specialist
Department of Sociology
University of California
Santa Barbara, California

Jack Bermingham
Lecturer in History
Department of History
University of the West Indies
Kingston, Jamaica

David Chanaiwa
Professor of History
Department of History
California State University
Northridge, California

Todd Carrell
Journalist
San Francisco, California

Sucheng Chan
Assistant Professor
Department of Ethnic Studies
University of California
Berkeley, California

Edwin Clausen
Assistant Professor
East Asian History
Department of History
Lafayette College
Easton, Pennsylvania

John F. Dovidio
Assistant Professor
Department of Psychology
Colgate University
Hamilton, New York

William Edwards
Lecturer
Department of Black Studies
University of California
Santa Barbara, California

Samuel L. Gaertner
Associate Professor
Department of Psychology
University of Delaware
Newark, Delaware

M. R. Karenga
Associate Professor
Black Studies Program
California State University
Long Beach, California

Douglas Lee
Assistant Professor
Asian American Studies Program
University of Washington
Seattle, Washington

Laura P. Miller
Assistant Professor
Graduate School of Education
University of California
Los Angeles, California

George O. Roberts
Professor of Comparative Culture
  and Social Sciences
University of California
Irvine, California